100 Commonly Asked Questions in Math Class

100 Commonly Asked Questions in Math Class

Answers That Promote Mathematical Understanding, Grades 6–12

Alfred S. Posamentier

William Farber

Terri L. Germain-Williams

Elaine Paris

Bernd Thaller

Ingmar Lehmann

CORWIN
A SAGE Company

CORWIN
A SAGE Company

FOR INFORMATION:

Corwin
A SAGE Company
2455 Teller Road
Thousand Oaks, California 91320
(800) 233-9936
www.corwin.com

SAGE Publications Ltd.
1 Oliver's Yard
55 City Road
London EC1Y 1SP
United Kingdom

SAGE Publications India Pvt. Ltd.
B 1/I 1 Mohan Cooperative Industrial Area
Mathura Road, New Delhi 110 044
India

SAGE Publications Asia-Pacific Pte. Ltd.
3 Church Street
#10-04 Samsung Hub
Singapore 049483

Acquisitions Editor: Robin Najar
Associate Editor: Desirée A. Bartlett
Editorial Assistant: Ariel Price
Production Editor: Melanie Birdsall
Copy Editor: Amy Rosenstein
Typesetter: C&M Digitals (P) Ltd.
Proofreader: Scott Oney
Indexer: Marilyn Augst
Cover Designer: Michael Dubowe

Copyright © 2013 by Corwin

Printed in the United States of America

Library of Congress Cataloging-in-Publication Data

Posamentier, Alfred S.

100 commonly asked questions in math class : answers that promote mathematical understanding, grades 6–12 / Alfred S. Posamentier, William Farber, Terri L. Germain-Williams, Elaine Paris, Bernd Thaller, Ingmar Lehmann.

pages cm
Includes bibliographical references and index.

ISBN 978-1-4522-4308-5 (acid-free paper)

1. Mathematics—Study and teaching (Middle school)
2. Mathematics—Study and teaching (Secondary)
3. Mathematics—Problems, exercises, etc. I. Title. II. Title: One hundred commonly asked questions in math class.
III. Title: Hundred commonly asked questions in math class.

QA139.P65 2013
510.71′2—dc23   2013022103

This book is printed on acid-free paper.

13 14 15 16 17 10 9 8 7 6 5 4 3 2 1

Contents

About the Authors

Alfred S. Posamentier is Dean of the School of Education and Professor of Mathematics Education at Mercy College, New York. Previously, he held these same positions for 40 years at The City College of The City University of New York. He began his professional career as a high school mathematics teacher for six years in New York City. He is the author and coauthor of more than 55 mathematics books for teachers, students, and the general readership. He is also a frequent commentator in newspapers on topics relating to education.

Dr. Posamentier has extended his reputation in mathematics education to Europe. He has been visiting professor at several European universities in Austria, England, Germany, and Poland, and at the University of Vienna, he was Fulbright Professor in 1990.

William Farber is an Associate Professor of Mathematics Education at Mercy College in New York. He presently serves as Director of the Graduate Level Clinically Rich Teacher Preparation Pilot Program, which was awarded to the School of Education of Mercy College to establish an ongoing partnership with participating high-need schools in the Yonkers School District. His professional experiences include serving as K–12 Mathematics Specialist for the New York City Department of Education's Department of Mathematics, Director of the Dr. Charlotte K. Frank Mathematics Education Center at The City College of New York, and a teacher of secondary school mathematics in the Bronx. He is the author and coordinator of many grant awards involving innovative professional development programs in mathematics education.

Terri L. Germain-Williams is an Assistant Professor of Mathematics Education at Mercy College. Prior to accepting the position with Mercy College Graduate School of Education, Germain-Williams worked as an Achievement Manager with the New York City Department of Education, supporting more than 25 K–12 schools in the areas of instruction, strategic planning, professional development, federal and state data and accountability, scheduling/programming, and student services. She has taught Grades 8–12 mathematics and served the New York City Department of Education as a high school Assistant Principal.

Elaine Paris holds BS and MA degrees in mathematics from Brooklyn College, CUNY, and a doctorate in mathematics education from Teachers College, Columbia University.

She began her teaching career at Erasmus Hall High School in Brooklyn as a math teacher. Later, Dr. Paris began teaching mathematics and computer programming at Mercy College. She coauthored the first computer manual used at Mercy College and published several math and computer texts and articles.

She has been a professor in the Department of Mathematics and Computer Information Sciences for more than 30 years, Assistant Chair and Chair, as well as the Director of the U.S. Department of Education federal grant McNair Post-Baccalaureate Scholar Program. Dr. Paris recently retired and holds the rank of Professor Emerita.

Bernd Thaller is a mathematical physicist and Associate Professor at the University of Graz, Austria, who has made contributions to quantum mechanical spectral and scattering theory. He has written several books on quantum mechanics, introducing and applying new visualization methods for quantum wave functions. In recent years, his focus has shifted toward educational math. He was coordinator of a European Community project for teaching math in secondary high schools between 2005 and 2008. In 2008, he founded and is currently the head of a regional educational competence center for mathematics and geometry, whose main task is the coordination of activities of the math teacher training institutions in the region.

Ingmar Lehmann is retired from the mathematics faculty at Humboldt University in Berlin. For many years, he led the Berlin Mathematics Student Society for gifted secondary school students, an organization with which he is still closely engaged today.

He is the author of numerous mathematics texts in Germany and the coauthor with Alfred S. Posamentier of some other books, including *The Secrets of Triangles, The Glorious Golden Ratio, Magnificent Mistakes in Mathematics,* and *The Fabulous Fibonacci Numbers.*

Introduction

It is well known that students will pose questions to teachers about a variety of topics. Oftentimes, these topics are related to what is being taught. Yet on occasion, students who hear about things mathematical from family, friends, or the media will not hesitate to ask their math teacher to explain something that may have been confusing to them. Most of the time, teachers can respond to these questions in proper fashion. However, there may be times when the question asked is not at ready reference for the teacher. We hope that this book will provide a resource for teachers who need a quick response to a variety of questions relating to school mathematics.

In general, mathematics education practitioners and researchers agree that teachers need to present mathematics as a motivating subject to their students—one that promotes and fosters thinking, and, at times, flexible and unrestricted inquiry. In fact, when explaining the Process Standard "Reasoning and Proof," the National Council of Teachers of Mathematics states thus: "The ability to reason systematically and carefully [in mathematics] develops when students are encouraged to make conjectures, are given time to search for evidence to prove or disprove them, and are expected to explain and justify their ideas." Clearly, this statement indicates a national imperative in mathematics education for teachers to emphasize the importance of process as well as mathematical thinking in their classes.

At the same time, students want—and need—to know the answers to their mathematics questions without the teacher telling them to think through the problem. In other words, although process in solving mathematical problems and conceptual understanding of mathematical topics are both important, students need to learn procedural methods that will help them solve problems efficiently and effectively.

In this book, the authors identify common mathematics content questions that students, almost exclusively at the secondary level, often ask in class. We then follow each question with clear and concise answers that are aligned with the Common Core State Standards. Although the question-answer dyads themselves will span the middle school and high school grade levels, some questions might be introduced in grade levels prior to middle school. Accordingly, secondary-level students frequently ask questions that appear to be late elementary in terms of content. Because of their seemingly elementary-level nature, teachers often dismiss such questions. Given the emphasis on secondary-school student mathematics questions, our focus is to tailor seemingly elementary-level questions toward secondary mathematics courses.

This book will help to prepare the novice mathematics teacher or serve as enrichment for the more experienced mathematics teacher in anticipating common content-related mathematics questions that students of all ages and grade levels will undoubtedly ask during the school year. In addition, the authors strive to provide efficient answers that encourage flexibility in ways of solving various mathematics problems. The topic of this book is of increasing importance so that teachers of mathematics answer students' questions effectively and anticipate what students will ask so that the presentation of answers is clear and concise. Of equal importance is the book's emphasis on answers to mathematical questions as they relate to efficient test-taking strategies in different assessments that students will need to take, especially at the secondary level.

Each chapter provides a detailed list of common mathematics questions along with their answers in the most comprehensive way possible. This book focuses on practical application in mathematics and highlights ways that teachers can engage and motivate students. At the same time, the practical nature of the book is supported by research in mathematics education and human development.

1 General Questions

1. WHY DO I HAVE TO LEARN MATHEMATICS?

The "why" question is perhaps the one encountered most frequently. It is not a matter of if but when this question comes up. And after high school, it will come up again in different formulations. (Why should I become a mathematics major? Why should the public fund research in mathematics? Why did I ever need to study mathematics?) Thus, it is important to be prepared for this question. Giving a good answer is certainly difficult, as much depends on individual circumstances.

First, you should try to find an answer for yourself. What was it that convinced *you* to study and teach mathematics? Why do *you* think that mathematics is useful and important? Have *you* been fascinated by the elegance of mathematical reasoning and the beauty of mathematical results? Tell your students. A heartfelt answer would be most credible. Try to avoid easy answers like "Because there is a test next week" or "Because I say so," even if you think that the question arises from a general unwillingness to learn.

It is certainly true that everybody needs to know a certain amount of elementary mathematics to master his or her life. You could point out that there are many everyday situations where mathematics plays a role. Certainly one needs mathematics whenever one deals with money—for example, when one goes shopping, manages a savings account, or makes a monthly budget.

Nevertheless, we encounter the "why" question more frequently in situations where the everyday context is less apparent. When students ask this question, it should be interpreted as a symptom indicating that they do not appreciate mathematics. This could have many reasons, but the common style of instruction certainly has an influence. Are we really doing our best to make sure that education in the classroom becomes an intellectually stimulating and pleasurable experience? If lessons can be attended without fear of failure and humiliation, it is more likely that mathematics gets a positive image. Try to create an atmosphere where curiosity will be rewarded and where errors and mistakes are not punished but rather are welcomed as a necessary part of acquiring competence. It is most important that you always try to enrich your lessons with interesting facts, examples, and problems showing that mathematics is fascinating and intriguing, and well worth the effort.

It is wrong to say that studying mathematics should always be fun and entertaining. Mathematics, like most worthwhile things, requires a great deal of effort to master. Mathematics is the science of structured thinking, logical reasoning, and problem solving. It requires commitment and time to acquire these skills. To solve a given problem, students have to concentrate on a task, devote attention to details, keep up the effort for some time, and achieve understanding. But the students will be rewarded: Practicing precise logical thinking as well as learning many problem-solving techniques will be useful for many different situations in many different aspects of one's life.

Often, the "why" question originates in a basic misunderstanding of what mathematics is about. The basic fact is that mathematics is useful because it solves problems. In fact, it has been developed for at least 4,000 years to solve problems of everyday life. In early times, mathematics was needed for trading, managing supplies, distributing properties, and even describing the motion of the stars and planets to create calendars and predict seasons for agricultural and religious activities.

Over time, the scope of the problems that can be solved by mathematics has widened considerably, and presently it encompasses all fields of human knowledge. Mathematics is not only useful for measurements and statistics; it also, in particular, is needed to formulate and investigate the laws of nature. With the help of computer technology, mathematics can deal even with very complicated real-world problems. Therefore, mathematical models provide us with useful and vital information about climate change, economic trends and predictions, financial crises, movements of the planets, and the workings of the human body, to name a few. Mathematics has played a major role in many technical developments; a few more recent examples are space exploration, CD players, mobile phones, Internet technologies (e.g., the compression algorithms used for storing music, pictures, and movies), and global positioning system technology for navigation.

So, one of the main reasons to learn mathematics is that it is useful. Today it is more useful than ever before, and it is of importance to more fields of knowledge than ever before. Correspondingly, mathematics is used in many different jobs by scientists, engineers, computer programmers, investment bankers, tax accountants, and traffic planners, to name just a few. Refusing to learn mathematics would mean closing off many career opportunities. Students will perhaps understand that it is important to keep their options open.

However, the comparatively simple mathematics problems prevailing in school are bound to create a wrong impression of the importance of mathematics in the modern world. For students, it may be impossible to understand what calculus has to do with meteorology or risk analysis or automotive engineering, unless you make some attempts to explain these connections. You should point out, for example, that the derivative of a function could be used to describe a rate of change. Differential calculus would be needed where we need precise information about the rate of change of some observable quantity. It should therefore become clear that even the basics of science and technology cannot be understood without a solid background in math.

There is a final, and perhaps the most important, reason why one should learn math, although it is difficult to communicate: Mathematics is a huge, logically and deductively organized system of thought, created by countless individuals in a continuous collective effort that has lasted for several thousand years and still continues at breathtaking pace. As such, mathematics is the most significant cultural achievement of humankind. It should be a natural and essential part of everyone's general education.

2. IS THERE A LANGUAGE CONNECTION BETWEEN MATHEMATICAL TERMS AND COMMON ENGLISH WORDS?

Many mathematical terms are seen by students as words whose definitions must be memorized. Students rarely see applications of these words outside their mathematical context. This is akin to having someone learn words from another language simply for use in that language and then avoiding tying the words back to their mother tongue, even when possible. To learn the meanings of the frequently used mathematical terms without connecting them back to common English usage deprives students of a genuine understanding of the terms involved and keeps them from appreciating the richness and logical use of the English language.

The term *perpendicular*, which everyone immediately associates with geometry, is also used in common English, meaning "moral virtue, uprightness, rectitude." The rays that emanate from the center of a circle to its circumference take on a name closely related, *radius*.

The rectangle is a parallelogram that stands erect. And the right angle, whose German translation is *rechter Winkel*, shows us the connection to the word rectangle. By itself, the word *right* has a common usage in the word *righteous,* meaning "upright, or virtuous."

The word *isosceles* typically is used in connection with a triangle or a trapezoid, as in *isosceles triangle* and *isosceles trapezoid*. The word *isosceles* evolved from the Greek language, with *iso* meaning "equal" and "skelos" meaning "leg." The prefix *iso* is also used in many other applications, as in isomorphism (meaning equal form or appearance, and in mathematics, two sets in a one-to-one onto relation that preserves the relation between elements in the domain), *isometric* (meaning equal measure), or *isotonic* (in mathematics sometimes used as isotonic mapping, referring to a monotonic mapping, and in music meaning that which is characterized by equal tones), just to name a few.

The word *rational* used in the term *rational number* (one that can be expressed as a ratio of two integers) means "reasonable" in our common usage. In a historical sense, a rational number was a "reasonable number." Numbers such as $\sqrt{2}$ were not considered as "reasonable" in the very early days of our civilization, hence the name irrational. The term *ratio* comes from the Latin *ratio,* meaning "a reckoning, an account, a calculation" from where the word rate seems to emanate.

It is clear, and ought to be emphasized, that natural numbers were so named because they were the basis for our counting system and were "nature's way" to begin in a study or buildup of mathematics. Real numbers and imaginary numbers also take their mathematical meanings from their regular English usage.

Even the properties called *associative, commutative*, and *distributive* have the meaning that describes them. The associative property "associates" the first pair of elements together (out of three elements) and then associates the second pair of these three elements. The commutative property changes position of the first element of two to the second position, much as one "commutes" from the first position (at home) to the second position (at work), and at the end of the workday, reverses the "commute" from work back to home. The distributive property "distributes" the first element to the two other elements.

It is clear that when we speak of *ordinal numbers,* we speak of the position or order of a number, as in first, second, third, and so on. The *cardinal numbers* refer to the size or magnitude of a number—that is, its importance. In this sense, one might say that the larger the number is, the more "important" it is. In English, we refer to something of "cardinal importance."

From the word *complete,* we get the term *complementary,* as a complementary item completes something. In its most common usage, an angle is the complement of another if it "completes" a right angle with it.

Once the prefix *con* meaning "with" is understood, terms such as *concentric* (circles having the same center), *coplanar* (in the same plane), or *concyclic* (points lying on the same circle) are easily defined. So just pointing out to students these small hints gives the mathematics terms more meaning.

The word *cave,* a hollow in a mountain, is related to the term *concave,* and one can draw a similar mental picture. The term *convex,* stemming from the Latin *convexus,* meaning "vaulted, arched, . . . drawn together to a point," refers to the opposite of concave.

Some words speak for themselves, such as a *bisector,* which sections something into two (equal) parts. The use of the prefix *bi* in mathematics is usually clear. For example, we have *biconditional* (conditional in two directions), *binomial* (having two names or terms), or *bilateral* (two sided). The word *triangle* also is self-descriptive: "three-angled polygon."

When one considers the definition of *factor* in its common English usage (i.e., "one of the elements contributing to a particular result or situation"), the mathematical definition of factor becomes clear (i.e., one of the numbers multiplied to get a product).

If we stretch the imagination just a bit, the term *fraction* also makes sense. It comes from the Latin *fractio,* meaning "a breaking in pieces," which is what a fraction represents: a piece. In some languages, such as German, a language with roots similar to those of English, the word for *fraction* is "Bruch," which also means "a break or piece," just as the Latin derivation of fraction does. When we fracture a bone, we break the bone.

In making students aware of the words used in mathematics, you also should make them aware of the prefixes that indicate magnitude, such as poly, bi, semi, tri, quad, pent, hex, sept, oct, non, dec, dodec, and so on. These prefixes, when combined with suffixes such as gon, hedron, and so on, allow students to determine a word's meaning.

Not to be overlooked is the term *prime number*, since it stems from the true definition of the word prime. As in the word *primitive,* referring to the basic elements, in a mathematical sense a prime number is one of the basic numbers from which, through multiplication, we build the other numbers.

Whenever a new word or term is introduced in mathematics, it should be related back to common English usage. This may require having a good dictionary at ready reference. The time it takes to tie mathematical terms back to ordinary English will help strengthen the mathematical understanding as well as enlarge a student's regular vocabulary. It is time well spent!

3. HOW MANY LEAVES ARE ON A TREE?

At first sight, this question does not seem to have much to do with mathematics. But it is about counting, and this is where mathematics starts. There is no need for special knowledge in biology, but it could be helpful to join forces with the biology teacher when attacking a problem like this in class.

First, we need to know what type of answer is expected. For a typical tree during the summer, the result will certainly be a very large number. It is fairly hopeless to determine this number exactly by counting the leaves one by one. And indeed, an exact answer (like 51,641) does not appear to be very useful. We would certainly be happy with a rough estimate like "about 50,000." Special techniques of estimating and guessing are needed to obtain a plausible answer, and it is well worth training these abilities, as they are important for applied science and technology.

There are several possible approaches to this problem, and for all of these approaches it is best to consider a real tree and eventually perform measurements on that tree, as it is difficult to obtain good estimates from pictures or memory alone.

One might start to estimate or count the number L of leaves on a typical twig. Next, we need to know the approximate number T of twigs on a branch, and a typical number B of branches on a main branch. Finally, we would count the number M of main branches of the tree. Then a reasonable guess for the number of leaves would be $L \cdot T \cdot B \cdot M$. Of course, the numbers will differ from branch to branch and from tree to tree. And it will be worth discussing what we mean by "typical values" for L, T, B, and M. Indeed, what is a typical branch? One could try to obtain several samples from a tree, count the number of leaves on each of these branches, and then compute the average (arithmetic mean). Depending on the situation and depending on whether you choose lower or higher numbers for these quantities, you will get probably something between 10,000 and 1,000,000 leaves. This should give you an idea of the order of magnitude (i.e., the power of 10) to be expected. It is a typical feature of this type of question that, no matter how we proceed, the final result will be far from unique. After all these estimates, we cannot say whether the result is right or wrong; we can at best judge the result as more or less plausible.

A rather ingenious method to estimate the number of leaves on a tree arises from some insight into the function of the leaves. Their main purpose is to collect sunlight for the process of photosynthesis. Therefore, the leaves are positioned to collect light from all directions, or at least from above. Assuming, for the sake of argument, that the crown of the tree is roughly a sphere, it would make sense to position the leaves in such a way that every point of the surface of this sphere (or at least the upper half of the sphere) is covered by one leaf (or perhaps by two leaves, but not many more, because the leaves outside would cast shadow on the leaves inside, thus making them rather useless for photosynthesis). So we could ask how many leaves are needed to cover the surface of a sphere that has the same diameter as the crown of our tree. To estimate the total number of leaves, we would (a) compute the size of the spherical surface exposed to the sun in square meters and

(b) determine the number of leaves needed to cover 1 square meter with not too much overlap (this can be determined experimentally or from an estimate of the surface area of one leaf, which is an interesting problem in itself).

As an example, consider a tree whose crown has a diameter of about 10 meters. For a sphere with a radius of $r \approx 5$ meters, we get a surface of $4\pi r^2 \approx 314$ m². Assuming, that about 1,000 leaves are needed to cover a square meter, we would need about 314,000 leaves to cover the surface of the crown.

There is another, related method. When the tree sheds its leaves in fall, we expect that the ground beneath the crown would be covered by leaves, probably by more than one layer. Assuming that the roughly spherical area under the crown (area $\pi r^2 \approx 78.5$ m²) is covered by four layers of leaves, we would get the same answer as above. Forestry scientists use a measure called Leaf Area Index (LAI). This is defined as the leaf area (one-sided) in the part of the crown above a unit of ground surface area. So LAI = 1 means that the leaves of the tree can be used to cover the ground just once, while LAI < 1 means that you can still see the ground between the leaves. LAI = 4 means that you can cover the area beneath the crown with four layers of leaves from that tree. In an oak wood, the LAI is typically 5 to 7; for a beach wood, the LAI is 6 to 8. Assuming a LAI of 6, a big old oak tree whose crown has a radius of 15 m could well have a total leaf surface of about $6 \times 15^2 \times \pi \approx 4{,}250$ m². If the area covered by one big oak leaf is about 50 cm², we would need about 200 leaves to cover 1 m² of ground, and therefore we get about $200 \times 4{,}250 = 850{,}000$ leaves for that oak tree.

Questions like this have come to be known as Fermi questions, named after the famous physicist and Nobel laureate Enrico Fermi, who liked to pose questions like "How many piano tuners are in Chicago?" to train his students' abilities to seek fast, rough estimates in situations where the available facts are incomplete or where a direct measurement seems to be difficult or impossible. Other examples of Fermi questions include the following:

"How many hairs are on your head?"

"How many drops of water are in the Atlantic ocean?"

"How many words have you said so far in your life?"

"How many golf balls will fit into your classroom?"

"How long is the queue if all the people living in New York would line up?"

"What is the weight of the U.S. public debt in 100 dollar bills?" and so on.

When approaching these questions, it is important to avoid giving up early with a shrug and the attitude "How could I know?" The main effect is that students will have to create a strategy, think in big numbers, learn to change units as needed, and learn to make estimates and reasonable guesses. In short, they are forced to employ everyday reasoning when doing mathematics.

4. WHY DO WE HAVE TO LEARN ABOUT THE HISTORY OF MATHEMATICS?

Students study a variety of mathematical topics throughout their secondary school experience. They learn about the Pythagorean theorem, Pascal's triangle, Euclidean geometry, the Cartesian plane, Platonic solids, Boolean algebra, Gaussian arithmetic, Diophantine equations, Euler's equation, Fibonacci numbers, and a multitude of other mathematical concepts and principles. You may notice that the 10 aforementioned topics are named after great mathematicians, whose work and discoveries contributed to the growth and development of mathematical ideas.

It is essential for students to go beyond the rote and procedures of learning mathematical skills in the classroom. Discovering where all of these mathematical rules, axioms, conjectures, and theorems came from will help reveal to students how the developments in mathematics have helped to shape the cultures of the world, and how the cultures of the world influenced mathematics, for example, how the growth of numbers and numeration is revealed in language, how the concept of quantification led to different theories of arithmetic, how the concept of informal measurement led to geometry, how early theories of astronomy led to trigonometry and logarithms, and how analytic geometry and calculus were developed to gain a better understanding of motion.

One reason why students should learn mathematics from a historical perspective is that mathematics has a rich cultural heritage. Studying the history of mathematics will help students appreciate this culture. Moreover, learning mathematics from a historical perspective will help students realize the connections of mathematics to other disciplines such as art, music, architecture, crafts, religion, and philosophy.

Learning about the history of mathematics can give students a deeper appreciation of mathematics, and therefore help them personalize mathematics. In addition, by learning about the great mathematicians, students can appreciate the contributions of different cultures throughout the world. Students can also learn to value the persistent efforts and collected genius of these influential mathematicians, and subsequently discover how mathematics evolved throughout the ages and how new branches of mathematics were developed. Moreover, students will be able to recognize the value of how the combined advances in mathematics transformed not only mathematics but also other sciences and civilization.

Learning about the history of mathematics motivates students and the mathematics becomes more functionally relevant to their lives, and in turn, they will become more interested, which helps to spur student achievement. Oftentimes, students take a small tidbit of historical facts revealed in the mathematics classroom to their history class, thereby forming a genuine link between the subjects. Each subject benefits from this connection.

5. WHO INTRODUCED THE HINDU-ARABIC NUMBERS TO THE WESTERN WORLD, AND WHEN?

In the early Middle Ages, Europeans still used the Roman numeral system for commerce and trade. The Roman numeral system was quite limited in that it lacked a real system of place value as well as a value of zero. There were only seven symbols, and each represented a different number:

$I = 1$

$V = 5$

$X = 10$

$L = 50$

$C = 100$

$D = 500$

$M = 1,000$

Numbers were read from the left to the right, with the largest valued symbol appearing in the leftmost position. In addition, there was a minimal placement agreement that if a smaller valued symbol preceded a larger valued symbol, one would subtract the smaller value from the adjacent larger value. For example, the year 2013 would be represented as MMXIII and the year 1942 would be MCMXLII. The only additional representation this system offered was that if a horizontal line was placed over a symbol, it was meant to multiply its face value by 1,000, so $\overline{V}$ would represent 5,000.

We retain Roman numerals for special uses today such as the numbering of preface pages in texts, memorializing the construction date of significant buildings, naming subsequent heirs to a throne or members of a family such as John Smith III, and recording the release dates for movies.

When working in Roman numerals, one would often need to do calculations on an abacus. You can imagine how long a process would be needed for very large numbers that are common today, such as the U.S. national debt, which as of the beginning of the year 2013 stood at $16,436,821,542,578 and is still growing.

One of the most famous mathematicians of the Middle Ages was Leonardo of Pisa (also known as Fibonacci; c. 1170–1250). He was born in Italy but grew up in North Africa, near Algiers, where his father, Guglielmo, was stationed as a trade representative for the city-state of Pisa. He travelled widely with his father in the Middle East and was exposed at an early age to the Arab system of numeration and the use of zero. He studied under the leading Arab mathematicians and quickly realized the advantage of the Hindu-Arabic place-valued decimal system over the Roman numeral system. In 1202, at the age of 32, Fibonacci wrote *Liber Abaci (The Book of Calculation),* which was well received by educated Europeans. It introduced them not only to the Hindu-Arabic system and the number zero but also to our current notations for fractions and square roots.

The Hindu-Arabic numeration system had 10 symbols, which have been modified and morphed from their appearances in the Middle Ages into our current mathematical number symbols. See the comparative chart of the 10 symbols from medieval times to modern times below.

Hindu-Arabic	٠	١	٢	٣	٤	٥	٦	٧	٨	٩
European	0	1	2	3	4	5	6	7	8	9

By using the 10 symbols called *digits* (0, 1, 2, 3, 4, 5, 6, 7, 8, 9) and a place-value system based on the powers of 10, numbers of any size could easily be represented and used in calculations.

The place-value system permitted the digits to carry the "weight of their place" times their face value. For example, in the number 123,056, we note the place value below the digit face value, beginning with the rightmost digit.

1	2	3	0	5	6
Hundred-thousands	Ten-thousands	Thousands	Hundreds	Tens	Ones
10^5	10^4	10^3	10^2	10^1	10^0

To evaluate, start from the right end and the first digit, 6:

Digit 6 is in the units or ones column and represents	$6 \times 1 = 6$
Digit 5 is in the tens place and represents	$5 \times 10 = 50$
Digit 0 is in the hundreds place and represents	$0 \times 100 = 000$
Digit 3 is in the thousands place and represents	$3 \times 1,000 = 3,000$
Digit 2 is in the ten-thousands place and represents	$2 \times 10,000 = 20,000$
Digit 1 is in the hundred-thousands place and represents	$1 \times 100,000 = 100,000$
Adding all these values gives us the original number	123,056

There is no limit to the size of the number you can represent using only the 10 digits and employing the zero as a placeholder.

The number above represents a whole number. If we expand to the right of the decimal point, the system works perfectly as digits that appear there have a place value continuing in order from left to right as 10^{-1}, 10^{-2}, 10^{-3} as tenths, hundredths, thousandths, and so on.

Acceptance and use of the Hindu-Arabic number system quickly spread and became practical and functional in everyday life as well as in spheres of trade and finance such as importing and exporting, banking, calculating interest, and money exchanges. These changes had a profound impact on all mercantile and merchandising activities throughout the European world.

6. WHAT ARE THE THREE FAMOUS PROBLEMS OF ANTIQUITY?

Unsolved problems have always fascinated people. The three geometric problems of antiquity are perhaps the most famous of all. They were posed by the ancient Greeks and remained unsolved for more than 2,000 years. The solution obtained in modern times, with the help of abstract algebra, was not quite satisfactory either.

The three problems are as follows:

1. *The trisection of an arbitrary angle*

   Given an angle, construct an angle one-third its measure.

2. *The doubling of a cube*

   Given a cube, construct a cube with double the volume.

3. *The squaring of a circle*

Given a circle, construct a square that has the same area as the circle.

But here is a hitch. The only tools allowed to accomplish these tasks are a compass and an unmarked straightedge (and a pencil, of course). Moreover, according to Euclidean geometry, the only operations that are allowed to be done with these tools are the following:

1. Drawing points

2. Connecting two points with a line segment

3. Drawing a circle centered at a given point with a given line segment as radius

4. Marking intersection points (of two lines, of a line and a circle, of two circles)

When we say that something can be done with compass and unmarked straightedge, we mean that the whole construction can be reduced to a finite sequence of the four steps listed above.

It turned out that the three problems of antiquity are impossible to accomplish with a compass and straightedge, and using only allowed operations. For a very similar reason, it is impossible to construct a regular heptagon (a seven-sided polygon).

The impossibility of these constructions follows from modern algebra and is rather difficult to prove at secondary-school level. The general result is the following:

Starting with a line segment of unit length, a line segment of length L can only be constructed (using compass and unmarked straightedge) if L can be obtained from the rational numbers by a finite number of steps involving the operations addition/subtraction, multiplication/division, and taking square roots. Using the theory of fields, one can show that whenever a number L is constructible in this sense, then L is an algebraic number (i.e., a root of a polynomial with integer coefficients), and that the degree of its minimal polynomial is a power of 2 (the minimal polynomial is the polynomial with the smallest degree that has L as a root). It can be seen that problems 1 and 2 lead to minimal polynomials of degree 3 and problem 3 would need the construction of the square root of π, which is a transcendental number (i.e., it is not the root of a nontrivial polynomial with integer coefficients).

Thus, all of these problems have been proven to be unsolvable. Of course, this result depends on the required usage of compass and unmarked straightedge only for its construction. It is possible to obtain solutions, if other tools are allowed or if the tools are used in nonstandard ways.

Here we will provide an example for a trisection of an angle that was described by Pappus around AD 320 but is certainly much older (probably the oldest known construction of this type).

We are given an angle with vertex at P, as indicated in Figure 1.1. Draw a point A on one of the legs of the angle, thus creating a line segment PA of length a. Through point A, draw one line g parallel to the other leg of the angle, and one line h perpendicular to g.

Figure 1.1

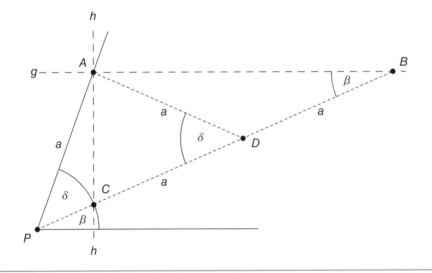

Next, draw a line through the vertex P intersecting h at C and g at B in such a way that the length of the segment CB is precisely $2a$. (This step can be achieved if we mark the length $2a$ on a ruler and move the ruler in the plane until it has the required position—unfortunately, this is not an allowed Euclidean operation.)

The line segment PB cuts the given angle into two parts, which we call β and δ. Obviously, the angle at B also equals β.

The midpoint D of segment BC defines an isosceles triangle DAP so that the angle δ also appears at D, as indicated. But the triangle ADB is also isosceles so that the angle δ is easily shown to be 2β. Hence the original angle at P is $\beta + \delta = 3\beta$. This shows that the newly constructed angle β trisects the given angle at P.

Another method was developed by Archimedes: Given an angle with vertex P, draw a circle with radius r around P. Let A be the intersection of that circle with one of the legs of the given angle. Through A, draw a straight line as in Figure 1.2, such that the segment CB has precisely the length r.

Then the indicated angle at C is precisely one-third of the given angle at P. This is rather easy to see and probably a good exercise for your students.

Fitting a line segment of a given length between two given lines in a certain way is called a "Neusis construction." It requires that two points on a straightedge are marked, and the straightedge is moved until the two points have the desired position. Unfortunately, this is not an allowed Euclidean operation.

Figure 1.2

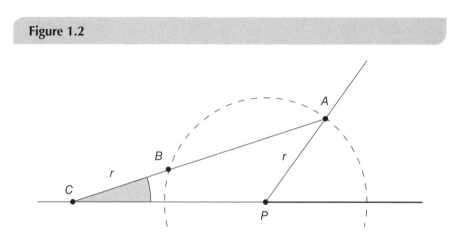

These famous problems have attracted amateurs who tried to find solutions, ignoring the proven fact that they cannot be solved. Even today, mathematicians are frequently approached by people who believe that they have a solution to one of these famous problems. What they really have is most probably either an approximate or a Neusis construction.

7. WHAT ARE THE FIBONACCI NUMBERS?

Leonardo of Pisa, called Fibonacci (1170–1250), was one of the best-known mathematicians of the Middle Ages. He lived in Bugia, a trading post in Algiers, where his father was probably the resident trade authority for the city-state of Pisa. Fibonacci travelled widely with his father and was exposed to Eastern mathematical thoughts and ideas, and he carried the accomplishments of Persian (Iranian), Indian, and Arabic mathematicians back to Western civilization. One of the most well-known examples of Eastern mathematics he worked with and introduced was the number sequence that bears his name.

The Fibonacci sequence[1] is defined by giving its initial value(s) and a rule that determines the next term in the sequence. The first two terms of the Fibonacci sequence are

$$F_1 = 1$$

$$F_2 = 1$$

Fibonacci Rule: Each proceeding [next] term is the sum of the previous two terms so that

$$F_3 = F_2 + F_1 = 1 + 1 = 2$$

$$F_4 = F_3 + F_2 = 2 + 1 = 3$$

$$F_5 = F_4 + F_3 = 3 + 2 = 5$$

$$F_6 = F_5 + F_4 = 5 + 3 = 8$$

And, in general: $F_n = F_{n-1} + F_{n-2}$ with $n \geq 3$

Obtaining the next dozen or so terms is usually easy for students, but it may be interesting to discuss whether there will be even and odd numbers, squares, cubes, primes, and composites coming up in the sequence. They quickly get 1, 1, 2, 3, 5, 8, 13, 21, 34, 55, 89, 144, 233, and they will ask, "So, what is so special about this sequence that it has enjoyed such long-lasting popularity?" The answer is to demonstrate the amazing beauty and wealth of applications that developed from this simple sequence known to Indian mathematicians in the sixth century but popularized in European culture by Fibonacci in his well-received book *Liber Abaci* (1202).

The Fibonacci numbers emanate from the discussion of the "Growth of a Pair of Rabbits," which appears in Chapter 12 of Fibonacci's book *Liber Abaci*: Here is a translation of the problem as it appeared in Fibonacci's book.

Beginning 1 First 2 Second 3 Third 5 Fourth 8 Fifth 13 Sixth 21 Seventh 34 Eighth 55	**"A certain man had one pair of rabbits together in a certain enclosed place, and one wishes to know how many are created from the pair in one year when it is the nature of them in a single month to bear another pair, and in the second month those born to bear also. Because the above written pair in the first month bore, you will double it; there will be two pairs in one month. One of these, namely the first, bears in the second month, and thus there are in the second month 3 pairs; of these in one month two are pregnant and in the third month 2 pairs of rabbits are born and thus there are 5 pairs in the month; in this month 3 pairs are pregnant and in the fourth month there are 8 pairs, of which 5 pairs bear another 5 pairs; these are added to the 8 pairs making 13 pairs in the fifth month; these 5 pairs that are born in this month do not mate in this month, but another 8 pairs are pregnant, and thus there are in the sixth month 21 pairs; to these are added the 13 pairs that are born in the seventh month; there will be 34 pairs in this month; to this are added the 21 pairs that are born in the eighth month; there will be 55 pairs in this month; to these are added the 34 pairs that are born in the ninth month; there**

(Continued)

(Continued)

Ninth 89 Tenth 144 Eleventh 233 Twelfth 377	**will be 89 pairs in this month; to these are added again the 55 pairs that are both in the tenth month; there will be 144 pairs in this month; to these are added again the 89 pairs that are born in the eleventh month; there will be 233 pairs in this month. To these are still added the 144 pairs that are born in the last month; there will be 377 pairs and this many pairs are produced from the above-written pair in the mentioned place at the end of one year.**
	You can indeed see in the margin how we operated, namely that we added the first number to the second, namely the 1 to the 2, and the second to the third and the third to the fourth and the fourth to the fifth, and thus one after another until we added the tenth to the eleventh, namely the 144 to the 233, and we had the above-written sum of rabbits, namely 377 and thus you can in order find it for an unending number of months."

The chart below summarizes this calculation.

Month	Pairs	Number of pairs of adults (A)	Number of pairs of babies (B)	Total pairs
January 1	A	1	0	1
February 1	A B	1	1	2
March 1	A B A	2	1	3
April 1	A B A A B	3	2	5
May 1	A B A A B A B A	5	3	8
June 1	A B A B A B A A B A A B	8	5	13
July 1		13	8	21
August 1		21	13	34
September 1		34	21	55
October 1		55	34	89
November 1		89	55	144
December 1		144	89	233
January 1		233	144	377

The number of pairs of mature rabbits living each month determines the Fibonacci sequence (column 1): 1, 1, 2, 3, 5, 8, 13, 21, 34, 55, 89, 144, 233, 377, . . .

Nature is full of examples of the Fibonacci sequence. Flowers of every sort have petals in the count of 5, 8, and even the popular "she loves me, she loves me not" daisy usually sports 34 petals (Figure 1.3). Knowing that even number, you should always begin with the situation you do ***not*** want to end with. Only an odd number of petals, such as 33 or 35, will produce the situation you start with. The spiral of a seashell is the shape of a spiral formed by the Fibonacci numbers (Figure 1.4).

A closely aligned integer sequence was introduced by Eduardo Lucas (1842–1891). His sequence began with the numbers 1, 3 instead of 1, 1, which is the beginning of the Fibonacci numbers. Therefore, given $L_1 = 1$, $L_2 = 3$, using the "familiar" rule $L_{n+2} = L_n + L_{n+1}$, the sequence of Lucas numbers would be 1, 3, 4, 7, 11, 18, 29, 47, . . .

The Lucas numbers are related to the Fibonacci numbers by several identities, one of which appears below:

$$L_n = F_{n-1} + F_{n+1} = F_n + 2F_{n-1}$$

Mathematicians worldwide are still fascinated by the Fibonacci number sequence and continue to do research work on the sequence and related mathematics, producing university-level articles that are reviewed and published by *the Fibonacci Quarterly*, the official publication of the Fibonacci Association. *The Fibonacci Quarterly* is a scientific journal that has been publishing articles since 1963. Research articles as well as those presenting and solving elementary and advanced problems in related fields dealing with

Figure 1.3

Source: Wikimedia Commons

Figure 1.4

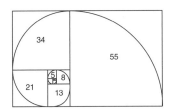

Source: Chris 73/Wikimedia

Lucas numbers, primes, the golden ratio, graph coloring, the Pythagorean triples, and topics in advanced mathematics, music, computers, and art are submitted to the journal editorial staff for distribution to interested readers.

8. WHAT IS THE GOLDEN RATIO?[2]

Students may be familiar with the golden rectangle and the architectural beauty of the ratio of its sides. Extending these wonders, have the students take the ratio of any pair of consecutive Fibonacci numbers and consider their value. As the students use the larger Fibonacci numbers to calculate the ratio, they will find themselves getting closer and closer to the "ideal" ratio found in the length/width ratio of the golden rectangle, which is known as the *golden ratio*.

Ratio of Consecutive Fibonacci Numbers	Value of Ratio
$\frac{5}{3}$	1.66667
$\frac{8}{5}$	1.60000
$\frac{13}{8}$	1.62500
$\frac{21}{13}$	1.61538
$\frac{34}{21}$	1.619048
$\frac{233}{144}$	1.618056
$\frac{987}{610}$	1.618033
$\frac{f_{n+1}}{f_n}$	1.61803398874989484820458868 . . .

Furthermore, the Fibonacci numbers can be used as square blocks to build a close approximation of a golden rectangle, which is shown in Figure 1.5.

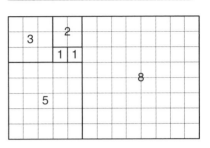

Figure 1.5

When we talk about the beauty of mathematics, we tend to think of the most beautiful rectangle. This is the golden rectangle, which has been shown by psychologists to be the most esthetically pleasing rectangle. We will now consider this golden ratio from the algebraic point of view.

Begin by having students recall the golden ratio: $\dfrac{1-x}{x} = \dfrac{x}{1}$.

This gives us $x^2 + x - 1 = 0$, and $x = \dfrac{\sqrt{5}-1}{2}$.

We let $\dfrac{\sqrt{5}-1}{2} = \dfrac{1}{\phi}$.

Not only does $\phi \cdot \dfrac{1}{\phi} = 1$ (obviously!), but $\phi - \dfrac{1}{\phi} = 1$.

This is the only number for which this is true.

Your students may want to verify this.[3]

By the way, students may want to know what value ϕ has. They can easily determine it with the help of a calculator:

$$\phi = 1.6160339887498948482045868343656381177203091798 0576\ldots$$

and $\dfrac{1}{\phi} = .6160339887498948482045868343656381177203091798 0576\ldots$

There are many other interesting features of ϕ. Your students ought to be guided to develop some after you give them the proper hints. They might want to show that this infinite continued fraction has the value ϕ.

$$\phi = 1 + \cfrac{1}{1 + \cfrac{1}{1 + \cfrac{1}{1 + \cfrac{1}{1 + \cfrac{1}{1 + \cfrac{1}{1 + \cfrac{1}{1 + \cdots}}}}}}}$$

To do this, students ought to realize that nothing is lost by truncating the continued fraction at the first numerator. This will give them the following:

$$\phi = 1 + \frac{1}{\phi}, \text{ which yields the golden ratio.}$$

Another curious relationship is

$$\phi = \sqrt{1+\sqrt{1+\sqrt{1+\sqrt{1+\sqrt{1+\sqrt{1+\sqrt{1+\sqrt{1+\cdots}}}}}}}}$$

Each of these is easily verifiable and can be done with a similar technique. We shall do the second one here and leave the first one to be justified by your students.

$$x = \sqrt{1+\sqrt{1+\sqrt{1+\sqrt{1+\sqrt{1+\sqrt{1+\sqrt{1+\sqrt{1+\cdots}}}}}}}}$$

$$x^2 = 1+\sqrt{1+\sqrt{1+\sqrt{1+\sqrt{1+\sqrt{1+\sqrt{1+\sqrt{1+\cdots}}}}}}}$$

$$x^2 = 1 + x$$

$x = \phi$ from the definition of ϕ.

It is fascinating to observe what happens when we find the powers of ϕ.

$$\phi^2 = \left(\frac{\sqrt{5}+1}{2}\right)^2 = \frac{\sqrt{5}+3}{2} = \frac{\sqrt{5}+1}{2} + 1 = \phi + 1$$

$$\phi^3 = \phi \cdot \phi^2 = \phi(\phi+1) = \phi^2 + \phi = (\phi+1) + \phi = 2\phi + 1$$

$$\phi^4 = \phi^2 \cdot \phi^2 = (\phi+1)(\phi+1) = \phi^2 + 2\phi + 1 = (\phi+1) + 2\phi + 1 = 3\phi + 2$$

$$\phi^5 = \phi^3 \cdot \phi^2 = (2\phi+1)(\phi+1) = 2\phi^2 + 3\phi + 1 = 2(\phi+1) + 3\phi + 1 = 5\phi + 3$$

$$\phi^6 = \phi^3 \cdot \phi^3 = (2\phi+1)(2\phi+1) = 4\phi^2 + 4\phi + 1 = 4(\phi+1) + 4\phi + 1 = 8\phi + 5$$

$$\phi^7 = \phi^4 \cdot \phi^3 = (3\phi+2)(2\phi+1) = 6\phi^2 + 7\phi + 2 = 6(\phi+1) + 7\phi + 2 = 13\phi + 8$$

and so on.

A summary chart reveals a pattern among the coefficients of ϕ.

$$\phi^2 = \phi + 1$$
$$\phi^3 = 2\phi + 1$$
$$\phi^4 = 3\phi + 2$$
$$\phi^5 = 5\phi + 3$$
$$\phi^6 = 8\phi + 5$$
$$\phi^7 = 13\phi + 8$$

These are the Fibonacci numbers (see page 14).

By this time, your students are probably thinking that there is no end to the connections that one can draw to the golden ratio. Indeed, they are correct!

9. IS THERE A SMALLEST NUMBER, AND IS THERE A LARGEST NUMBER?

Before we can find the smallest or largest natural number, we have to define what we mean by natural number. Here we have two opinions. Some mathematicians define $\mathbb{N}$, the set of natural numbers, as the set of nonnegative integers, while others call only the positive integers the natural numbers. If we take the first definition, then $\mathbb{N} = \{0, 1, 2, 3, \ldots\}$ and the smallest natural number is zero. If we take the second definition, then $\mathbb{N} = \{1, 2, 3, 4, \ldots\}$ and the smallest natural number is one. In either case, there is a definite number we can identify as the smallest in the set of natural numbers.

If we now look for the largest number in the set $\mathbb{N}$, using either definition, we see that no matter what natural number we pick, there will always be a larger one as the members of the natural numbers differ from each other by one; thus, it is easy to create "the next natural number." So if you say that "n" is the largest, one can counter that by creating the natural number "$n + 1$" and $n + 1 > n$, and we now have found a number that is definitely bigger than n. Therefore, there is no largest natural number. When this happens, we say that the set goes on forever or that its members increase without bound. When considering a largest value in sets that have this concept of *unboundedness*, we note a largest value by the symbol $+\infty$, which is translated as *positive infinity* and means that the set has no identifiable value as the largest, as the members of the set continue to grow in a positive direction. Think of standing on the natural number line and looking toward the right where the "horizon" lies. Looking toward the horizon, you begin to walk in that direction while focused on reaching the horizon. But you never actually get there since the horizon continues to stretch to the right, beyond where you are.

It would be the same as we turn our attention to the set of positive real numbers, $\mathbb{R}^{positive}$, and look for a largest member. We see that the set $\mathbb{R}^{positive}$, as with the set $\mathbb{N}$, grows without an upper bound, and for every real number, there will always be a larger one. We say the upper limit of $\mathbb{R}^{positive}$ is also $+\infty$, which implies that the positive real numbers increase without bound.

Continuing, we look in the other direction to see if the set of positive real numbers, $\mathbb{R}^{positive}$, has a smallest member, and we meet the concept of *boundedness*. Before we begin our search, consider this task: You are standing about 20 feet from the door. The door is point "0" and you must move toward that door by halving your distance from it in each move. Your first move brings you to 10 feet from the door, then 5 feet, then 2.5 feet, then 1.25 feet, and now you are close. Your next move brings you to .625 feet (almost $7\frac{1}{2}$ inches) from the door, and then you are .3125 feet (less than 4 inches) from the door. Watch out that you do not bump your nose as you move this close to the "zero" point! In theory, you get closer and closer to that door but you never really will be at the exact zero place—the door.

We can now form an analogy with the positive real numbers. The set, $\mathbb{R}^{positive}$, has a lower bound of zero that is *not* a member of this set since zero is in a class by itself and is neither positive nor negative. The positive numbers begin to the right of the zero point. As we find smaller and smaller positive real numbers, we are moving closer toward zero. We can always get a bit closer by halving the smallest real number we have, but we will never hit the zero. So there is no smallest positive real number.

Moving on, let us consider the smallest number in the set of all the real numbers, $\mathbb{R}$, which would include all the negative numbers and zero, along with all the positive numbers. As the positive real numbers increase without bound, the negative real numbers decrease without bound. Taking all the real numbers into consideration, for every real number, you can find one less than it by just subtracting any positive amount from it. So if one claims that x is the smallest real number, you can offer $x - .001$ as smaller: $x - .001 < x$. Likewise, looking for the largest real number, if one claims that y is the largest, then you can offer $y + .001$ as a larger number. So the set of real numbers, $\mathbb{R}$, increases and decreases without bounds and ranges from "that horizon off to the left" known as negative infinity, $-\infty$, to "that horizon off to the right" known as positive infinity, $+\infty$. In interval notation, we write that $\mathbb{R} = (-\infty, +\infty)$. This is an "open" interval, meaning the $+\infty$ and the $-\infty$ represent the concept of the set of real values, having no bounds in either direction and having no smallest and no greatest real number.

10. WHY IS INFINITY NOT A NUMBER?

This problem arises in calculus, where the symbol ∞ (infinity) appears in the description of certain limits. Compare, for example, the two equations:

$$\lim_{x \to 0} \frac{1}{x^2} = \infty$$

and

$$\lim_{x \to 1} \frac{1}{x^2} = 1$$

The first equation means that as x approaches 0, the value $\frac{1}{x^2}$ increases without bound. And this is written in the same way as a regular limit, for which the second equation is an example. This shows that the symbol ∞ sometimes appears in places where one usually finds quite ordinary numbers. This naturally creates the (wrong) idea that the symbol ∞ can be treated like any other number.

The symbol ∞ is a mathematical concept that is related to numbers, but it is not a number itself, neither a natural number nor a real number, and not even a complex number. In some mathematical contexts, various types of infinite objects are still called "numbers." For example, there are Cantor's transfinite cardinal numbers, or the set of hyperreal numbers of nonstandard analysis, which contains infinite numbers as well as their inverses, the infinitesimal numbers. These objects, however, differ very much from usual numbers (and even from the symbol ∞, as used in calculus), and we will not discuss them here. Hence, it is best to state it clearly and to repeat it often: ∞ is not a number.

One introduces the symbol infinity mainly to have a convenient way of writing infinite limits. In calculus, the main use of ∞ is to describe the behavior or trend of sequences or of functions. Actually, in real calculus, one needs two such symbols, and they are called $+\infty$ and $-\infty$ (positive infinity and negative infinity). If these two symbols are added to the set of real numbers, one frequently calls this new set the (affinely) extended real numbers, and this set is sometimes written with a bar:

$$\overline{\mathbb{R}} = \mathbb{R} \cup \{-\infty, \infty\}$$

One defines $+\infty$ as something bigger than any real number and $-\infty$ as something less than any (negative) real number, so one has the ordering relation

$$-\infty < a < +\infty \text{ for all } a \text{ in } \mathbb{R}.$$

Still, $\pm\infty$ are not real numbers because they fail to obey many basic rules of arithmetic. Special rules apply when using these symbols, and these rules have their natural origin in the mathematical results and theorems for the limits of combined sequences.

We have, for example,

$$\infty + a = a + \infty = \infty, \qquad \text{for every } a \text{ with } -\infty < a \le \infty,$$
$$a - \infty = -\infty, \qquad \text{for every } a \text{ with } -\infty \le a < \infty,$$
$$a \cdot \infty = \infty, \qquad \text{for every } a \text{ with } 0 < a \le \infty,$$
$$a \cdot \infty = -\infty, \qquad \text{for every } a \text{ with } -\infty \le a < 0, \text{ and}$$
$$\frac{a}{\infty} = 0, \qquad \text{for every } a \text{ with } -\infty < a < \infty.$$

The relation with limits is the following: Consider, for example, a sequence (a_n) with limit a, and a second sequence (b_n), which diverges toward $+\infty$. Then you can form the sum $(a_n + b_n)$ of the two sequences (by adding them elementwise), and you will get another sequence that diverges toward $+\infty$. Thus, we can write

$$\infty = \lim_{n \to \infty} (a_n + b_n) = \lim_{n \to \infty} (a_n) + \lim_{n \to \infty} (b_n) = a + \infty.$$

This remains true even if $a = +\infty$. And this is our first rule from the list above.

When dealing with the extended real numbers, you are allowed to form the expression $\infty + \infty$ (which again gives ∞), but you are not allowed to form $\infty - \infty$. And the reason is clearly the following: Given two sequences, each going to $+\infty$, one cannot tell in advance what the limit of their difference would be. Anything could happen: $(a_n + b_n)$ could converge to some real number, or it could diverge to $\pm\infty$, or it might happen that the limit does not exist at all. Consider, for example, $a_n = n$ and $b_n = \frac{n}{2}$. Then $a_n - b_n = \frac{n}{2}$ again goes to $+\infty$. In this case, $\infty - \infty$ would be ∞. Choose instead $b_n = 2n$ to obtain $a_n - b_n = -n$, which goes to $-\infty$. In this case, $\infty - \infty$ would be $-\infty$. Choose $b_n = a_n$ to obtain 0 as the difference, and $\infty - \infty$ would be 0. Or take (b_n) to be the sequence $(1, 1, 3, 3, 5, 5, \dots)$ to obtain the sequence $(a_n - b_n) = (0, 1, 0, 1, 0, 1, \dots)$, which has two accumulation points and hence the limit does not exist at all. Hence, one cannot set up a general rule for $\infty - \infty$, because the result depends on the chosen sequences. There is no consistent way to associate an element of the extended real number set with the expression $\infty - \infty$. In general, this expression is just meaningless.

In the same sense, it is impossible to associate a unique meaning to $\frac{\infty}{\infty}$, or to $0 \cdot \infty$ (let your students explain why this is the case), or to $\frac{a}{0}$. For the last expression, you need to divide a by a sequence b_n with limit 0. But when b_n goes to zero, $\frac{a}{b_n}$ could go to $+\infty$, if $b_n > 0$, or to $-\infty$, if $b_n < 0$, or not exist at all if b_n alternates. Therefore, the expression $\frac{a}{0}$ must remain undefined. Mathematicians call expressions like this "indeterminate forms." In some cases, they can be thought of as having a certain value, while in other cases, as having another value or none at all.

11. HOW LARGE IS INFINITY?

The first real opportunity where even young children can experience a "sense of wonder" in a mathematical context is when they make the basic observation that counting never ends. Typically, children are fascinated by very large numbers, and so was the 9-year-old Milton Sirotta, who became famous for inventing the name googol for the number 10^{100} in 1920. Later on, his uncle, the mathematician Edward Kasner (1878–1955), wrote about this in a book *Mathematics and the Imagination,* and still later, other imaginative young fellows named their company Google after the number googol to indicate the large amount of data handled by Internet search engines.

Although the number googol is already unimaginably large, we can easily think of even larger numbers, for example, googol + 1 or 10^{googol} (which has been called googolplex), or even the factorial of googol, or googol^{googol}. The process of generating larger numbers from any given number obviously has no end. Therefore, the set of integers certainly cannot be finite. If it were, then there would be a largest number, which is impossible, because for any given number we can immediately find a bigger one just by adding 1. Therefore, the sequence of natural numbers has no end and we say that it goes to infinity, because anything that has no end or grows without limit is referred to as infinite. Thus, infinity is not a number in the usual sense—it is rather an idea or concept. And thinking about infinity is one of the most intriguing aspects of mathematics.

Already in Greek philosophy, Aristotle (384 BC–322 BC) distinguished between potential infinity and actual infinity. The process of generating larger and larger integers is an example leading to potential infinity. Potential infinity refers to an endless procedure, like counting, that can be continued indefinitely. No matter how far you go, you can still go further. This is the type of infinity encountered in calculus, when one deals with limits of sequences. We say that a sequence (α_n) goes to *infinity*, which we write symbolically as $\lim_{n \to \infty} \alpha_n = \infty$, if the sequence grows without bounds. The precise definition is the following: Whenever we assume a bound M, no matter how large, we can always find an index n_0 so that starting with this index, all the remaining a_n are bigger than M. It is important to notice that this definition only mentions finite numbers M and n_0 and refers to a procedure that can be repeated in the same way when M is made larger and larger. This is characteristic of potential infinity—it always refers to finite quantities, which, however, may be arbitrarily large.

In contrast, actual infinity (or completed infinity) refers to mathematical situations where infinity is actually achieved. This notion has been rejected by Aristotle and other mathematicians until modern times, where, for example, Carl Friedrich Gauss (1777–1855) vehemently protested against the usage of infinity in the sense of a completed quantity. But when Georg Cantor (1845–1918) invented set theory, he also felt the need to deal with actual infinities. In set theory, actual infinity is just the number of elements (the cardinality) of infinite sets, and an infinite set can simply be defined as one that is not finite. For example, the set of all natural numbers is considered as a single, well-defined mathematical object that is given once and for all and does not change any more. It is an infinite set as has been shown before. Here infinity has been reached, as it refers to a property of a completely well-defined set. Cantor introduced the symbol $\aleph_0$ (aleph-null) to describe the (infinite) cardinality of the set of all natural numbers, and he was even able to distinguish among different types of infinity. In this context, the cardinality $\aleph_0$ of the integers is also called "countable infinity."

Actual infinity may lead to statements that appear paradoxical at first sight. Two sets are said to have the same cardinality when there exists a one-to-one mapping (a bijection) between them. For infinite sets, this notion leads to some quite amazing and unexpected results: An infinite set A will have a proper subset B that has the same cardinality as the set A. For example, the set of square integers $\{0, 1, 4, 9, 16, 25, \ldots\}$ has the same cardinality as the set $\mathbb{N} = \{0, 1, 2, 3, 4, 5, \ldots\}$ of all nonnegative integers (because there is a one-to-one correspondence between nonnegative integers and their squares, $n \leftrightarrow n^2$). Indeed, Cantor (and before him Dedekind) used this property to give an alternative definition of infinite sets: An infinite set is one that has the same cardinality as one of its proper subsets.

Another strange result is that an infinite set A has the same cardinality as the Cartesian product $A \times A = \{(x, y) | x, y \in A\}$. An example of a one-to-one mapping between $\mathbb{N} \times \mathbb{N}$ and $\mathbb{N}$ is $(n, m) \leftrightarrow 2^n(2m+1)$, because every natural number can be written in a unique way as a product of a power of two and an odd number. Similarly, the one-dimensional line $\mathbb{R}$ contains the same number of elements as the two-dimensional plane $\mathbb{R}^2 = \mathbb{R} \times \mathbb{R}$. Of course, this could not happen with a finite set.

The counterintuitive aspects of (countable) infinite sets are paraphrased in the story of Hilbert's hotel: In a world inhabited by infinitely many people, in one of its infinitely many cities there is a hotel called Hilbert's Grand

Hotel after the famous mathematician David Hilbert (1862–1943). Hilbert's Grand Hotel has infinitely many rooms (consecutively numbered as 1, 2, 3, . . .). All rooms are occupied when a new guest arrives. The manager now has a simple idea that enables him to accommodate the new guest in the hotel. He moves the guest occupying room 1 to room 2, the guest occupying room 2 to room 3, and so on. This will leave room 1 empty for the newcomer. (Do not try to imagine the noise in the lobby, when infinitely many guests complain that they have to change room because of a single newcomer.) Actually, if the manager had told everybody to move from the room with number n to the room with number $2n$, this would even have emptied infinitely many rooms (all those with odd room numbers) and still no one would be without accommodation.

It should be noted that actual infinity is still a mathematical concept and the word actual does not imply that anything infinite exists in the real world. Although infinity is used as a mathematical concept in theoretical physics, physicists generally believe that nothing in the physical world can be infinite. For example, the number of protons in the whole universe is estimated at about 10^{80}, which is much less than a googol. On philosophical grounds, one might even argue that enormously big numbers do not exist at all except as a mathematical idea. Except for those special numbers for which we have an explicit algorithm or notation (like, for example, 10^{googol}), there is no way to write an arbitrary number that has googol decimal digits. The whole universe would not provide sufficient space, time, and material to do that, not even if we place a digit on every single elementary particle of all the galaxies in the universe. One could not represent this number in any way or compare it with others or do any computation with it. In short, there is nothing in reality that corresponds to such a number. And in mathematics, even these large numbers are infinitely tiny against infinity.

12. IS THERE ANYTHING LARGER THAN INFINITY?

The mathematical concept of infinity is tricky, but interesting. In calculus, the symbol ∞ is defined as something that is bigger than any real number, hence we have $a < \infty$ for all real numbers a. In that sense, no number is larger than infinity. But wait, mathematics is full of surprises!

In number theory, we encounter the concept of infinity as the number of elements, or cardinality, of an infinite set. An example of an infinite set is the set of all natural numbers, $\mathbb{N} = \{1, 2, 3, \ldots\}$, whose cardinality is denoted by $\aleph_0$ (pronounced "aleph-null," where aleph is the first letter in the Hebrew alphabet). In fact, most of the sets that are of interest in mathematics are infinite: the set of rational numbers, the set of real numbers, the set of points in a plane, and so on.

It is quite natural to ask if all these infinities are the same size. The answer is "no." It turns out that some infinities are bigger than others! But this is not at all easy to see.

Actually, many infinite sets have the same cardinality as the natural numbers although they appear to be much larger. For example, it turns out that the set $\mathbb{Z} = \{0, \pm1, \pm2, \pm3, \ldots\}$ of all integers has exactly the same size (cardinality) as the set $\mathbb{N} = \{1, 2, 3, \ldots\}$ of positive integers. This is quite surprising, because, after all, the set of positive integers is a proper subset of the set of all integers. So, what exactly do we mean by saying that two sets have the same size?

In mathematics, we say that two sets have the same cardinality if we can find a one-to-one correspondence between these sets. A one-to-one correspondence pairs every element of the first set with precisely one element of the second set, and vice versa. Let us illustrate this with the set of integers. Here the arrows indicate a possible pairing between natural numbers and integers:

$$
\begin{array}{ccccccccccccc}
\mathbb{N}: & 1 & 2 & 3 & 4 & 5 & 6 & 7 & 8 & 9 & 10 & 11 \ldots \\
& \downarrow & \downarrow & \downarrow & \downarrow & \downarrow & \downarrow & \downarrow & \downarrow & \downarrow & \downarrow & \downarrow \ldots \\
\mathbb{Z}: & 0 & 1 & -1 & 2 & -2 & 3 & -3 & 4 & -4 & 5 & -5 \ldots
\end{array}
$$

Obviously, in that way, every element of $\mathbb{Z}$ can be associated (or "counted") with a natural number, and none is left out. Counting all elements of the infinite set actually puts these elements in an ordered list (a sequence):

$$0 \to 1 \to -1 \to 2 \to -2 \to 3 \to -3 \to 4 \to -4 \to \ldots$$

Setting up a one-to-one correspondence of a given set with the natural numbers (or a subset thereof) thus amounts to counting the elements of that set. Any set that has the same cardinality as the set of natural numbers is therefore called countable. The set of integers is countable in that sense.

Here we show that the rational numbers too can be counted. We show this for the positive rational numbers by putting them into a two-dimensional array as follows:

$$
\begin{array}{cccccc}
1/1 \to 1/2 & 1/3 \to 1/4 & 1/5 \to 1/6 & \ldots \\
\swarrow \quad \nearrow & \swarrow \quad \nearrow & \swarrow \quad \nearrow \\
2/1 \quad 2/2 & 2/3 \quad 2/4 & 2/5 \quad 2/6 & \ldots \\
\downarrow \nearrow \quad \swarrow & \nearrow \quad \swarrow & \nearrow \\
3/1 \quad 3/2 & 3/3 \quad 3/4 & 3/5 \quad 3/6 & \ldots \\
\swarrow \quad \nearrow & \swarrow \quad \nearrow \\
4/1 \quad 4/2 & 4/3 \quad 4/4 & 4/5 \quad 4/6 & \ldots \\
\downarrow \nearrow \quad \swarrow & \nearrow \\
5/1 \quad 5/2 & 5/3 \quad 5/4 & 5/5 \quad 5/6 & \ldots \\
\swarrow \quad \nearrow \\
\ldots \quad \ldots
\end{array}
$$

The arrows in this diagram indicate how we can put the rational numbers into an ordered list. Just follow the arrows as you count:

$$\frac{1}{1} \to \frac{1}{2} \to \frac{2}{1} \to \frac{3}{1} \to \frac{1}{4} \to \frac{2}{3}$$

$$\to \frac{3}{2} \to \frac{4}{1} \to \frac{5}{1} \to \frac{5}{1} \to \dots$$

Sometimes you find a number (such as $\frac{2}{2} = 1$, or $\frac{4}{2} = \frac{2}{1}$, etc.) that you have already counted and that you can simply omit. In that way, every positive rational number will be paired with a natural number. No rational number is left out, and all natural numbers get used. This proves that the set of all positive rational numbers has the same cardinality as the set of natural numbers.

The examples above show that it is far from trivial to prove that there are sets that are not countable. The cardinality of such a set would be larger than $\aleph_0$, the cardinality of the natural numbers. It was Georg Cantor, the founder of set theory, who gave an ingenious proof for the fact that the set of real numbers is uncountable. This proof shows that any listing of real numbers (i.e., any attempt to establish a one-to-one correspondence with natural numbers) is incomplete.

Any attempt to count the real numbers between 0 and 1 would put these numbers into an ordered list, as explained above. The list would certainly be infinitely long, and in decimal notation, most numbers would contain infinitely many nonzero digits. The list could begin, for example, as follows:

$1 \to 0.35$

$2 \to 0.1$

$3 \to 0.14159. \dots (= \pi - 3)$

$4 \to 0.61803. \dots$ (golden ratio)

$5 \to 0.41215$

$6 \to 0.999999 \dots (= 1)$

The new number, which will not be in that list, is constructed in the following way. The digit before the decimal point will be zero to guarantee that the number is between 0 and 1. For its first decimal place, we choose any digit that is different from the corresponding digit of the first number in the list. This digit is 3, so we may choose, for example, 4 as the first decimal digit of our new number. This ensures that the new number is different from the first number in our list. For the second decimal place, we choose a digit that is different from the digit on the second decimal place of the second number in the list (the second number in the list is 0.1, and the digit on the second decimal place is 0). We may choose the number 1 (or anything else that is different from 0), so that our new number starts with 0.41..., and hence it is different from the first two numbers of the given list. If we continue to construct our new number in that way, with the nth digit being different from the nth digit of the nth number in the list, we obtain a number that is certainly different from all numbers in the given list. In our example, the new number could begin with, say, 0.412160..., but it is clear that, actually, an awful lot of numbers are not in the given list, because we can choose among nine different digits for each decimal place. This holds for every conceivable listing of real numbers. Hence, none of these listings would be complete. Consequently, there is no one-to-one correspondence between natural numbers and the real numbers in the interval [0,1].

Thus, there are certainly more real numbers than one can count by natural numbers. Cantor denoted the cardinality of real numbers by $\aleph_1$, and this type of infinity is certainly larger than $\aleph_0$. The big question now was whether there exists any set that has a cardinality strictly in between $\aleph_0$ and $\aleph_1$. Cantor conjectured that there is no such set, and this assumption has become widely known as the "continuum hypothesis" (the name referring to the "continuum" of real numbers). Cantor tried for many years to prove it, without success. In the following, the continuum hypothesis became the first problem of David Hilbert's famous list of important open questions in mathematics. Meanwhile, it has been shown by Kurt Gödel and Paul Cohen that it can be neither proved nor disproved, as it is independent from the other axioms of formal set theory. Questions surrounding the continuum hypothesis are still an important topic of contemporary research.

In simpler terms, if you want to create a set larger than a given infinite set, then the set of all subsets of the given infinite set would be a larger infinite set.

13. CAN THE UNION OF TWO SETS EVER BE EQUAL TO THE INTERSECTION OF THE TWO SETS?

Let us start by exploring the vocabulary of this question. We find the notions of "sets" and "unions" and "intersections."

Sets are collections of objects, defined in a way that it is known which elements belong to the set and which elements do not belong to the set. Sets can be described verbally or by using curly brackets. For example, the set of all positive even numbers can be written as {2, 4, 6, 8, ... }.

The *union* of two sets can be described as the collection of all elements from both sets and uses the notation $\cup$. Here are some examples of the union of two sets:

A	B	A$\cup$B
{!, @, $}	{q, r, s}	{!, @, $, q, r, s}
{0, 1, 2, 3, . . . }	{ . . . , −3, −2, −1, 0}	{ . . . , −3, −2, −1, 0, 1, 2, 3, . . . }
{2, 4, 6, 8}	{1, 2, 3, 4}	{1, 2, 3, 4, 6, 8}
{vowels}	{consonants}	{all letters of the alphabet}

The *intersection* of two sets is the set of all elements that both sets have in common. The notation for the intersection is $\cap$. Using the same sets, we can find the intersections:

A	B	A$\cap$B
{!, @, $}	{q, r, s}	Ø
{0, 1, 2, 3, . . . }	{ . . . , −3, −2, −1, 0}	{0}
{2, 4, 6, 8}	{1, 2, 3, 4}	{2, 4}
{vowels}	{consonants}	Y

Now, to answer the question at hand, we need to find a set A and a set B for which the union and the intersection are the same. By glancing at the above sets, we notice that none of the unions match the intersections.

At second glance, we notice there are elements that show in both tables. For example, 0 in the second row as well as 2 and 4 in the third row are found in both the union and the intersection. Is there a pattern that we can find? Well, these elements are found in both set A and set B of their respective rows. It would seem that for the union of two sets to be equal to the intersection, all elements must be in both sets, or the sets would have to be exactly the same. And this is, indeed, the case: For two sets A and B, we have

$$A\cup B = A \cap B \text{ if and only if } A = B.$$

14. HOW CAN WE DETERMINE HOW MANY SUBSETS A GIVEN SET HAS?

This question poses a great opportunity for students to investigate through an inquiry process and create a conjecture about what they think happens. Compared with the origins of mathematics, which date to the dawn of humankind, set theory is a rather recent topic in mathematics. Georg Cantor

(1845–1918) developed rules and ideas for working with sets but was not looked upon favorably by the public for his work. He suffered a great deal of trauma from what he called attacks from mathematicians who did not agree with his assertions involving set theory, and he passed away in a mental hospital at the age of 72.

We can begin by understanding what a set is and what a subset is. A set is a collection of items. The items in the set are called elements or members. The word is akin to the colloquial word "set" that we use to describe collections, such as a set of baseball cards or a set of tires. Braces {} are used to enclose the list of elements in a set, which are not to be interchanged with other symbols such as [ ] or ( ) or | |, each of which carries a different meaning in mathematics.

A subset can be created by any combination of the elements in a set. More formally, given any two sets A and B, if every element in A is also in B, then A is a subset of B. All sets have at least two subsets, namely the empty set and the set itself (unless those two sets are actually the same set).

Students can start with a set of any number of elements, and we will begin with the smallest set possible, or the empty set. The empty set is notated as Ø or {}.

Set	Subsets	Number of Subsets
{}	Ø	1
{1}	Ø {1}	2
{a, b}	Ø {a} {b} {a, b}	4
{☼, ♠, ❁}	Ø {☼} {♠} {❁} {☼, ♠}{☼, ❁}{♠, ❁} {☼, ♠, ❁}	8
{\$, #, %, &}	Ø {\$} {#} {%}{&} {\$, #} {\$, %} {\$, &} {#,%} {#, &} {%, &} {\$, #, %} {\$, #, &} {\$, %, &} {#, %, &} {\$, #, %, &}	16

The following chart summarizes the above one.

Number of Elements	Number of Subsets	
0	1	2^0
1	2	2^1
2	4	2^2
3	8	2^3
4	16	2^4

Let us see if there is a pattern here. The empty set has 1 subset. A set with 1 element has 2 subsets, and so on as you can see. In reviewing the pattern, we now determine that the number of subsets in a set with n elements is 2 to the power that is the number of elements in the set: 2^n.

By the way, the set of all subsets of a given set A is denoted by P(A) and is called the power set of A.

15. HOW CAN WE AVOID MAKING AN ERROR IN A "PROOF" THAT LEADS TO A GENERALIZATION?

The following proof should cause students some discomfort, since we begin with a true statement and end up with a ridiculous result. The question is how can this be avoided, and where is the mistake?

We begin by accepting the fact that $\sqrt[3]{3} > \sqrt[2]{2}$ is true. (That is, 1.4422 > 1.4142.)

Raising both sides of $\sqrt[3]{3} > \sqrt[2]{2}$ to the sixth power $\left(\sqrt[3]{3}\right)^6 > \left(\sqrt[2]{2}\right)^6$ and then writing the radical expression with a fractional exponent, we get $\left(3^{\frac{1}{3}}\right)^6 > \left(2^{\frac{1}{2}}\right)^6$.

Now simplifying gives us $3^{\frac{6}{3}} > 2^{\frac{6}{2}}$, which is $3^2 > 2^3$, and simplifying we get a sensible result, namely, $9 > 8$.

At this point, we actually haven't proven anything; however, if we work backwards we can substantiate that this is correct, since using a calculator we would find that $\sqrt[3]{3} \approx 1.442249570 > 1.414213562 \approx \sqrt[2]{2}$, which we actually knew from the start.

The temptation here is to generalize the pattern and form some sort of conclusion. This is where the danger begins. This time, let us consider the following question: Which is larger, $\sqrt[5]{5}$ or $\sqrt[4]{4}$?

Using our above result, we would speculate that $\sqrt[5]{5} > \sqrt[4]{4}$. However, using the procedure we used before, we would take each side of the inequality $\sqrt[5]{5} > \sqrt[4]{4}$ to the 20th power to get $\left(\sqrt[5]{5}\right)^{20} > \left(\sqrt[4]{4}\right)^{20}$, and then as before change the radical to fraction form for convenience so that we have $\left(5^{\frac{1}{5}}\right)^{20} > \left(4^{\frac{1}{4}}\right)^{20}$.

This gives us $5^{\frac{20}{5}} > 4^{\frac{20}{4}}$, which is then $5^4 > 4^5$. The result is a surprising $625 \ngtr 1024$.

So we see that by generalizing a pattern, we need not necessarily have established one if our conjecture was wrong.

Another example where a check is necessary is the following:

Consider the inequality $\sqrt{x^2 - 3} < x$ (in **R**, the set of real numbers).

To prove this inequality, one might have the idea to square both sides to get $x^2 - 3 < x^2$, and then by adding $-x^2 + 3$ to both sides of the inequality we get $0 < 3$, which is true. Left alone, this would appear to prove that the given inequality is correct for all real numbers x. However, upon further analysis, there is a mistake here in applying a squaring procedure to the inequality, because $a^2 < b^2$ does not imply that $a < b$ (unless a and b are both positive).

Let us take a closer look. If $|x| < \sqrt{3}$, we then have $x^2 < 3$, we have $|x| < \sqrt{3}$, and the expression $\sqrt{x^2 - 3}$ becomes imaginary because the radicand is now negative, and so the inequality is not defined in the real number system. When $x \leq -\sqrt{3}$, then $\sqrt{x^2 - 3} > x$. Therefore, the correct statement is that $\sqrt{x^2 - 3} < x$ is only true for real numbers x where $x \geq \sqrt{3}$.

It is always a good idea to check your proof of an inequality by working your arguments backwards.

16. HOW DOES A CALCULATOR FUNCTION?

A pocket calculator belongs to the everyday tools that are nowadays used by schoolchildren, even at a very young age. Among the handheld devices used for mathematics education, we find anything ranging from a classic pocket calculator to a multipurpose smartphone with a touch screen. These devices miraculously perform difficult computations that are very tedious or even impossible to do by hand. So the question "How does it work?" will come up inevitably, and some kind of answer will be expected, in particular, from the mathematics teacher. But even the simplest pocket calculator is a very complicated electronic device, and one cannot hope to give a comprehensive answer (particularly for a mathematics teacher who usually lacks the necessary background in engineering). Nevertheless, one could offer some enlightening bits and pieces of information. Moreover, calculators provide an excellent motivation for discussing the binary number system and elementary logic in high school.

A vintage pocket calculator has a comparatively simple structure. It consists of several well-distinguished components: A unit for input (keyboard), a unit for output (display), and a so-called processing unit inside. Pressing the keys activates electrical circuits that pass the information on to the processing unit on the calculator's main board. The processing unit is a microchip containing many electronic switches and circuits, which process the data, store the input and intermediate results, and pass the processor's output on to the liquid crystal display, where the results of the data processing gets translated back into human-readable form.

To perform computations, a microchip has to contain a very complicated network of electric circuits. But these circuits are not assembled from individual electronic components (like transistors and diodes); rather, they are printed as a whole on a piece of semiconducting material (a silicon wafer) using a technique that is called photolithography. When printed directly rather than being assembled, the electronic circuits can be made much smaller, and they consume very little power. Presently, integrated electronic circuits may contain about 9 million transistors on a single square millimeter.

Internally, calculators (like any computer) represent numbers and instructions using a so-called *binary code*. In binary code, every entry of information is translated into a sequence of zeros and ones. The reason for doing this is that binary information can be realized easily with electric circuits. In digital electronics, electric wires are always in one of two possible states: Either they carry voltage or they do not. These two states may be called "on" and "off." Switching electricity on is represented by the number "1," and switching it off is represented by the number "0." A bit is the smallest unit of information. It tells us about two alternatives, like "yes/1" or "no/0." The entry information is stored in a series of these bits. You will need a whole array of electric wires that can be switched on or off independently to store a number in the binary system: For example, using an array of four wires, we could store the number: on-on-off-on = 1101 in base $2 = 1 \times 2^3 + 1 \times 2^2 + 0 \times 2^1 + 1 \times 2^0 = 8 + 4 + 1 = 13$ in our base 10 number system.

Whatever you type into a calculator is transformed into such a sequence of on-off states of the electric circuits in a microchip inside the calculator.

To perform a computation, the digital signals representing numbers and instructions will be transmitted to a "processing unit." The processing unit then transforms the input signals internally to produce an output (i.e., it performs a computation). The output again consists of digital signals (1 or 0) that will be transmitted to other data processing circuits or to the display unit. For example, a certain unit might receive the input 10000101 and produce the output 1101. This would correspond to the binary computation 1000 + 0101 = 1101 (which means 8 + 5 = 13).

An electronic circuit performing an elementary computation is usually called a "logical gate." A logical gate can be considered a black box with several connectors. Some of these connectors are used for receiving input, and some other connectors produce output that logically depends on the received input. In practice, input as well as output consists of digital signals, that is, electric voltage (on or off) at the connectors.

When you have occasion to discuss elementary logic in your class, the remarks above should provide enough motivation to present in more detail how binary computations can be performed by logical gates. A logic gate that is able to perform binary addition of two bits is the exclusive OR (=XOR) circuit that has two input connectors and one output connector (see Figure 1.6). The output connector is turned on (i.e., it produces the output "1") whenever one and only one of its inputs is 1, and it is switched off (output "0") otherwise.

Figure 1.6

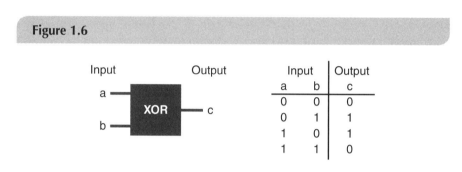

Binary addition of longer numbers has to perform an XOR operation on every bit of a binary number, and it has to take care of carrying digits over to the next place, if necessary (in a quite similar way as you are used to in ordinary addition). For every bit of the number, this is done with an "XOR and carry" gate (better known as a "1-bit adder"). It uses three bits of input (one bit from each of the numbers to be added and one "carry" bit) and produces two bits of output (one bit giving the result and one bit to be carried over to the next digit of the number). The output depends on the values of the input bits according to the following table.

Input			Output	
a	*b*	carry	*c*	carry
0	0	0	0	0
0	0	1	1	0
0	1	0	1	0
0	1	1	0	1
1	0	0	1	0
1	0	1	0	1
1	1	0	0	1
1	1	1	1	1

A series of binary adders can now be used to add two numbers with several binary digits. It is a good exercise to discuss this process with some examples. Figure 1.7 shows the addition of the two numbers 010 and 011, which results in 101 (in decimal notation, 4 + 5 = 9). Here we start at the right with the digits having the lowest value and the initial carry bit 0.

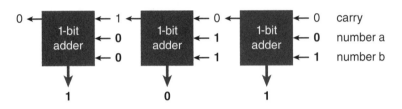

Figure 1.7 The binary addition of 010 and 011

The result of the calculation is finally sent to the display unit, where individual pixels are switched on (thus turning black) or off to form human readable numbers. Early calculators had a seven-segment display, where each digit was written lighting some or all of the seven segments (see Figure 1.8). Here, certain logic circuits take care that, for example, the number "2" (= 10 in binary representation) is displayed by activating the segments A, B, G, E, D.

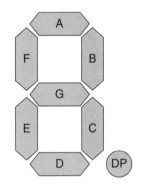

Figure 1.8

17. WHICH IS CORRECT—MY CALCULATING, THE CALCULATOR, OR THE COMPUTER?

Using a calculator can present some challenges. If you key in a number that is too large, or perhaps too small, the calculator will return the answer: "overflow," "underflow," or "error." For example, a calculator with eight places, when one inputs 12!, will return the answer as $4.7900 \cdot 10^8$. The correct answer is 479,001,600. A calculator with more decimal places to offer can also present problems when input is $20! \approx 2.4329 \cdot 10^8$. Thus, the correct answer is 20! = 2,432,902,008,176,640,000. When the calculator returns an answer of ERROR, then students become aware that there is a problem. Otherwise, students are apt to just accept what the calculator offers as an answer.

A similar problem arises when we compare two algebraically equivalent terms that yield different results on the calculator. Consider the algebraic expression $\dfrac{1}{\sqrt{a+b}-\sqrt{a}}$ and its equivalent at the end of the following series of equalities:

$$\dfrac{1}{\sqrt{a+b}-\sqrt{a}} = \dfrac{1}{\sqrt{a+b}-\sqrt{a}} \cdot \dfrac{\sqrt{a+b}+\sqrt{a}}{\sqrt{a+b}+\sqrt{a}} = \dfrac{\sqrt{a+b}+\sqrt{a}}{\left(\sqrt{a+b}\right)^2 - \left(\sqrt{a}\right)^2}$$

$$= \dfrac{\sqrt{a+b}+\sqrt{a}}{(a+b)-a} = \dfrac{\sqrt{a+b}+\sqrt{a}}{b}.$$

That is, we have the two equivalent algebraic expression: $\dfrac{1}{\sqrt{a+b}-\sqrt{a}}$ and $\dfrac{\sqrt{a+b}+\sqrt{a}}{b}$.

The table below shows the discrepancy between the two equivalent algebraic expressions.

		$\dfrac{1}{\sqrt{a+b}-\sqrt{a}}$	$\dfrac{\sqrt{a+b}+\sqrt{a}}{b}$
$a = 1{,}000$ $b = 0.001$	A calculator with eight digit places	63,**291.139**	63,**245.569**
	DERIVE 6 (20 places)	63,245.5690147519**92618**	63,245.5690147519**34636**
$a = 100$ $b = 0.01$	A calculator with eight digit places	2000.**048**	2000.**05**
	DERIVE 6 (20 places)	2000.04999875006249**68**	2000.04999875006249**60**

A calculator can also do some rather weird things. Take for example the series $a_n = \dfrac{1}{3} + \dfrac{(11-n)^9}{(9+n)^9}$.

In the table on the next page, notice what happens to the value (a_n) as n increases. At first it appears that the sequence has a limiting value of 0.333333. However, the table shows that as n increases, this is clearly not the case.

If we were to do this on a 10-place calculator, the results would be analogous. However, the results of a pseudo-convergence remain the same. In short, we must be careful about accepting calculator results as they can produce puzzling results as well.

n	a_n
0	6.41960
1	1.33333
2	0.497637
3	0.359345
4	0.337138
5	0.333821
6	0.333384
7	**0.333333**
. . .	. . .
17	**0.333333**
18	0.333328
. . .	. . .
1,000	−0.501781
1,000,000	−0.666486
100,000,000	**−0.666666**

18. WHAT ARE CONIC SECTIONS?

Students are familiar with the cone as the shape that holds one of their favorite desserts, ice cream, and also as hazard warnings and perhaps as a party hat (see Figure 1.9).

Figure 1.9

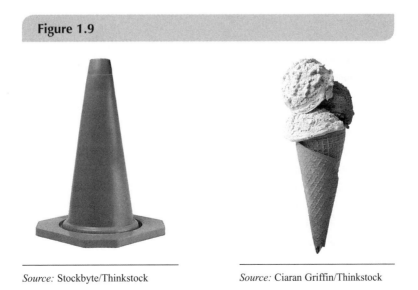

Source: Stockbyte/Thinkstock   *Source:* Ciaran Griffin/Thinkstock

Since this is a solid (three-dimensional) shape students may best appreciate the form of a right circular cone by generating one themselves. Ask them to hold their pen or pencil in the middle, and to rotate the bottom point on a sheet of paper to draw a circle on a sheet of paper. The pencil will move creating one cone below their fingers and another one above them. The "point" where fingers hold the writing instrument is called the *apex* of the shape. The two cone shapes are called *nappes* (see Figure 1.10).

The cone has a circular base and its height (vertical axis) is determined by a line drawn from its upper point, called the *apex*, falling perpendicular to a diameter of the circular base (and to its center); hence the full name of this shape is the *right circular cone*.

The conic sections are the two-dimensional nondegenerate curves or conic paths formed when a plane "cuts" through one or two nappes of a right circular cone. The four main curves formed by the plane as it cuts across one or two of the nappes are the circle, the ellipse, the parabola, and the hyperbola (see Figures 1.11–1.14).

The Circle

If the "cutting" plane is held parallel to the base (or perpendicular to the vertical axis) of the cone, the curve formed is a *circle*. The center of the circle will lie on the vertical height line of the cone, and the diameter will be determined by how far from the apex point the cut is made. The further from the apex point the parallel cut is made, the larger the diameter of the circle. This cut will be in only one nappe of the cones (see Figure 1.11). The circle is often considered a special case of the ellipse.

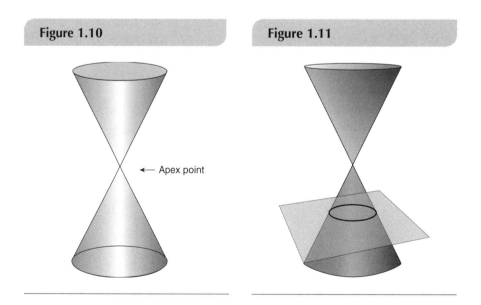

Figure 1.10

← Apex point

Figure 1.11

The Ellipse

Tilting the "cutting" plane so that it is not perpendicular to the axis of the cone, nor parallel to a straight line on the surface of the cone, and doesn't cut the upper nappe, will form the shape of an ellipse. Again, this shape is wholly contained in the single nappe (see Figure 1.12).

The Parabola

Holding the "cutting" plane so that it is parallel to a straight line on the surface of the cone (the edge) will produce a parabola. And, like in the previous examples, this cut is again in only a single nappe (see Figure 1.13).

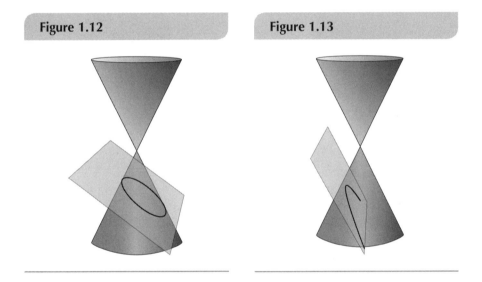

Figure 1.12 **Figure 1.13**

The Hyperbola

Now we see a cut that involves both the upper and lower nappes. Holding the "cutting" plane parallel to the axis (or at an angle less than a line on the surface of the cone makes with the axis) will produce a shape called a hyperbola. This cut will form the two branches, or two arcs, of the hyperbola—one in each nappe (see Figure 1.14).

So by changing the angle and location of the plane-cone intersection, we can produce a circle, ellipse, parabola, or hyperbola. We should also view three cases of special, or degenerate, shapes that can result from very specific cuts. These occur when the plane passes through the apex point (see Figures 1.15–1.17).

If the plane cut is parallel to the base of the cone and intersects the axis point, the ellipse/circle degenerates into a point, namely the axis point itself.

Figure 1.14

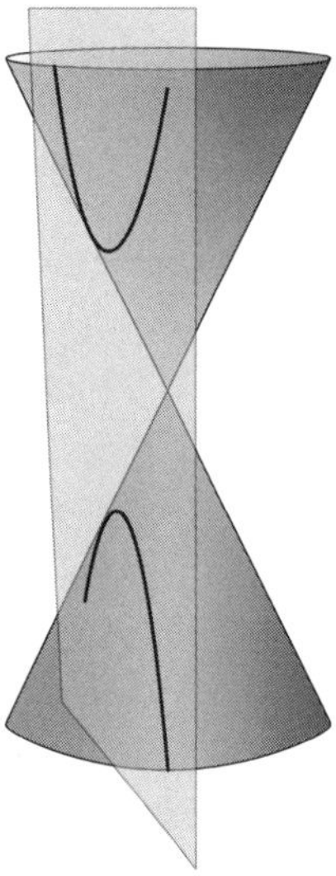

Figure 1.15

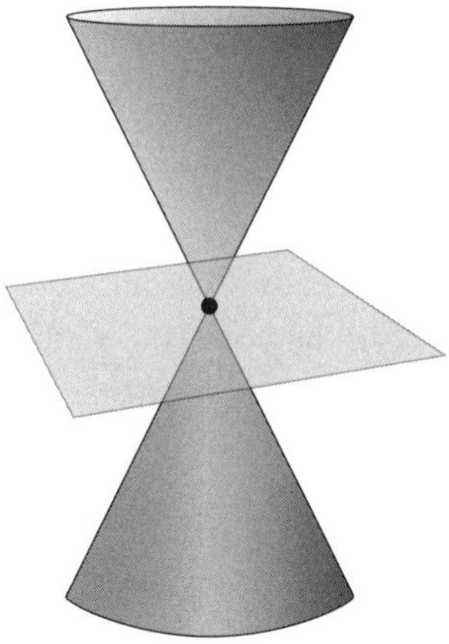

In another degenerate case, the parabola would become a straight line when the cutting plane is tangential to the surface of the nappes.

In a third such case, the degeneration of the hyperbola would occur. If the plane cut is less than the tangential angle and goes through the apex point, the hyperbola will degenerate into two straight lines intersecting at the apex point.

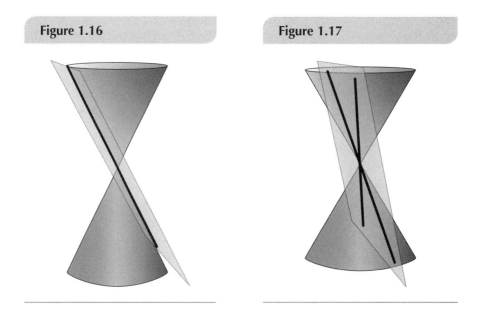

Figure 1.16

Figure 1.17

19. WHAT IS A MATHEMATICAL GROUP?

There are many common words that exist in the world outside of mathematics whose meanings are quite different from the ones they have within mathematics. The word "group" is one of these words. You have the group you "friended" on Facebook and a group who "friended" you; there are religious groups and food groups, as well as a group hug and a group project. Although groups are not all the same, there is a definite similarity in how the word is used. You can determine if you are in or out of the "group" according to some rule of admittance. In mathematics, groups are a similar construct. Mathematical groups are defined as *algebraic structures* made up of a set of elements (finite or infinite) with a binary operation, which is defined on every two elements of that set such that the elements along with the operation satisfy the requirements of four operating rules called axioms. If they do, we have a group.

Let us use the capital letters, such as S, to represent sets and lowercase letters, such as x, for elements in the set. If an element "x" is in the set, we write $x \in S$, and if an element "y" is not in a set, we write $y \notin S$. The binary operation defined on elements of the set is represented by a symbol. Addition is our most familiar binary operation, so we will begin with the set S and the operation of "+," addition. Using set notation, $(S, +)$ forms a group if the following four axioms hold true:

Axiom 1: **Closure:** For every $x, y \in S$ if $x + y = z$, then $z \in S$. The set is said to be closed under addition.

Axiom 2: **Associativity:** For every $x, y, z \in S$,

$$x + (y + z) = (x + y) + z.$$

Axiom 3: **Identity:** There exists an identity element $I \in S$ such that for every $x \in S$

$$x + I = I + x = x.$$

Axiom 4: **Invertibility (existence of additive inverses):** For every $x \in S$ there exists an inverse element, let it be denoted as $\underline{x} \in S$, such that $x + \underline{x} = \underline{x} + x = I$.

Let us view the set of integers, $S = \mathbb{Z}$, to see if it forms a group under the operation "addition."

For Axiom 1: Yes, the integers are closed under addition. The sum of every pair of integers is an integer.

$$1 + 2 = 3 \text{ and } 3 \text{ is an integer.}$$

For Axiom 2: Yes, the integers are associative under addition.

$$1 + (2 + 3) = (1 + 2) + 3, \text{ using Axiom 1}$$

$$1 + (5) = (3) + 3, \text{ again using Axiom 1}$$

$$6 = 6, \text{ both sums are the same}$$

For Axiom 3: Yes, there is an identity element for every $x \in \mathbb{Z}$ under addition. That identity element is 0 and $0 \in \mathbb{Z}$.

$$x + 0 = 0 + x = x$$

$$4 + 0 = 0 + 4 = 4$$

For Axiom 4: Yes, there is an inverse for every $x \in \mathbb{Z}$ under addition. The inverse of x is $-x$ and $-x \in \mathbb{Z}$

$$x + (-x) = (-x) + x = 0$$

$$2 + (-2) = (-2) + 2 = 0$$

Our conclusion is that the set of integers forms a group under addition. Furthermore, the set of integers is commutative under the binary operation addition, and such groups are called *Abelian groups.*

Looking further at our set of integers to see if they form a group under other binary operations, we find the following:

- $\mathbb{Z}$ does not form a group under subtraction, failing Axiom 3.
- Under the operation of division, the integers do not always produce an integer ($3 \div 4 = \frac{3}{4}$), thus failing to satisfy Axiom 1. The set of integers do *not* form a group under division.
- Under the operation of multiplication, the set of integers does not satisfy Axiom 4, since the multiplicative inverse of an integer, except for one and zero, is a fraction, which is not an element of the set of integers. Moreover, the inverse of zero is undefined. So, the integers do *not* form a group under multiplication.

By eliminating the "problem" element from a set, we may be able to form a group with the remaining set elements. Look at the next example with the set of real numbers excluding the element zero. We denote that set as $\mathbb{R}^{nonzero}$. Let us see if it forms a group under the operation "multiplication."

For Axiom 1: Yes, the set is closed under multiplication. The product of every pair of real numbers is a real number: $(-2) \cdot (-3) = 6$, and $6 \in \mathbb{R}^{nonzero}$.

$$\left(\frac{-3}{5}\right)\left(\frac{2}{7}\right) = \frac{-6}{35}, \text{ and } \frac{-6}{35} \in \mathbb{R}^{nonzero}$$

For Axiom 2: Yes, the set is associative under multiplication:

$$(1)(2 \cdot 3) = (1 \cdot 2)(3)$$

$$(1)(6) = (2)(3)$$

$$6 = 6, \text{ both products are the same.}$$

For Axiom 3: Yes, there is an identity element for every $x \in \mathbb{R}^{nonzero}$ under multiplication, and the identity element $I = 1 : (x)(1) = (1)(x) = x$,

$$\frac{2}{7}(1) = (1)\frac{2}{7} = \frac{2}{7}$$

For Axiom 4: Yes, there is an inverse for every $x \in \mathbb{R}^{nonzero}$ under multiplication, and the inverse of x is $\frac{1}{x} : (x)\left(\frac{1}{x}\right) = \left(\frac{1}{x}\right)(x) = 1$

$$\frac{2}{7}\left(\frac{7}{2}\right) = \frac{7}{2}\left(\frac{2}{7}\right) = 1$$

$$4\left(\frac{1}{4}\right) = \frac{1}{4}(4) = 1$$

$$(-.23)\left(-\frac{100}{23}\right) = (-\frac{100}{23})(-.23) = 1$$

Note: You can now see why zero was removed from the set of real numbers: The inverse of zero would be $\frac{1}{0}$, which is undefined.

Our conclusion is that the set $\mathbb{R}^{nonzero}$ forms a group under multiplication.

The study of groups began in the 1830s with the work of Evariste Galois and is viewed today in many different contexts both within and outside of mathematics. Advanced group study in mathematics may work with sets consisting of permutations, transformations, and complex numbers. We have subgroups, simple groups, and Abelian groups. Since the idea of a group is somewhat abstract, it can be thought of as a conceptual model, and we can see the same group structure in different settings and apply what we learn about the structure in one setting to the same structure in other settings, spreading the properties to new environments with different perspectives.

20. WHAT IS A MATHEMATICAL RING?

The word "ring" is a common noun and even a common verb: "What?? He gave you a ring? For your finger, or on the telephone?" However, in branches of mathematics, such as geometry, analysis, and abstract algebra, where ambiguity is not tolerated, a *ring* is a concept that is clearly defined by the following:

Mathematical rings are defined as *algebraic structures* made up of a set of elements (finite or infinite) together with *two binary operations* defined on every pair of elements of that set. Let us use the notation of capital letters such as S to represent sets and lowercase letters such as x and y to represent elements of the set. If an element "x" is in the set, $x \in S$, and if an element "y" is not in a set, $y \notin S$. The two binary operations are defined on every pair of elements of the set and are represented by the symbols + and *. The non-empty set S, together with two binary operations, + and *, noted as $(S +, *)$, form a ring if the following six axioms hold true:

Axiom 1: **Associativity under +:** For any $x, y, z \in S$,

$$(x + y) + z = x + (y + z).$$

Axiom 2: **Existence of an identity under +:** There exists an element $I \in S$, such that for every $x \in S$,

$$x + I = I + x = x.$$

Axiom 3: **Invertibility under + (existence of additive inverses):** For each $x \in S$, there exists an element $-x \in S$, such that

$$x + (-x) = (-x) + x = I.$$

Axiom 4: **Commutativity under +:** For any $x, y \in S$,

$$x + y = y + x.$$

Axiom 5: **Associativity under *:** For any $x, y, z \in S$,

$$(x * y) * z = x * (y * z).$$

Axiom 6: **Left and right distribution under + and *:** For any $x, y, z \in S$,

(a) $x * (y + z) = x * y + x * z$ and

(b) $(y + z) * x = y * x + z * x$.

Example 1:

Does the set of integers, $\mathbb{Z}$, with the operation of addition and multiplication form a ring? Since the operation of addition on the set of integers is closed and associative, there is an identity element, 0, which is an integer, and each integer, x, has an additive inverse, $-x$, which is an integer, it is a *group* (see Question 19). Furthermore, since the operation of addition is commutative, we have an *Abelian group*. Examining the second binary operation, the integers under multiplication satisfy associativity and the multiplication is distributive over addition. In fact, the ring of integers is a *commutative ring* since the second operation, multiplication, is also commutative.

Example 2:

Another familiar set we can examine is the set of even integers, $\mathbb{Z}^{even}$. Let us demonstrate that this set is also a ring.

For Axiom 1: The integers are associative under +.

$(2 + 4) + 6 = 2 + (4 + 6)$, the sum of two even integers is always an even integer and therefore, an element of $\mathbb{Z}^{even}$.

$$6 + 6 = 2 + 10$$

$$12 = 12$$

For Axiom 2: The identity element under + is zero, which is an even integer and in the set $\mathbb{Z}^{even}$.

$$2 + 0 = 0 + 2 = 2$$

For Axiom 3: The inverse under + is the negative of the even integer, and negative even integers are elements of the set $\mathbb{Z}^{even}$.

$$2 + (-2) = (-2) + 2 = 0$$

For Axiom 4: Reversing the positions of the integers does not change their sum. The operation is commutative.

$$2 + 4 = 4 + 2 \text{ (Both sums are equal to six.)}$$

$$6 = 6$$

For Axiom 5: The $\mathbb{Z}^{even}$ are associative under *.

$$(2 * 4) * 6 = 2 * (4 * 6)$$

$$(8) * 6 = 2 * (24)$$

$$48 = 48$$

For Axiom 6: Multiplication distributes over addition.

$$(a)\ 2 * (4 + 6) = 2 * 4 + 2 * 6$$

$$2 * (10) = 8 + 12$$

$$20 = 20$$

$$(b)\ (4 + 6) * 2 = 4 * 2 + 6 * 2$$

$$10 * 2 = 8 + 12$$

$$20 = 20$$

Example 3:

Consider the four-element set known as $\mathbb{Z}_4 = \{0, 1, 2, 3\}$, where addition and multiplication are defined as x mod 4. In other words, the results of both operations would be the remainder when x is divided by 4.

So for any $x, y \in S$, their sum would equal $(x + y)$ mod 4 and their product would equal $(x * y)$ mod 4.

We express the additive structure of our set in the table on the left. Select a top row element and a first column element. The element in the intersection of the row and column is their sum mod 4.

Using this table, we can see that $\mathbb{Z}_4$ is closed under addition; associativity and commutativity follow from the set of all integers; the additive identity is 0; and each element has an inverse, which produces the 0 under addition. Select a top row element and a first column element. The element in the cross of the row and column is their sum mod 4.

We express the multiplicative structure of our set in the second table shown. Again, select a top row element and a first column element. The element in the cross of the row and column is their product mod 4.

Similarly, for our set $\mathbb{Z}_4$, the associativity of multiplication as well as the closure and distributivity of

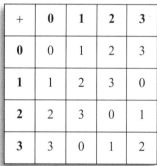

+	0	1	2	3
0	0	1	2	3
1	1	2	3	0
2	2	3	0	1
3	3	0	1	2

*	0	1	2	3
0	0	0	0	0
1	0	1	2	3
2	0	2	0	2
3	0	3	2	1

multiplication over addition follows from the set of all integers. Our multiplication is also commutative, which is easily seen by the symmetry in the above table of the elements about the main diagonal. Therefore, $\mathbb{Z}_4$ does form a ring under the given operations of addition and multiplication.

Ring theory was established in the late 19th century by Richard Dedekind (1880) and David Hilbert (1892) and expanded in the 1920s by Emmy Noether, one of the first renowned female mathematicians. In the branches of higher mathematics, researchers are able to apply elementary algebra theorems and concepts to rings consisting of noninteger elements such as matrices, modular groups, quantum groups, and transformations, to name a few. Today, ring theorists study rings that are noncommutative and similar structures whose operations do not satisfy all the axioms listed above.

21. WHAT IS A MATHEMATICAL FIELD?

The word "field" is a common noun and even a common verb. We can admire a *field* of daisies, or know someone who is romantically playing the *field,* or we can be given a command from our coach to *field* a ball. However, in branches of mathematics such as geometry, analysis, and abstract algebra, ambiguity is not tolerated; therefore, a *field* is a mathematical concept that is clearly defined below. Mathematical *fields* like groups and rings are defined as *algebraic structures* made up of a **set** of elements (finite or infinite) together with two binary operations. Let us use the notation of capital letters such as S to represent sets, and lowercase letters, such as x and y, to represent elements of the set. If an element "x" is in the set, we will write it as $x \in S$, and if an element "y" is not in a set, we will write it as $y \notin S$. The two binary operations are defined on every pair of elements of the set and are represented by the symbols + and *. The nonempty set S, together with two binary operations, + and *, inverses for both operations, and identity elements for both operations $(S, +, \cdot, -, ^{-1}, 0, 1)$, forms a field if the following nine axioms hold true:

The first six axioms are the same as rings and to those we add three more:

Axiom 1: **Associativity under +:** For any x, y, and $z \in S$, $(x + y) + z = x + (y + z)$.

Axiom 2: **Existence of an identity element under +:** There exists an element $I_+ \in S$, such that for every $x \in S$, $x + I_+ = I_+ + x = x$.

Axiom 3: **Invertibility under + (existence of additive inverses):** For each $x \in S$, there exists an element $-x \in S$ such that $x + (-x) = (-x) + x = I_+$, where "$I_+$" is the identity element under +.

Axiom 4: **Commutativity under +:** For any $x, y \in S$, $x + y = y + x$.

Axiom 5: **Associativity under *:** For any $x, y, z \in S$, $(x * y) * z = x * (y * z)$.

Axiom 6: **Left and right distribution under + and *:** For any $x, y, z \in S$,

(a) $x * (y + z) = x * y + x * z$ and

(b) $(y + z) * x = y * x + z * x$.

Axiom 7: **Commutativity under *:** For any $x, y \in S$, $x * y = y * x$.

Axiom 8: **Existence of an identity element under *:** There exists an element $I_* \in S$, such that for all $x \in S$, $x \neq 0$, $I_* * x = x * I_* = x$.

Axiom 9: **Invertibility under * (existence of multiplicative inverses):** For each $x \in S$, $x \neq 0$, there exists an element, called $x^{-1} \in S$ such that

$x * x^{-1} = x^{-1} * x = I_*$, where "$I_*$" is the identity element under *.

Example: Let us see if the set of rational numbers, $\mathbb{Q}$, form a field.

All elements of set $\mathbb{Q}$ can be expressed as a fraction $\frac{x}{y}$, where x and y are integers and $y \neq 0$.

Now is a good time to review the process of combining and multiplying fractions with the students as it will be necessary to do so to establish the veracity of several of the field axioms. So we will process the axioms in a different order from the one initially presented. We begin with Axiom 4 in which you have to combine two fractions.

When adding two fractions, you need to find a common denominator and convert each fraction to that denominator. When the denominators are the same, you can combine the numerators and place the sum over that common denominator. In addition, we need to remember that our numerators and denominators are integers and the set of integers is commutative under addition and multiplication; so we can rearrange the factors in a product and not change its value.

Let us begin.

For Axiom 4: The rational elements are commutative under +. (Juxtaposition infers multiplication.)

Note: As the members of the set of integers are commutative under multiplication and addition, the integer factors in the sums and products of the numerators and denominators can be reordered. Recall that denominators are never zero.

$$\frac{x}{y} + \frac{a}{b} = \frac{a}{b} + \frac{x}{y}$$

$$\frac{x \cdot b}{y \cdot b} + \frac{a \cdot y}{b \cdot y} = \frac{a \cdot y}{b \cdot y} + \frac{x \cdot b}{y \cdot b}$$

$$\frac{xb + ay}{yb} = \frac{ay + xb}{by}$$

$$\frac{xb + ya}{yb} = \frac{ay + xb}{by}$$

$$\frac{xb + ya}{yb} = \frac{xb + ya}{yb}$$

In Axiom 7, you are required to multiply two fractions. When we multiply fractions, we can multiply their numerators and then their denominators, forming a new fraction.

For Axiom 7: The set $\mathbb{Q}$ is commutative under $\cdot$.

$$\frac{2}{3} \cdot \frac{4}{5} = \frac{4}{5} \cdot \frac{2}{3}$$

$$\frac{2 \cdot 4}{3 \cdot 5} = \frac{4 \cdot 2}{5 \cdot 3}$$

$$\frac{8}{15} = \frac{8}{15}$$

$$\frac{x}{y} \cdot \frac{a}{b} = \frac{a}{b} \cdot \frac{x}{y}$$

$$\frac{xa}{yb} = \frac{ax}{by}$$

$$\frac{xa}{yb} = \frac{xa}{yb}$$

Again, the numerators and denominators are integers, so their products are commutative and the factors can be rearranged so they "match." Now we are ready to address the other axioms.

For Axiom 1: The set of rational numbers, $\mathbb{Q}$, is associative under +.

Let $\frac{x}{y}, \frac{a}{b}, \frac{c}{d}$ be rational numbers, $y, b, d \neq 0$. Remembering that integers are commutative under both addition and multiplication and multiplication is distributive over addition, we can rearrange our final answers to be identical.

$$\left(\frac{x}{y}+\frac{a}{b}\right)+\frac{c}{d}=\frac{x}{y}+\left(\frac{a}{b}+\frac{c}{d}\right)$$

$$\left(\frac{xb+ya}{yb}\right)+\frac{c}{d}=\frac{x}{y}+\left(\frac{ad+bc}{bd}\right)$$

$$\frac{d(xb+ya)+ybc}{ybd}=\frac{xbd+y(ad+bc)}{ybd}$$

$$\frac{dxb+dya+ybc}{ybd}=\frac{xbd+yad+ybc}{ybd}$$

$$\frac{dxb+dya+ybc}{ybd}=\frac{dxb+dya+ybc}{ybd}$$

For Axiom 2: The identity element in $\mathbb{Q}$ under + is zero, which is a rational number.

$$\frac{2}{3}+0=0+\frac{2}{3}=\frac{2}{3}$$

$$\frac{x}{y}+0=0+\frac{x}{y}=\frac{x}{y}$$

For Axiom 3: Each rational element in $\mathbb{Q}$ has an inverse under + that is also in $\mathbb{Q}$.

The inverse of $\frac{x}{y}$ is $-\frac{x}{y}$. By the definition of a rational number, $y \neq 0$.

The minus sign in front of the fraction can be moved to the numerator. Keep the denominator and combine the numerators.

$$\frac{2}{3}+\left(-\frac{2}{3}\right)=\left(-\frac{2}{3}\right)+\frac{2}{3}=0$$

$$\frac{x}{y}+\left(-\frac{x}{y}\right)=\frac{x-x}{y}=\frac{0}{y}=0$$

For Axiom 5: The elements in set $\mathbb{Q}$ are associative under multiplication.

$$\left(\frac{x}{y}\cdot\frac{a}{b}\right)\cdot\frac{c}{d}=\frac{x}{y}\cdot\left(\frac{a}{b}\cdot\frac{c}{d}\right)$$

$$\left(\frac{xa}{yb}\right)\cdot\frac{c}{d}=\frac{x}{y}\cdot\left(\frac{ac}{bd}\right)$$

$$\frac{xac}{ybd}=\frac{xac}{ybd}$$

For Axiom 6: Left and right distribution under + and *.

$$\frac{x}{y} \cdot \left(\frac{a}{b} + \frac{c}{d} \right) = \left(\frac{a}{b} + \frac{c}{d} \right) \cdot \frac{x}{y}$$

$$\frac{x}{y} \cdot \left(\frac{ad + bc}{bd} \right) = \left(\frac{ad + bc}{bd} \right) \cdot \frac{x}{y}$$

$$\frac{x \cdot (ad + bc)}{ybd} = \frac{(ad + bc) \cdot x}{bdy}$$

$$\frac{xad + xbc}{ybd} = \frac{adx + bcx}{bdy}$$

For Axiom 8: The identity element under * for the set of $\mathbb{Q}$ is "1," which is a rational number that can be written as $\frac{1}{1}$.

$$\frac{2}{3} \cdot 1 = 1 \cdot \frac{2}{3} = \frac{2}{3}$$

$$\frac{x}{y} \cdot 1 = 1 \cdot \frac{x}{y} = 1$$

For Axiom 9: The multiplicative inverse of $\frac{x}{y}$, $y \neq 0$ is another rational element $\frac{y}{x}$ in $\mathbb{Q}$.

$$\frac{-2}{3} \cdot \frac{3}{-2} = \frac{-2 \cdot 3}{3 \cdot (-2)} = \frac{-6}{-6} = 1$$

$$\frac{x}{y} \cdot \frac{y}{x} = \frac{xy}{yx} = 1$$

We have satisfied all nine field axioms and have proved that the set of rational numbers form a field under the operations of addition and multiplication.

Fields at one time were called *integral domains,* but under either name fields must have the identity elements for the two operations. Usually they are required to be different (0 for addition, and 1 for multiplication in our example above), implying that every field must have a minimum of two elements. Other examples of fields are the sets of complex numbers and the real numbers but not the integers, which lack the inverses under multiplication.

Fields are studied within a branch of mathematics known as *Galois Theory,* which focuses on the roots and coefficients of polynomials and has produced proofs for the impossibility of trisecting an angle and squaring a circle with a compass and ruler—two of the three famous problems of antiquity.

22. WHAT ARE THE THREE FAMOUS LAWS THAT JOHANNES KEPLER DISCOVERED ABOUT PLANETARY MOTION INVOLVING THE ELLIPSE?

An ellipse is a closed curve in which the sum of the distances from every point on the curve to two points, called foci, is a constant. After painstakingly analyzing planetary data gathered (prior to regular use of the telescope to study celestial bodies), Johannes Kepler proposed three laws:

1. The Law of Ellipses. The path of the planets about the sun is elliptical in shape, with the center of the sun being located at one focus (Figure 1.18).

Figure 1.18

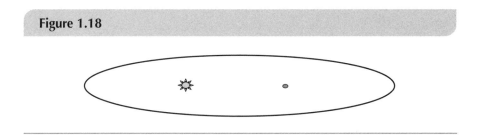

2. The Law of Equal Areas. An imaginary line drawn from the center of the sun to the center of the planet will sweep out equal areas in equal intervals of time (Figure 1.19).

Figure 1.19

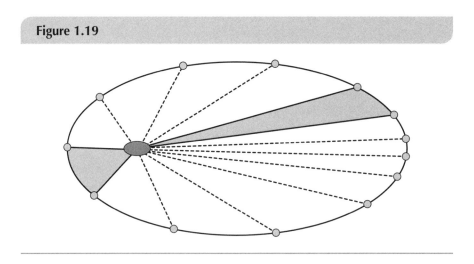

3. The Law of Harmonies. The ratio of the squares of the periods (one complete cycle) of any two planets is equal to the ratio of the cubes of the semi-major axes of their orbits.

Kepler published this law, discovered between 1609 and 1618, a year later in his book *Harmonices Mundi*. This discovery, not the legendary falling apple, is what led Sir Isaac Newton to his law of gravity.

NOTES

1. Interested readers may wish to pursue this topic further; see Posamentier, A. S., & Lehmann, I. (2007). *The fabulous Fibonacci numbers.* Amherst, NY: Prometheus Books.

2. Interested readers may wish to pursue this topic further; see Posamentier, A. S., & Lehmann, I. (2012). *The glorious golden ratio.* Amherst, NY: Prometheus Books.

3. Here is the result derived:

$$\text{If } \frac{1}{\phi} = \frac{\sqrt{5}-1}{2}, \text{ then } \phi = \frac{2}{\sqrt{5}-1} \cdot \frac{\sqrt{5}+1}{\sqrt{5}+1} = \frac{\sqrt{5}+1}{2}$$

$$\text{and } \phi - \frac{1}{\phi} = \frac{\sqrt{5}+1}{2} - \frac{\sqrt{5}-1}{2} = 1.$$

2 Arithmetic Questions

23. WHAT IS THE DIFFERENCE BETWEEN A *NUMBER* AND A *DIGIT*?

The difference between a number and a digit is similar to the difference between a word and a letter or a character. Alphabetical letters make up words, and digits make up numbers, which represent numbers.

Historically, the first numeral system—as we know it today—is believed to be the Hindu-Arabic numeral system, established in the seventh century, which used both numbers and digits. However, the use of the digit zero was not widely accepted. In fact, a space was used in place of zero. By the 13th century, Hindu-Arabic numerals were recognized in European mathematical circles. In fact, these numerals first appeared in the European world in *Liber Abaci* (1202), which is a book on arithmetic applications by Leonardo of Pisa, known later as Fibonacci. In addition, the Hindu-Arabic numerals were recognized and used commonly by the 15th century. By the end of the 20th century, nearly all noncomputerized calculations in the world were done with these Hindu-Arabic numerals.

Numbers

In ancient times, people needed to count objects. Therefore, numbers were introduced for counting and measuring items used in barter such as chickens, cows, and barrels of rum. They required only whole numbers. Later on, rational numbers (i.e., fractions) were introduced. In modern mathematics, we talk about different categories of numbers, such as real numbers, complex numbers, rational and irrational numbers, and so on.

Digits

A digit is a single symbol in a numeral representation of a number. A digit can have both place value and face value. Both 2 and 246 are numbers. The 2 is a single-digit number, but 246 is a three-digit number. The value of a number is unique, but the value of a digit can be different depending upon the position it occupies in the number. In other words, a digit holds a position value as well as a face value.

A digit is a single symbol in the set {0, 1, 2, 3, 4, 5, 6, 7, 8, 9}. These are the 10 digits in the base-ten system that are used to form numerals. For example, the digit 2 and the digit 9 when used in combination form either 29 or 92, which are represented in a positional numeral system.

The word *digit* is derived from the ancient Latin *digita,* which means fingers of the hands. Thus our fingers easily correspond to the symbols of the base-ten numerical system.

A *numeral* is a symbol or name that represents a number. In our decimal system, the digits 0 through 9 are called numerals.

A *number* is a mathematical object used to count or quantify (measure). A number is an idea that we discuss in terms of numerals, such as "7" or "seven."

Examples of digits: 4, 8

Example of a number: 48

Moreover, the definition of number also includes zero, negative numbers, rational numbers, irrational numbers, and complex numbers.

24. WHAT ARE THE DIFFERENCES BETWEEN CARDINAL, ORDINAL, AND NOMINAL NUMBERS?

Cardinal Numbers

The idea of cardinality was developed by Georg Cantor, the originator of set theory, between 1874 and 884. Cantor first recognized cardinality as a method to compare sets; for example, the sets {1, 2, 3} and {3, 4, 5} are not equal, but they have the same cardinality—three. That is, cardinal numbers are numbers that indicate quantity, such as one, two, three, four, five, and six. Cardinal numbers are natural numbers. For example, the cardinality of a set of six objects is the natural number 6, indicating six elements in the set. See Figure 2.1.

In general, when the question of "How many?" is posed, a cardinal number is the response.

Figure 2.1

Ordinal Numbers

In 1883, Georg Cantor also introduced ordinal numbers to accommodate infinite sequences and to arrange sets with selected kinds of order. In fact, he derived them by chance while working on a problem involving trigonometric series. Ordinal numbers state the position of something in a list, such as first, second, third, fourth, fifth, and so on. For example, Barbara is the second person on line.

The illustration in Figure 2.2 indicates an example where ordinal numbers are used.

Figure 2.2

Source: © Getty Images

Nominal Numbers

A nominal number is a number that represents a name or that is used to identify something that does not have a value that can be used in arithmetic operations. For example, a zip code such as 10522, a telephone number such as 914-555-1234, or the model number of an item, such as 634, are all examples of nominal numbers.

25. WHAT ARE THE NATURAL NUMBERS, AND DOES THE NUMBER ZERO BELONG TO THE NATURAL NUMBERS?

We can conceive of mathematics being born out of necessity to count and track items. The natural numbers are sometimes called the counting numbers, or positive whole numbers. The smallest natural number is 1, and there is no largest number. No matter how big a number we can name, there will always be a larger one, which is why we call the set of natural numbers infinite. The natural numbers are closed under addition as well as multiplication, which means that when we add or multiply two or more natural numbers, the result will always be another natural number. However, we find that the closure property does not hold under subtraction: $5 - 7 = -2$, and -2 is *not* a natural number. Nor does closure hold under division: $\frac{3}{5}$ is a fraction, and fractions are *not* natural numbers. Zero is usually not included in the set of natural numbers, and so $5 - 5 = 0$ and $\frac{0}{5} = 0$ would also yield invalid results for the set of natural numbers.

26. HOW CAN WE REMEMBER THE ORDER OF OPERATIONS USING PEMDAS?

The mnemonic PEMDAS represents the hierarchy of arithmetic operations when evaluating an expression moving from left to right. The letters stand for **P**arentheses, **E**xponents, **M**ultiplication/**D**ivision, **A**ddition/**S**ubtraction. Many students memorize the saying **P**lease **E**xcuse **M**y **D**ear **A**unt **S**ally to help them remember the correct order of operations.

Remember to work from left to right and scan the line three times as a computer would do: first to do all exponents, second to do the multiplying and dividing, and third to do all the adding and subtracting. Work inside parentheses must be done first. See Examples 1 and 2 below.

Example 1: $\dfrac{(8+12)}{5} \cdot 5 = \dfrac{20}{2} \cdot 5 = 10 \cdot 5 = 50$

Example 2: $\dfrac{(8+12)}{2 \cdot 5} = \dfrac{20}{10} = 2$

Nested parentheses present a challenge. Proper matching of the parentheses, starting with the rightmost left parentheses with the leftmost right parentheses, must be done first. Do the calculations in the innermost parentheses and then move to the next pair of parentheses and so on. Parentheses can override the usual order of operations. See Example 3, where exponentiation becomes the last operation.

Example 3:

$$\left(\frac{\left[\left(4^2 - 3\right) + 7\right]}{2} - 5 \right)^2 = \left(\frac{(16-3)+7}{2} - 5 \right)^2 = \left(\frac{[13+7]}{2} - 5 \right)^2 =$$

$$\left(\frac{[20]}{2} - 5 \right)^2 = (10-5)^2 = (5)^2 = 25$$

Extra care must be used when entering arithmetic expressions into a calculator. Entering $13 - 5^2$ will get the correct answer, -12, as the calculator "knows" the correct order of operations, but ignoring the parentheses in $(13 - 5)^2$ will also get -12, when the correct answer is $(8)^2 = 64$.

27. WHAT IS A FRACTION?

A fraction is a numerical or algebraic expression with a numerator and a denominator, such as $\dfrac{2}{3}$, where the denominator is never allowed to be zero. The etymology comes from the Latin root *fractus,* which means "broken." Perhaps include English words like fracture, fragment, and fractal to show the connection to everyday words. Some of the linguists in your class might find this interesting as they think of fractions as parts of a whole. There are numerical fractions and algebraic fractions, so fractions can include both constants and variables.

28. WHAT IS A RATIONAL NUMBER?

A rational number is any number that can be expressed as a fraction. More formally, we would say that a rational number is a number that can be written as $\dfrac{a}{b}$, where a and b are both integers, and where b is not zero.

The set of all rational numbers has the following symbol: **Q**. In the late 19th century Italian mathematician Peano wrote the set notation of the set based on the Italian word *quoziente*. Fractions are also called "quotients" since they have a numerator and a denominator. The denominator cannot be 0 since we would then have an invalid fraction.

Rational numbers can be represented in a variety of forms, including neat fractions such as $\frac{1}{2}$ whose decimal equivalent is .5, which we call a terminating decimal. On the other hand, we can identify fractions such as $\frac{2}{3}$, whose decimal equivalent is .666666 . . . and which is called a nonterminating, infinite, or repeating decimal.

The rational numbers are closed under addition, multiplication, and subtraction. This means that whenever you add, subtract, or multiply any rational number, the result will also be a rational number.

The rational numbers would also be closed for division, with one exception: zero cannot be in the divisor. Division is closed for all nonzero rational numbers. The set of nonzero rational numbers is generally symbolized by $\mathbf{Q^*}$.

29. HOW CAN ONE CONVERT A DECIMAL NUMBER TO A FRACTION?

Before we discuss the procedure for converting a decimal to a fraction, it is important to first establish whether the decimal can, in fact, be converted to a fraction. To establish this, let us look at three types of decimal numbers that are representative of the real number system.

The first type of decimal number is the terminating decimal, where the decimal ends at a certain place. Some common examples of finite decimals include 0.5, 0.25, and 0.250.

The second type of decimal is the repeating decimal. A repeating decimal is a way of representing a rational number that at some point becomes periodic—there is a group of one or more digits repeated infinitely. Examples of repeating decimals are 0.333333333 . . . and 0.3636363636 . . . .

The third type of decimal is the nonterminating, nonrepeating decimal, where there is never a repeated pattern. Examples of nonterminating, nonrepeating decimals include π, $\sqrt{2}$, and $\sqrt{3}$.

The first two types of decimal numbers are called *rational numbers*, and these numbers can be expressed as a fraction. The third type of decimal numbers are called *irrational numbers* and cannot be converted into a fraction.

To convert a terminating decimal to a fraction, simply write it as a fraction and reduce to lowest terms:

$$.625 = \frac{625}{1000} = \frac{5}{8}.$$

To convert a repeating decimal to a fraction, let $x =$ the decimal number, determine the number of decimal places (digits) that repeat the pattern, and then multiply both sides of the equation by 10, 100, or 1000 (or a higher power of 10), depending on whether 1, 2, or 3 (or more) decimals repeat. For example, to convert 0.777777 . . . , we would follow this procedure:

First, to make matters simpler, a repeating decimal can be expressed using a bar notation, such as with $0.777777\ldots$, expressed as $.\overline{7}$.

Let $x = .\overline{7}$. Since only 1 digit repeats, we multiply by 10 to get $10x = 7.\overline{7}$. Then subtracting $x = .\overline{7}$ from this equation, we have $9x = 7$. When we divide both sides by 9, the result is $x = \dfrac{7}{9}$.

As another example, we will change $.\overline{36}$ to fraction form.

$$x = .3636363636\ldots$$

$$100x = 36.363636\ldots$$

$x = .363636\ldots$, subtract the last two equations to get

$$99x = 36$$

$$x = \frac{36}{99} = \frac{4}{11}.$$

The third type of decimal, the irrational decimals, are so "irrational" that they do not end nor do they display any repeating sequence and therefore cannot be converted to fraction form.

30. WHAT IS SO SPECIAL ABOUT THE PASCAL TRIANGLE?

The Pascal triangle is an inexhaustible source of fascinating mathematical discoveries. It is most noted for its use in the binomial formula

$$(a+b)^n = \sum_{k=0}^{n} \binom{n}{k} a^{n-k} b^k,$$

where the binomial coefficient $\binom{n}{k}$ is the number at the kth position in the nth row of Pascal's triangle (see Chapter Five, Question 96, "What is the Pascal triangle?"). Here are a few properties that you might find surprising.

The Sums of the Rows

For $a = 1$ and $b = 1$, the binomial formula reads: $(1 + 1)^n = 2^n = \sum_{k=0}^{n} \binom{n}{k}$, which shows immediately that the sum of all numbers in the nth row of the Pascal triangle gives 2^n. For example,

$2^5 = 1 + 5 + 10 + 10 + 5 + 1 = 32$ (the sum of the numbers in the fifth row) and

$2^6 = 1 + 6 + 15 + 20 + 15 + 6 + 1 = 64$ (the sum of the numbers in the sixth row).

The Powers of 11

Inspection of the results for $(10 + 1)^n$ reveals the following curious fact:

If one reads the nth row of the Pascal triangle as a single number whose digits are the elements of that row, we get the nth power of 11. For example, the digits in the third row are 1, 3, 3, and 1. And indeed, $1331 = 11^3$! Similarly, the fourth row $(1, 4, 6, 4, 1)$ becomes $14641 = 11^4$.

But there is one caveat: Whenever the element in the Pascal triangle has more than one digit, one has to carry over to the previous digit. To make this clear, let us arrange, for example, the numbers 1, 5, 10, 10, 5, 1 of the fifth row in the following way:

$$1\,5$$

$$1\,0$$

$$\underline{1\,0\,5\,1}$$

$$1\,6\,1\,0\,5\,1$$

As you can easily check, $161051 = 11^5$. In a similar way, the sixth row $(1, 6, 15, 20, 15, 6, 1)$ becomes $1771561 = 11^6$, and so on.

Figure 2.3

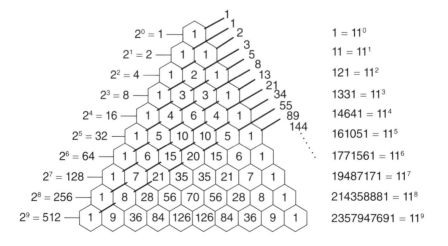

Fibonacci Numbers

The famous Fibonacci sequence 1, 1, 2, 3, 5, 8, 13, 21, 34, . . . , where every number is the sum of the two preceding numbers, can also be found in the Pascal triangle. The Fibonacci numbers appear as the sums along the shallow diagonals, as shown in Figure 2.3 on the previous page.

Multiples of Prime Numbers

You may have noticed that the number at position 1 in the nth row is n (remember that the "1" at the beginning of the row is at position 0). Whenever n is a prime number, all the remaining numbers in that row (except the 1's) can be divided by n. For example, in the seventh row (1, 7, 21, 35, 35, 21, 7, 1), the numbers 21 and 35 are all divisible by 7.

Triangular Numbers

The numbers in the diagonal with $k = 1$ are simply the natural numbers. The numbers in the diagonal with $k = 2$ are known as triangular numbers: 1, 3, 6, 10, 15, 21, ... They count the vertices of the triangular patterns in Figure 2.4.

Figure 2.4

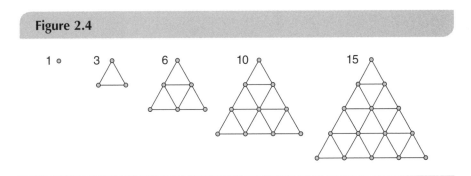

Similarly, the numbers in the diagonal with $k = 3$ are tetrahedral numbers, which count the vertices of tetrahedrons stacked in three dimensions.

Number of Cyclic Polygons

If you draw some points (all different from each other) on a circle, you can create various figures (triangles, quadrilaterals, etc.) by joining the points through line segments. For example, with five points on a circle, you could draw five different cyclic quadrilaterals, because you can choose four of the five points in $\binom{5}{4} = 5$ different ways (here we exclude any self-intersecting figures, hence we have just one figure for every choice of points).

We can set up the following table, which again contains the numbers of the Pascal triangle (except the leading 1's).

	Points	Line Segments	Triangles	Quadrilaterals	Pentagons	...
	1	—	—	—	—	—
	2	1	—	—	—	—
	3	3	1	—	—	—
	4	6	4	1	—	—
	5	10	10	5	1	—
	...					

31. HOW CAN THE PRODUCT OF TWO NUMBERS BE SMALLER THAN BOTH OF ITS FACTORS?

This phenomenon is encountered first when teaching the multiplication of fractions. For example, $\frac{1}{2}$ times $\frac{1}{2}$ equals $\frac{1}{4}$, which is clearly smaller than both of the factors. But do your students really know what is going on here? To understand this phenomenon on a formal level, one would need to know about two methods:

1. How to multiply fractions: $\frac{a}{b} \cdot \frac{c}{d} = \frac{a \cdot c}{b \cdot d}$.

2. How to compare the size of two fractions: $\frac{a}{b} > \frac{c}{d}$ if and only if $a \cdot d > b \cdot c$ (assuming that all numbers are positive).

However, there is little value in presenting formal algebraic manipulations too early. Your students would not be able to appreciate an argument based on formal reasoning, unless they have developed true understanding and familiarity with the underlying thought processes.

Therefore, let us start with what students are likely to know about multiplication of whole numbers (positive integers) when they start learning about fractions. They should understand, for example, that multiplication is repeated addition. For example, to obtain 4 times 3 you need to form four groups of three; that is, you add the number 3 four times: $4 \cdot 3 = 3 + 3 + 3 + 3 = 12$.

Your students should also know that the result remains the same if you exchange the two factors. Moreover, they should be familiar with the interpretation of multiplication as the area of a rectangle (see Figure 2.5).

Figure 2.5

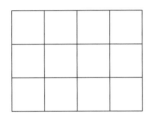 4×3

$=$

3×4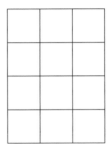

The topic of this section arises from a conflict with the following basic observation about positive integers:

"The product of two numbers is always larger than the factors, unless one of the factors is 0 or 1."

Certainly, it is possible to build on these basic elements of understanding when introducing the multiplication of fractions. $4 \cdot \frac{1}{2}$ means adding $\frac{1}{2}$ four times: $\frac{1}{2} + \frac{1}{2} + \frac{1}{2} + \frac{1}{2} = 1 + 1 = 2$. (Take four times one-half of a cake—how many cakes will you have?)

$\frac{1}{2} \cdot 4$ is perhaps more difficult, because of the meaning of adding 4 one-half times ("Take one-half times four cakes" simply does not sound right). It is useful to call this "$\frac{1}{2}$ of 4," so we take one-half of four cakes, which is again two.

Students should try to visualize this operation with rectangles. Instead of $4 \cdot \frac{1}{2}$, start with $4 \cdot 1$ and erase one-half of each square (see Figure 2.6).

Figure 2.6

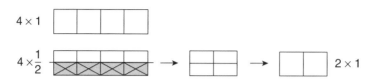

Let us try it again with $\frac{1}{2} \cdot 4$ (see Figure 2.7). Start with $1 \cdot 4$ and erase one-half of each unit square. Make sure your students agree with every single step:

Figure 2.7

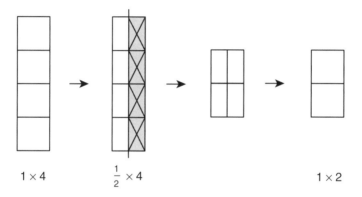

In the same way, and by analogy, you can now explain the idea behind $\frac{1}{2} \cdot \frac{1}{2}$. One-half times one-half is the same as "one-half of one-half," as shown in Figure 2.8. Your students should now understand that multiplication by $\frac{1}{2}$ means to erase one-half of each unit (horizontally or vertically):

Figure 2.8

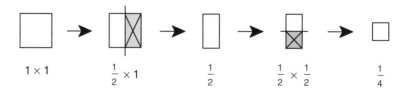

You might wish to do further examples. Finally, you could ask your students whether the statement about the product of numbers being larger than the factors remains correct for fractions. How would it have to be modified? How about the following:

> "The product of two numbers is always larger than the factors, unless one of the factors is 0 or 1 or a fraction between 0 and 1."

32. IF THE TEMPERATURE RISES FROM 80°F TO A TEMPERATURE OF 88°F, WHY IS IT WRONG TO SAY IT BECAME 10% WARMER?

Recently a headline in a British newspaper stated that Madagascar has experienced a 10% increase in temperature in the past 50 years.[1] What does this mean? Presently, the average temperature in Madagascar is 65°F. So if the temperature has risen by 10%, the average temperature would have been $\frac{100}{110} \cdot 65°F = 59.09°F$ in the past. But wait! Temperature in Madagascar and in Great Britain is measured in the Celsius scale. You can use the formula $C = \frac{5}{9}(F - 32)$ to convert between the Fahrenheit and Celsius scales. Measured in Celsius, the average temperature in Madagascar is 18.3°C. Therefore, an increase of 10% would mean that 50 years ago the average temperature would have been about 16.63°C. But this corresponds to 61.93°F, which is different from the earlier result. So which one is true?

This example shows us that the statement "it became 10% warmer" is useless. It is about as meaningless as saying that the year 1100 occurred "10% later" than the year 1000.

The problem is the type of data represented by a temperature scale. The temperature scale is an example of an *interval scale*. Temperature differences are meaningful, and the temperature difference between 10 and 20 degrees represents the same change in heat as the difference between 80 and 90 degrees. But the zero point of the temperature scale is arbitrary and is merely a matter of convention. Zero temperature does not mean that there is "no temperature." Consequently, a temperature change described as a percentage (of either Fahrenheit or Celsius values) does not correspond to any physical phenomenon that changes by that percentage.

Clearly distinguishing the kinds of variables one might want to analyze is essential for a proper application of statistical methods. Therefore, many statistics books begin by defining the different types of values that occur in the applications:

- Nominal variable: Each value has a unique meaning, but the values are not ordered and they do not describe a magnitude. Examples are color, gender, place of birth, and so on.
- Ordinal variable: Here the values describe an order or magnitude, but the differences of the values are meaningless. An example is the star rating of hotels.
- Interval variable: The order and the difference of the values are meaningful, but there is no natural zero point. Examples include the temperature in Fahrenheit or Celsius, years, and dates.
- Ratio variable: This variable is like an interval variable with a natural definition of zero. Typical examples include length and weight.

Which statistical quantities one is allowed to compute depends on the type of variables.

	Nominal	Ordinal	Interval	Ratio
Compute relative and absolute frequencies	Yes	Yes	Yes	Yes
Compute median and percentiles	–	Yes	Yes	Yes
Add or subtract, mean, standard deviation	–	–	Yes	Yes
Compute ratios, coefficient of variation	–	–	–	Yes

In physics, temperature describes the intensity (average kinetic energy) of the thermal molecular motion. Physicists use the Kelvin scale, which has an absolute zero corresponding to no molecular motion at all—this is really a state without temperature, and there exist no temperatures below zero Kelvin. Thus, temperature measured in Kelvin is a ratio variable.

33. HOW DO THE VALUES OF THE FOLLOWING DIFFER: ab^c, $(ab)^c$, $(a^b)^c$, a^{b^c}?

It is obvious that the differences come from the placement of the exponent and the parentheses. As students of mathematics, we follow established rules (algorithms) that dictate the steps in our solutions and that ensure we all get the same answer when we do the same calculation. One of the most basic is the "Order of Operations" that dictates which of the five arithmetic operations are performed first, which is second, and so on. Furthermore, we need to remember that addition and multiplication are commutative operations and that subtraction and division are left-associative and not commutative as is exponentiation, which is right-associative. Most students still remember the mnemonic device PEMDAS, which represents the following:

1st **P**lease   **P**—Do work inside **P**arentheses first.

2nd **E**xcuse   **E**—Next do **E**xponentiation.

3rd **M**y ⎤ **M** & **D**—Next do **M**ultiplication and **D**ivision, reading
3rd **D**ear ⎦ from left to right.

4th **A**unt ⎤ **A** & **S**—Last do **A**ddition and **S**ubtraction, reading from
4th **S**ally ⎦ left to right.

It is important to remember that the exponent is applied only to what is exactly in front of the exponent. It is the one operation of the five that is right-associative only. Therefore, there is a clear difference between $-a^2$ and $(-a)^2$. In the first case, the minus sign is independent of the exponent, so it is excluded from the operation, and in the second case, the minus sign is enclosed within the parentheses and the right parenthesis is exactly in front of the exponent, so it is included in the operation.

For example, $-4^2 = -(4)(4) = -16$, while if we insert parentheses $(-4)^2 = (-4)(-4) = +16$.

Therefore in ab^c the exponent "c" refers only to the "b" in front of it, and

$$ab^c = a \cdot b \cdot b \cdot b \cdot b \cdot \ldots \cdot b \text{ (with } c \text{ factors of } b\text{)},$$

while in $(ab)^c$ the exponent now refers to the contents of the parentheses, which are directly in front of it, and the product of a and b is calculated first (rule #1), and then that value is raised to the c power:

$$(ab)^c = ab \cdot ab \cdot ab \cdot ab \cdot ab \cdot \ldots \cdot ab \text{ (with } c \text{ factors of } ab\text{)} = a^c b^c.$$

Continuing on to $(a^b)^c$, we see a power being raised to a power, so first we do the work inside the parentheses: raise a to the b power, and then use that result as a new base and raise it to the c power:

$$(a^b)^c = a^b \cdot a^b \cdot a^b \cdot a^b \cdot a^b \cdot \ldots \cdot a^b \text{ (with } c \text{ factors of the value of } a^b\text{)} = a^{bc}.$$

Note: A shortcut method of calculating $(a^b)^c$ would be to multiply the powers first, bc, and raise the base a to that power obtaining the same answer, $a^{bc} = a \cdot a \cdot a \cdot a \cdot a \cdot ... \cdot a$ (using a as a factor bc times).

In the last case, a^{b^c}, we have a value being raised to an exponent that is itself being raised to another exponent. This type of exponentiation is still right associative, and we make sure that the evaluation takes place from right to left; that is, we begin with the outermost right-hand operation, which would be the exponentiation using the exponent c, and apply it to what is directly in front of it—the base b—obtaining a new exponent b^c and then raise the a, which is now the base, to the exponent, b^c, to get the final answer. You are actually raising the base a to that new exponent:

$$a^{b^c} = a \cdot a \cdot a \cdot a \cdot a \cdot ... \cdot a \text{ (using } a \text{ as a factor } b^c \text{ times).}$$

In applications such as code programming or in e-mails or texting, there is no way to insert a natural exponent (superscript). All the input has to appear on a linear coded line. Donald Knuth (1938–), famed computer scientist and professor emeritus at Stanford University, introduced the up arrow, $\uparrow$, or the circumflex, $\wedge$ (located on the keyboard as a SHIFT/6), to substitute for the words "to the power of," which permits placement of the exponent on the same line as the base.

Take for example that $a = 2$, $b = 3$, and $c = 4$, and evaluate the following four expressions:

$ab^c = ab^\wedge c$	$(ab)^c = (ab)^\wedge c$	$(a^b)^c = (a^\wedge b)^\wedge c$ $= a^\wedge(bc)$	$a^{b^c} = (a)^\wedge b^\wedge c$
$= (2)(3^4) = 2(3)(3)(3)(3)$ $= 2(81)$ $= 162$	$= (2 \cdot 3)^4$ $= (6)^4$ $= (6)(6)(6)(6)$ $= 1296$	$\left(2^3\right)^4 = (2)^{3 \cdot 4}$ $(8)^4 = (2)^{12}$ $= 4096$	$= 2^{3^4}$ $= 2^{81}$ $= 2.417851639 \times 10^{24}$

The result of the last calculation is so large it can only be expressed in scientific notation. As natural number exponentiation grows at a faster rate than multiplication, which grows at a faster rate than addition, a "tower of exponents" grows a value faster than all operations, as in the fourth column in above chart.

Now with a^{b^c} we have extended the ordinary arithmetical operations of addition (or subtraction), multiplication (or division), and exponentiation to a level known as *hyperoperations,* or *repeated exponentiation,* or *tetration.*

As we can see from the definition, when evaluating a tetration expressed as our "exponentiation tower," the exponentiation is done at the deepest level first (in the notation, at the highest level). In other words,

$$2^{2^{2^2}} = 2^{(2^{[2^2]})} = 2^{(2^4)} = 2^{16} = 65,536.$$

Remember that exponentiation is right associative, so evaluating the expression in the other order, from the left, will lead to a different and erroneous answer:

$$2^{2^{2^2}} \neq [(2^2)^2]^2 = 2^{2 \cdot 2 \cdot 2} = 2^8 = 256.$$

34. WHY IS DIVISION BY ZERO NOT PERMISSIBLE?

Division by zero is forbidden. In fact, on the list of mathematical commandments this is on top. But why is division by zero not permissible? We in mathematics take pride in the order and beauty with which everything in the realm of mathematics falls neatly into place. When something arises that could spoil that order, we simple *define* it to suit our needs. This is precisely what happens with division by zero. You give students a much greater insight into the nature of mathematics by explaining why "rules" are set forth. So let us give this "commandment" some meaning.

Consider the quotient $\dfrac{n}{0}$, where $n \neq 0$. Without acknowledging the division-by-zero commandment, let us speculate (i.e., guess) what the quotient might be. Let us say it is p. In that case, we could check by multiplying $0 \cdot p$ to see if it equals n as would have to be the case for the division to be correct. We know that $0 \cdot p \neq n$, since $0 \cdot p = 0$. So there is no number p that can be the answer to this division. For that reason, we define division by zero to be invalid.

A more convincing case for defining away division by zero is to show students how it can lead to a contradiction of an accepted fact, namely, that $1 \neq 2$. We will show them that were division by zero acceptable, then $1 = 2$, which is clearly an absurdity!

Here is the "proof" that $1 = 2$:

$$\text{Let } a = b$$
$$\text{Then } a^2 = ab \qquad \text{[multiplying both sides by } a]$$
$$a^2 - b^2 = ab - b^2 \qquad \text{[subtracting } b^2 \text{ from both sides]}$$
$$(a - b)(a + b) = b(a - b) \qquad \text{[Factoring]}$$
$$a + b = b \qquad \text{[Dividing by } (a - b)]$$

$$2b = b \qquad \text{[Since } a = b, \text{ replace } a \text{ by } b]$$
$$2 = 1 \qquad \text{[Divide both sides by } b]$$

In the step where we divided by $(a - b)$, we actually divided by zero, because $a = b$, so $a - b = 0$. That ultimately led us to an absurd result, leaving us with no option other than to prohibit division by zero. By taking the time to discuss this rule about division by zero with your students, you will give them a much better appreciation for mathematics.

35. WHY IS $x \cdot 0 = 0$?

Most people will not remember how they felt when they heard about this for the first time. Consequently, they find it very difficult to explain this apparently elementary fact to others. Students are then simply told to learn it and accept it as truth. Of course, this is bound to create an uneasy feeling later and the vague idea of having missed out on an explanation: "If I hold a dollar in my hand and multiply it by zero, is it really gone? Who took it?"

One has to be aware that—when encountered for the first time—the fact $x \cdot 0 = 0$ might appear unusual and strange and that it takes some time for a student to grasp its meaning. When we try to come up with explanations, we should, as always, be patient and appeal to the student's basic understanding. And, most important, while talking to the student, one should try to figure out the sources of possible misunderstandings. First, make sure the student knows that "0" is a symbol meaning the absence of something or that it simply means "nothing." To do something zero times means not doing it at all. Next, the student must have a basic understanding of products: for example, 6 times 3 means to take six groups of three, or equivalently, three groups of six. If one takes zero groups of six, that means one takes no group at all, and that leaves one with nothing, that is, "0." The same result is obtained if one takes six groups of zero, meaning that one takes six times nothing and that remains nothing.

This might still be difficult to grasp for a student who is not used to the way of speaking like "take zero groups of something." It is important to know in which ways this could be misunderstood and to be able to offer alternative explanations. One might be asked "If I have 6 and add it three times, I get $6 + 6 + 6 = 6 \cdot 3$. But if I add it zero times, I do nothing at all to the original 6 and therefore I'm still left with the group of 6. So why isn't $6 \cdot 0 = 6$?" Here we see that the problem is probably one of rhetoric. It has more to do with our way of speaking than it does with mathematics: "Doing nothing, shouldn't that leave you with what you have?" But what do you "have" to start with? $6 \cdot 0$ just means that you "have" zero groups of 6, that is, nothing. Thus, multiplying by 0 is not equivalent to "doing nothing" (which would leave 6 as it is).

Sometimes it helps to change the picture. Think of 6 times 3 as taking 6 steps of length 3. If you take a step of length 0 you remain where you are. You can take as many steps of length zero as you want without moving forward. Or, to the same effect, you can take zero steps of an arbitrary length— that is, no steps at all—and again you will not change your position.

At a much later stage, when we start teaching mathematical proofs, one might bring up this question again. There is, indeed, a mathematical proof of this fact, which is not an axiom. A formal proof would have to be based on the basic properties ("axioms") concerning the operations "+" and "·". For elementary arithmetic of integers we have, in particular, the following axioms:

1. The addition "+" operation is both commutative (meaning: $x + y = y + x$) and associative (meaning: $x + (y + z) = (x + y) + z$)), the multiplication "·" operation is associative.

2. The multiplication "·" operation is distributive over "+" (meaning: $x \cdot (y + z) = x \cdot y + x \cdot z$ and $(x + y) \cdot z = x \cdot z + y \cdot z$).

3. There is a neutral (identity) element for addition (called "0") such that $x + 0 = x$.

4. For every x there exists an additive inverse, called $-x$, such that $x + (-x) = 0$.

Now, the proof is as follows. We consider $x \cdot 0$ and replace 0 by $0 + 0$ (axiom 3) and obtain with the help of the distributive law (axiom 2) the following:

$$x \cdot 0 = x \cdot (0 + 0) = x \cdot 0 + x \cdot 0.$$

We next add the inverse element $-x \cdot 0$ to both sides of this equation,

$$x \cdot 0 + (-x \cdot 0) = (x \cdot 0 + x \cdot 0) + (-x \cdot 0).$$

Axiom 3 states that the left side of this equation is 0 and hence

$$
\begin{aligned}
0 \ &= (x \cdot 0 + x \cdot 0) + (-x \cdot 0) \\
&= x \cdot 0 + (x \cdot 0 + (-x \cdot 0)) \quad \text{(using the associative law, axiom 1)} \\
&= x \cdot 0 + 0 \quad \text{(using axiom 4)} \\
&= x \cdot 0 \quad \text{(using axiom 3)}
\end{aligned}
$$

which completes the proof of $x \cdot 0 = 0$.

The proof also works for vectors and scalar multiplication, for which similar rules as the ones stated above apply. Let x be a vector, let $\mathbf{0}$ be the zero vector (to be distinguished from the scalar 0), and assume that "·" is the operation of multiplying a vector by a scalar. Then the corresponding result would be

$$x \cdot 0 = 0 \cdot x = 0,$$

that is, multiplying an arbitrary vector by the scalar 0 gives the zero vector.

The axioms (1–4) stated above are the axioms of a ring. Examples of rings are the set of integers, the sets of rational, real, or complex numbers, and the set of square matrices, each with their usual operations of addition and multiplication.

Note that the equation $x + 0 = x$ belongs to the axioms and need not be proved within ring theory. On the other hand, the equation $-(-x) = x$ does not appear in the list of axioms and thus has to be proved. Fortunately, the proof is simple: This equation states that x is the additive inverse of $-x$, and this means $(-x) + x = 0$. But using the commutativity of "+", this is just the statement of axiom 4, and this completes the proof of $-(-x) = x$.

36. WHAT IS 0!?

Factorials and factorial notation play a significant role when learning about combinations and permutations. Let us first define what a factorial is and how it is used. In general, factorials are merely products, and the symbol used to indicate a factorial is an exclamation point. For example, "five factorial" is written as 5! and equals $1 \cdot 2 \cdot 3 \cdot 4 \cdot 5 = 120$.

Note: $n!$ means the product of all the positive integers less than or equal to n; that is, $n! = 1 \cdot 2 \cdot 3 \cdot \ldots \cdot n$.

In general, $n! = 1 \cdot 2 \cdot 3 \cdot 4 \cdot \ldots \cdot (n-2) \cdot (n-1) \cdot n$.

Therefore, we can express $n!$ as $n \cdot (n-1)!$

This will help us to justify the value of 0!

Although we define 0! to equal 1, the following example will help to justify this definition:

From our version of $n! = n \cdot (n-1)!$, we can apply this to the situation when $n = 1$ to get $1! = 1 \cdot (1-1)! = 1 \cdot 0! = 0!$, which simplifies to $1 = 0!$

Perhaps a bit of a "stretch," but you can present another way of looking at 0! by considering the number of permutations in a set.

If n represents the number of elements in a set, say $n = 1$, then the number of permutations, $n! = 1! = 1$.

If $n = 2$, then the number of permutations is equal to $2! = 2$ or looking at the arrangements of the elements of the set: (2, 1), (1, 2).

If $n = 3$, then the number of permutations is equal to $3! = 6$ or (1, 2, 3), (1, 3, 2), (2, 1, 3), (2, 3, 1), (3, 1, 2), (3, 2, 1).

Therefore, for $n = 0$, $0!$ is equivalent to the number of permutations of the empty set, which is ordered in only one way, so $0! = 1$.

37. WHAT IS THE LARGEST NUMBER THAT CAN BE REPRESENTED IN THE DECIMAL SYSTEM WITH THREE DIGITS (AND WITHOUT USING ANY OTHER SYMBOLS)?

The answer to this question is simple. The largest number that can be written using only three digits is 9^{9^9}.

This can be evaluated as follows:

$$9^{9^9} = 9^{(9^9)} = 9^{387,420,489} \approx 4.281247731 \cdot 10^{3.69693099}.$$

If we were to evaluate this, we would find the number is one consisting of 369,693,100 digits, with the last few digits being . . . 2,627,177,289.

In comparison we could have written this progression of powers in the following way: $\left(9^9\right)^9 = 9^{81}$, which is equal to 19662705047555291361807590852691211628310345094421476692731541553379663911196809

$\approx 1.966270504 \cdot 10^{77}$—a number consisting of 78 digits. This number, $\left(9^9\right)^9$, is actually smaller than 9^{99}.

In summary, we can state the following: $99^9 < \left(9^9\right)^9 = 9^{81} < 9^{99} < 9^{9^9} = 9^{(9^9)}$.

Bear in mind we were not able to use $9!^{9!^{9!}}$ because of the additional symbols (!).

38. WHAT IS A PRIME NUMBER?

The term *prime number* stems from the true definition of the word *prime.* As with the word *primitive,* referring to the basic elements, in a mathematical sense a prime number is one of the basic numbers from which, through multiplication, we build the other numbers. By definition, a number greater than 1 is prime if it is evenly divisible by only itself and one: for example, 2, 3, 5, 7, 11. Numbers that are not prime are known as *composite numbers.* For example, 12 can be divided evenly by 1, 2, 3, 6, and 12, so it is a composite number.

The crucial importance of prime numbers to number theory and mathematics in general stems from the fundamental theorem of arithmetic, which states that every positive integer larger than 1 can be written as a product of one or more primes in a way that is unique (except for the order of the prime factors). Prime numbers can thus be considered the "basic building blocks" of the natural numbers. To illustrate: $23,244 = 2 \cdot 2 \cdot 3 \cdot 13 \cdot 149$, or $23,244 = 2^2 \cdot 3 \cdot 13 \cdot 149$.

It is interesting to note that Euclid may have been the first to develop a proof indicating that there are infinitely many primes. Even after 2000 years, it stands as an excellent model of critical thinking.

39. DOES THE NUMBER 1 BELONG TO THE PRIME NUMBERS?

The number 1 does not belong to the prime numbers. By definition, an integer greater than 1 is called a prime number, if its only positive factors are 1 and itself.

For example, the number 15 can be factored as $3 \cdot 5$ or $1 \cdot 3 \cdot 5$. If 1 were deemed a prime, the above examples would be considered different factorizations of 15 into prime numbers, so the definition would have to be modified.

It should be noted, however, that in earlier times, the Greeks did not even believe 1 to be a number, and therefore, did not deem it a prime. However, during the 19th century, mathematicians did regard the number 1 as a prime number.

To illustrate, Derrick Norman Lehmer (1867–1938), an American mathematician and number theorist, listed primes up to 10,006,721; his list was reproduced in 1956, and the list began with 1 as its first prime. Also, Henri Lebesgue (1875–1941), a French mathematician, was the last mathematician to call 1 a prime number.

40. HOW MANY PRIME NUMBERS ARE THERE?

How do you "prove" there is no end to finding prime numbers? A review of the definition of prime and composite numbers and how to find them along with a "lemma" that establishes that every natural number greater than 1 is divisible by a prime would lay a firm foundation for discussing such a proof.

Prime numbers are natural numbers that have exactly two divisors, themselves and 1. Numbers that have more than two divisors are called *composite numbers*. The number 1 is neither prime nor composite, since the only number that divides 1 is 1. So we begin with the smallest prime, 2, since its divisors are only 2 and 1. Then 3 is our next prime with exactly two divisors, 3 and 1. However, 4 is a composite number since it has more than two divisors, specifically 4, 2, and 1. The number 5 is prime, 6 is composite, and 7 is prime. Since all *even* numbers after 2 have 2 as a divisor, they are composite. However, not all *odd* numbers are prime. The number 9 is the first odd number we find that is a composite number having 9, 3, and 1 as divisors.

Eratosthenes (c. 276–195 BC) was a Greek mathematician, philosopher, and poet. Although none of his work survived, he is cited in other texts as having created a simple method called the "Sieve of Eratosthenes" for finding the primes: Create a list of natural numbers, test each to see if it is a prime, and if it is, cancel out all multiples of that prime as you move through your list. The list, of course, would be endless, and you would be spending all your time determining if a large value is a prime before you can move on to test the next number.

2	3	4	5	6	7	8	9	10	11	12	13	14
15	16	17	18	19	20	21	22	23	24	25	26	27
28	29	30	31	32	33	34	35	36	37	38	39	40
41	42	43	44	45	46	47

Crossing out all multiples of the prime 2, eliminating all the remaining multiples of the prime 3, and removing all the residual multiples of the primes 5 and 7, we are left with the following primes among the first 50 natural numbers: 2, 3, 5, 7, 11, 13, 17, 19, 23, 29, 31, 37, 41, 43, 47.

Actually, you just have to test all the primes up to the square root of the value you are checking, and if none of those primes divides evenly into your selected value, you have found another prime for the list. This would be an endless pursuit, since there is an endless list of natural numbers. As you will notice, there does not seem to be any pattern in their appearance. One may ask how many prime numbers there are. Are there a finite number of them? One can just try to find one greater than all the ones found so far. However, attempting to prove that there is no limit to the number of prime numbers by using this "Method of Exhaustion" would lead to a process of discovery that would go on infinitely. To prove the *infinitude of the primes*, we move into the branch of mathematics called abstract number theory and review a proof that has been credited to Euclid and that is presented in his *Book IX* as Proposition 20 (c. 300 BC).

To work on this proof, we set the groundwork by demonstrating that every natural number *n* is divisible by a prime number. Consider this a preamble, or lemma, to proving that there are an infinite number of primes.

We use an indirect proof; a proof by contradiction, in which we list all possible outcomes, assume the opposite of what we want to prove, and show the assumption leads to a contradiction and therefore is impossible. We reject the assumption so that the only possibility left is the result we are seeking.

Lemma: If *n* is a natural number and *n* > 1, then *n* is divisible by a prime. Either *n* is divisible by a prime or it isn't. These are the only two possibilities.

Assumption: Let us assume *n* is *not* divisible by a prime:

Then *n* cannot be a prime number. If it were, it could be divided by a prime, namely by itself. Hence *n* must be a composite number. Let $n = p \cdot q$, where *p* and *q* are natural numbers, neither of which is a prime and with *p* the smallest divisor of *n* other than 1. Since *p* is a composite number, it can be rewritten as the product of two divisors, both smaller than *p*, and greater than 1. We shall call those values *j* and *k* so that $p = j \cdot k$. Now *j* must be between the values of 1 and *p*, $1 < j < p$, so *j* is smaller than *p*, and *j* divides *p*. Since *p* divides *n* and *j* divides *p*, we have *j* dividing *n*. However, since *p* was defined as the smallest divisor of *n*, we have a *contradiction*. We just found a smaller divisor of *n*, namely, *j*. Therefore we reject the assumption that *n* does not have prime divisors. Hence, every natural number greater than 1 is divisible by a prime.

Now we can proceed to prove the theorem, again using our indirect method.

Theorem: There are infinitely many primes.

Assumption: There are a finite number, *n*, of primes. Let us call them $p_1, p_2, p_3, \cdots p_n$.

Let *X* equal the product of all those primes plus one, that is, $X = p_1 \cdot p_2 \cdot p_3 \cdots p_n + 1$.

Now *X* is not divisible by any of those *n* primes, since no matter which one you would try to divide by there would always be a remainder of 1. However, *X* must be divisible by a prime according to our lemma. This result is a contradiction of our initial assumption that there are only *n* primes, and therefore the only possibility left is that there are an infinite number of primes.

Let us test this approach: We will assume we know the first three primes (2, 3, 5) and the list of primes is complete. $N = (2)(3)(5) + 1 = 31$. Testing 31 for a prime divisor that is less than or equal to its square root has us testing all the primes up to 5. None divides evenly into 31, and so 31 is a new prime. Could this be all the primes that exist? Assuming we know the four primes and the list of primes is complete, we can state that $N = (2)(3)(5)(31) + 1 = 931$. Have we then discovered another new prime? Yes, but it is not the value of *N*.

It is one of the factors of the composite number $N =$ 931 = (19)(49). Therefore, 19 is added to our list of primes. So this method does not always yield a prime in the calculated value N, but it does yield a prime in the divisors of that value N that is not on our prime list.

Figure 2.9

Knowing that there are infinitely many primes has created a desire to pursue ever greater primes. The search, supported by a contest with prize money, has encouraged many mathematicians to join the hunt. Since the contestants can employ those never-complaining, never-bored computers at the University of California, Los Angeles, and elsewhere that are run continuously and perform 29 trillion calculations per second, the search has produced primes of millions of digits.

We can see a prime number displayed on postage stamps from Liechtenstein (2004) recognizing the largest prime number found as of 2001 in celebration of the discoveries of such large prime numbers (see Figure 2.9). This particular prime belongs to a special group of primes called the Mersenne Primes that have the form $2^n - 1$ and is composed of 4,053,946 digits. By 2008, it was relegated to ninth place when the prime $2^{43112609} - 1$, which has 12,978,189 digits, was discovered in the Great Internet Mersenne Prime Search, which began in 1996. The discovery qualified for a $100,000 research award.

41. WHAT IS A PALINDROME?

No matter what area of mathematics is being studied, students have a built-in, natural fascination for numbers and how numbers behave. Whether they are learning the concepts of odd and even numbers, counting strategies, or number patterns (like Fibonacci numbers), it is important to capitalize on and encourage the natural curiosity that students possess. To illustrate, during a lesson on prime and composite numbers, a student noticed the number 2442 was written on the board. The student acknowledged that the number was a composite number but also observed that when the digits of 2442 are reversed, you end up with the same number 2442. One student became very curious about the number 2442 and other numbers that read the same when the digits are reversed. Is this a special type of number?

The student's curiosity, observation, and question were noted. Here you ought to take the time to digress and explain what such a number is. The reply to the student's question is that numbers that read the same when the digits are reversed are special types of numbers and are known as *palindromes*. A palindrome is a number, word, or expression that reads the same way in either direction, that is, from left to right and from right to left. Palindromes can also be considered symmetrical numbers or words. Single-digit numbers and single-letter words are also considered palindromes.

The following are examples of palindromes:

RADAR

REVIVER

ROTATOR

LEPERS REPEL

MADAM I'M ADAM

STEP NOT ON PETS

NEVER ODD OR EVEN

NO LEMONS, NO MELON

DENNIS AND EDNA SINNED

ABLE WAS I ERE I SAW ELBA

A MAN, A PLAN, A CANAL, PANAMA

SUMS ARE NOT SET AS A TEST ON ERASMUS

Therefore, the number 2442, which appears on the board, is an example of a palindrome, because it reads the same from left to right and right to left. In addition, there are interesting facts about palindromes.

For example, if the digits of any number are reversed and added to the original number, and this process is repeated, the outcome will eventually be a palindromic number. This is known as the *reverse and add* process.

Using the reverse and add process, let us consider the following examples:

Example 1: Beginning with the number 62, to generate a palindromic number we use the reverse and add process:

62 + 26 = 88, which is a palindrome. Using the *reverse and add* process the palindrome 88 occurred in one step, but this does not necessarily happen with all numbers.

Example 2: Beginning with the number 149, we will apply the reverse and add process to get

149 + 941 = 1090; this is not a palindrome. However, if we continue the reverse and add process and add 0901 (which is actually 901) to 1090,

we get 1991, which is a palindrome. This time it took us two steps to arrive at a palindrome. However, it should be noted that in the examples above, using the reverse and add process, a palindrome came about at the first or second addition; however, other times a palindrome may occur after many more additions. For example, the number 473 will require five additions as shown below:

$$473 \quad 847 \quad \mathbf{1595} \quad \mathbf{7546} \quad \mathbf{14003}$$
$$\underline{+374 \quad +748 \quad +5951 \quad +6457 \quad +30041}$$
$$847 \quad \mathbf{1595} \quad 7546 \quad \mathbf{14003} \quad 44044 \rightarrow \text{Palindrome}$$

It is interesting to note that when using the reverse and add process, there exist numbers that produce a palindrome following many additions. For example, if the reverse and add process is used on the number 89, a palindrome does not occur until the 24th addition. Moreover, another conundrum is the number 196, where it is not known whether a palindrome will ever appear. This is one of those unsolved situations in mathematics!

You might also mention to students that the first few powers of 11 will produce palindromic numbers:

$$11^1 = 11$$
$$11^2 = 121$$
$$11^3 = 1331$$
$$11^4 = 14641$$

It is important to urge students to observe numbers that are unique and interesting found in a real-world context, such as those that appear as serial numbers on dollar bills, telephone numbers, birth dates, and license-plate numbers. These numbers may have strange and wonderful properties. All students should be encouraged to search for other such number patterns.

42. WHAT ARE SUCCESSIVE PERCENTAGES?

Percentage problems have long been the nemesis of most students. Problems get particularly unpleasant when multiple percentages need to be calculated in the same problem. We will begin by considering the following problem:

Wanting to buy a coat, Lisa is faced with a dilemma. Two competing stores next to each other carry the same brand coat with the same list price, but at two different discount offers. Store A offers a

10% discount year-round on all its goods, but on this particular day offers an additional 20% on top of the already discounted price. Store B offers a discount of 30% on that day in order to stay competitive. How many percentage points difference is there between the two options open to Lisa?

At first glance, students will assume there is no difference in price, since 10 + 20 = 30, yielding the same discount in both cases. The clever student will see that this is not correct, since in store A only 10% is calculated on the original list price, with the 20% calculated on the lower price, whereas at store B, the entire 30% is calculated on the original price. Now the question to be answered is, what percentage difference (with respect to the original list price) is there between the discount in store A and store B?

One typical procedure would begin by having the student assume the cost of the coat to be $100. For store A, calculating the 10% discount (yielding an intermediate price of $90) followed by calculating an additional 20% off the $90 price (or $18) would bring the final price down to $72. In store B, a 30% discount on $100 would bring the price down to $70, giving a discount difference of $2, which in this case is 2%. This procedure, although correct and not too difficult, is a bit cumbersome and does not always yield a full insight into the situation.

An interesting and quite unusual procedure[2] is provided for entertainment and fresh insight into this problem situation:

Here is a mechanical method for obtaining a single percentage discount (or increase) equivalent to two (or more) successive discounts (or increases).

1. Change each of these percentages involved into decimal form:

.20 and .10.

2. Subtract each of these decimals from 1.00:

.80 and .90 (for an increase, add to 1.00).

3. Multiply these differences:

(.80)(.90) = .72.

4. Subtract this number you obtained (i.e., .72) from 1.00:

1.00 − .72 = .28, which represents the combined *discount.*

(If the result of step 3 is greater than 1.00, subtract 1.00 from it to obtain the percent of *increase.*)

When we convert .28 back to percentage form, we obtain 28%, the equivalent of successive discounts of 20% and 10%.

This combined percentage of 28% differs from 30% by 2%; therefore, store B offers a better "deal."

This procedure can also be used to combine more than two successive discounts. In addition, successive increases, combined or not combined with a discount, can also be addressed with this procedure by adding the decimal equivalent of the increase to 1.00 (where by comparison the discount was subtracted from 1.00), and then continuing in the same way. If the result comes out greater than 1.00, then this reflects an overall increase rather than a discount, as was found in the above problem.

This procedure not only streamlines a typically cumbersome situation but also provides some insight into the overall picture. Take, for example, the following question: "Is it advantageous to the buyer in the above problem to receive a 20% discount and then a 10% discount, or the reverse—that is, a 10% discount and then a 20% discount?" The answer to this question is not intuitively obvious. Yet, since the procedure just presented shows that the calculation is merely multiplication, a commutative operation, we find immediately that there is no difference between the two.

So here you have a delightful algorithm for combining successive discounts or increases, or combinations of these. Not only is it useful, but it will enchant your students (and probably your colleagues as well).

NOTES

1. Smith, D. (2009, October 23). Ravaged by drought, Madagascar feels the full effect of climate change. *The Guardian*. Retrieved from http://www.guardian.co.uk/world/2009/oct/23/madagascar-drought.

2. It is provided without justification of its validity so as not to detract from the solution of the problem. However, for further discussion of this procedure, the reader is referred to Posamentier, A. S., Smith, B. S., & Stepelman, J. (2014). *Teaching secondary mathematics: Techniques and enrichment units* (9th ed.). Boston, MA: Allyn & Bacon.

3 Algebra Questions

43. WHY IS THE PRODUCT OF TWO NEGATIVE NUMBERS POSITIVE?

It is easy to give students the rules for multiplication of signed numbers: *If the two signs match, the product is positive, and if the two signs do not match, the product is negative*, and expect them to be memorized. However, it is another thing to have the students understand them and be able to recall examples that substantiate the rules.

One of the rules that makes the least "sense" to the algebra student is that the product of two negatives yields a positive. Of course, they have already heard this in their English classes and probably could easily correct anyone who says, "Do not tell me no bad news!" But can they correct someone who multiplies (–4) times (–3) and gets (–12)?

Let our first look at this rule be an example from daily life. Suppose the Nosuch City Weather Bureau reports that—as amazing as it might be—the temperature in the city has been decreasing by 2°F every day in the month of November. There are 30 days in November and today is November 15, and you learn that the city temperature was recorded at 40°F. What was the temperature 10 days ago? The solution involves going back 10 days, so the number of days is (–10) and for each of those days the temperature went "down by 2°F," meaning that the daily change in temperature is –2°F. Calculation becomes (Number of Days) × (Daily Temperature Change) = Total Temperature Change. Looking at the change in temperature from November 15 back to November 5, we multiply (–10) × (–2°) = +20°, which means that it was warmer earlier in the month. It was 60°F on November 5 in Nosuch City and went down to 40°F by November 15.

Another popular application comes from daily life and involves money. Suppose you set up a monthly reduction from your bank account to pay for your car loan. The bank is to deduct $100 every month from your checking account to pay for your loan. One month the bank makes an error and deducts $100 twice: –$100 and then another –$100. You immediately notify them of their error and they take away one (–1) of those deductions (–100) and so return (+100) to your account: (–1)(–100) = +100. The bank has negated a debit, which is the same as two negative values multiplying and you have an increase (a plus) in your account.

Here is a third example students may enjoy. Remember that Distance = Speed × Time. Suppose you are standing on a road at zero position, facing north—distances to your right [east] are positive distances and distances to your left [west] are negative. An auto traveling to the east of you at 30 mph is traveling at +30 mph while an auto traveling west of you going 30 mph is traveling –30 mph. So if a car passes you at 50 mph going east, in 2 hours it will be +100 miles: (+2)(+50) = +100 = 100 miles east. And if a car passes you at 50 mph and is traveling west for two hours it will be –100 miles: (+2)(–50) = –100 = 100 miles west. Now suppose you have a car that passes you and is going west at 50 mph. Where was it 2 hours ago? Time equals –2 hours and the speed is –50, so we have (–2)(–50) = +100 = 100 miles east. Two hours ago, the car was 100 miles east of you!

We can also begin the discussion by showing a number pattern that establishes the rule that (–)(–) = (+). Start with what the student accepts, namely that a positive times a negative gives a negative, (+)(–) = (–), and that zero times anything is zero, (0)(x) = (0), and then go on from there:

$$3 \times (-2) = -6$$

$$2 \times (-2) = -4$$

$$1 \times (-2) = -2$$

$$0 \times (-2) = 0$$

Now move into the negative multipliers and continue using the pattern:

$$-1 \times (-2) = +2$$

$$-2 \times (-2) = +4$$

$$-3 \times (-2) = +6$$

This establishes a pattern but still does not "prove" the convention we ask the students to use: a negative times a negative equals a positive. Perhaps a more sophisticated approach using the order of operations (PEMDAS) and the Distributive Law may be more convincing.

Let m and n be any two real numbers and let the number

$$A = mn + (-m)(n) + (-m)(-n).$$

Now factor out the (n) from the first two terms on the right side of the equal sign:

$$A = mn + (-m)(n) + (-m)(-n)$$
$$A = (n)[(m) + (-m)] + (-m)(-n)$$
$$A = (n)[0] + (-m)(-n)$$
$$A = 0 + (-m)(-n)$$

Therefore

$$A = (-m)(-n).$$

Now use the same definition for A but factor out the $(-m)$ from the last two terms on the right side of the equal sign:

$$A = mn + (-m)(n) + (-m)(-n)$$
$$A = mn + (-m)[(n) + (-n)]$$
$$A = mn + (-m)[0]$$
$$A = mn + 0$$

Therefore

$$A = mn.$$

Well, now we have $A = (-m)(-n)$ and $A = mn$.

Thus, because two values are equal to the same value, they are equal to each other, and we have shown that

$$(-m)(-n) = mn,$$

which shows that the product of two negative numbers is positive.

44. WHY MUST a AND b BE POSITIVE IN ORDER FOR THE FOLLOWING TO HOLD TRUE? $\sqrt{a} \cdot \sqrt{b} = \sqrt{a \cdot b}$?

The Product Rule for Radicals states that if $\sqrt{a}$ and $\sqrt{b}$ are real numbers, then $\sqrt{a} \cdot \sqrt{b} = \sqrt{a \cdot b}$.

Implicit in this rule is that in order for $\sqrt{a}$ and $\sqrt{b}$ to be real values, both a and b must be nonnegative. If either is zero, the problem is trivial as the square root of zero is zero, and the product of zero and any other value is zero. Let us concentrate on positive a's and b's, which are the values within the radical sign and are called *radicands*.

The principal square root of a negative number is defined as follows: For any positive real number b, the principal square root of the negative number is defined by $\sqrt{-b} = i\sqrt{b}$, where "i" represents $\sqrt{-1}$, a mathematical construct called an imaginary number, and $i^2 = -1$.

In general the definition of the principal nth root of a real number a is $\sqrt[n]{a} = b$ which means that $b^n = a$. If n, the index, is even, and a is nonnegative ($a \geq 0$), then b is also nonnegative ($b \geq 0$). If n is odd, a and b can be any real numbers. In general, when n is even, the nth root of a negative radicand does not exist in the set of real numbers.

Consider the following:

$$(1)\ \sqrt{25} \cdot \sqrt{4} = \sqrt{25 \cdot 4} = \sqrt{100} = 10$$
$$(2)\ \sqrt{25} \cdot \sqrt{4} = 5 \cdot 2 = 10$$

In the above, both radicands, 25 and 4, are positive, so their square roots are real and the problem can be done two different ways using either approach (1) or (2).

However, consider the following:

$$(1)\ \sqrt{-25} \cdot \sqrt{-4} = \sqrt{(-25)(-4)} = \sqrt{100} = 10$$
$$(2)\ \sqrt{-25} \cdot \sqrt{-4} = i\sqrt{25} \cdot i\sqrt{4} = i^2\sqrt{(25)(4)} = i^2\sqrt{100} = (-1)(10) = -10$$

Using the same first approach in this case leads to an erroneous answer. The square roots of -25 and -4 are *not* real and so the rule that permits multiplying of the radicands before taking the square root does not apply. The second solution is the only correct way to do the multiplication when dealing with imaginary values.

We see this in the following that shows that if we violate this rule, we will have $-1 = +1$, which is clearly absurd.

Consider $\sqrt{a \cdot b} = \sqrt{a} \cdot \sqrt{b}$ to be true for $a = b = -1$. Now consider this:

$$\sqrt{a \cdot b} = \sqrt{(-1) \cdot (-1)} = \sqrt{1} = 1, \text{ but also consider}$$

$$\sqrt{a} \cdot \sqrt{b} = \sqrt{-1} \cdot \sqrt{-1} = \left(\sqrt{-1}\right)^2 = -1.$$

This "proves" that $1 = -1$.

By the same token, using exponents we have the same dilemma:

On the one hand, $((-1)^2)^{\frac{1}{2}} = (-1)^{2 \cdot \frac{1}{2}} = (-1)^1 = -1$, and on the other hand $((-1)^2)^{\frac{1}{2}} = (+1)^{\frac{1}{2}} = 1$.

Again, $-1 = +1$.

45. WHY IS IT ADVANTAGEOUS TO RATIONALIZE THE DENOMINATOR?

Rationalizing the denominator is a process that helps change fractions to a simpler form and thereby enables a simpler way to evaluate fractions.

A class of algebra students was solving equations containing rational expressions. One student was about to evaluate $\dfrac{1}{\sqrt{3}}$ when the teacher suggested to the student to first "rationalize the denominator," and then evaluate the expression. She said, "When you have a single square root in the denominator you just multiply the fraction by 1—written in the form of the numerator and denominator having the same radical expression as the original denominator."

Therefore, $\dfrac{1}{\sqrt{3}}$ becomes $\dfrac{1}{\sqrt{3}} \cdot \dfrac{\sqrt{3}}{\sqrt{3}} = \dfrac{\sqrt{3}}{3}$.

The student then asked the teacher, "Isn't $\dfrac{1}{\sqrt{3}}$ just as good as $\dfrac{\sqrt{3}}{3}$?"

The teacher replied, "The two expressions are equivalent, but in this case, the product yields an equivalent expression that does not have any radicals in the denominator, which makes it easier to calculate and evaluate, since you need only divide 1.732 by 3 to get 0.5773, which is easier than dividing 1 by 1.732." However, with today's technological tools the difference of division may not be so dramatic. Yet when we have the following expression, $\dfrac{8\sqrt{3}}{\sqrt{2}} = \dfrac{8\sqrt{3}}{\sqrt{2}} \cdot \dfrac{\sqrt{2}}{\sqrt{2}} = \dfrac{8\sqrt{6}}{2} = 4\sqrt{6}$, it simplifies much more easily when the denominator is rational. In short, we rationalize a denominator because having an irrational number in the denominator makes it harder to work with than having an irrational number in the numerator.

46. WHAT IS MEANT BY THE "ABSOLUTE VALUE" OF A VARIABLE?

The absolute value of a number x is denoted by $|x|$, and it is defined as the distance of the number x from zero on the number line. A distance is always a nonnegative number, so the absolute value is always nonnegative. For example, the absolute value of 6 is 6, and the absolute value of -6 is also 6, because both 6 and −6 are just 6 units away from 0 on the number line. The absolute value makes a negative number positive while leaving positive numbers unchanged.

In other words, the absolute value of a number is just its magnitude, ignoring its sign. It is a common mistake to assume that the absolute value of a variable is computed just by dropping the minus sign. Ignoring the sign of a variable is not the same as dropping the sign. The variable x could stand for a positive as well as a negative number. Whenever x is negative, the quantity $-x$ would be positive and in this case $|x| = -x$.

The following is the formal definition of the absolute value of a variable:

$$|x| = \begin{cases} x & \text{for } x \geq 0 \\ -x & \text{for } x < 0 \end{cases}$$

It is a function that maps real numbers onto the nonnegative real numbers, and its graph is depicted in Figure 3.1.

Figure 3.1

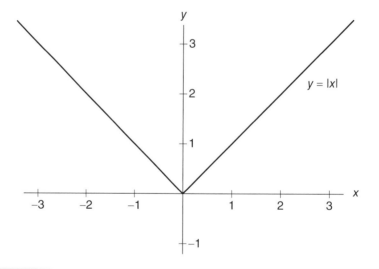

The most important properties of the absolute value can be deduced from the definition above:

1. $|0| = 0$

2. $|-x| = |x|$. It is acceptable to drop or change signs inside the absolute value bars. Hence, for example, $|x - 9| = |9 - x|$.

3. $|xy| = |x|\,|y|$. In particular, $|-x| = |(-1)x| = |-1|\,|x| = |x|$.

Here are some additional hints you might want to pass on to your students:

a. In some cases, the absolute value is also denoted by abs(x), for example, on a pocket calculator.

b. Try to make your vertical lines denoting absolute value somewhat longer than a 1 so as to avoid confusion.

c. For any number x, the quantity $-|x|$ is always negative, if $x \neq 0$. Just putting a minus sign in front of x does not make it negative (since x is a variable and cannot be assumed to be positive).

Whenever you have to solve an equation involving absolute values of the variable, you have to distinguish two cases and actually solve the equation twice! Consider, for example,

$$|x + 10| = 4.$$

We cannot just drop the bars, because we do not know whether $x + 10$ is positive or negative. The only way to solve this equation is to consider both possibilities and perform the computation twice:

First case: $x + 10 \geq 0$.

In this case, $|x + 10| = x + 10$. Hence the equation becomes $x + 10 = 4$ or $x = -6$.

Second case: $x + 10 < 0$.

In this case, $|x + 10| = -(x + 10) = -x - 10$. Then we obtain $-x - 10 = 4$ or $x = -14$.

Therefore, the equation $|x + 10| = 4$ has two solutions: $x_1 = -6$ and $x_2 = -14$. Insert these solutions into the original equation to see if both work!

For complex numbers, the absolute value is defined as the distance from 0 (the coordinate origin) in the complex plane. Using the Pythagorean theorem, we find that the absolute value of a complex variable is given by

$$|z| = \sqrt{x^2 + y^2}, \text{ for all } z = x + iy \in \mathbb{C}.$$

This is also a valid definition for real numbers, that is,

$$|x| = \sqrt{x^2}, \text{ for all real numbers } x.$$

On a more advanced level, it is useful to note the following inequalities (called triangle inequalities):

$$|x + y| \leq |x| + |y|$$

$$|x + y| \geq ||x| - |y||,$$

which also hold for complex numbers or n-dimensional vectors. Equality occurs whenever $y = \lambda x$ with some $\lambda \geq 0$ (for real variables, equality holds, in particular, whenever x and y are both positive, or both negative).

47. WHAT IS A VARIABLE? A TERM? AN EXPRESSION? AN EQUATION?

As students begin to explore concepts in algebra, they are met with new ideas and new vocabulary that they will be seeking to understand and apply. What might be helpful in answering some of these questions would be providing definitions as well as illustrations and also comparisons of the terminology they will see and need to use.

To begin, the "numbers" they have become accustomed to using and have understood in arithmetic are now called "constants." The constants never change their values. Algebra introduces the idea of a *variable* quantity, which will be quite different from the constant where 1 is always 1. The value of a variable, as its name implies, can change in each given problem. Therefore we represent a variable by a letter or a symbol as x, y, a, Ω, β, $\aleph$, or such that is unknown to us until we "solve" the problem.

When we have any combination of constants and variables joined by multiplication or division (but not addition or subtraction), the grouping is called a *term*. Terms do not have to include both constants and variables but can be simply a singular constant or variable as well. The juxtaposition of constants and variables implies they are multiplying each other in the algebraic term. Remember, terms may include exponents because exponents represent a shortened form of multiplication, where the base is multiplied the number of times in the exponent: a^3 can be written as $(a)(a)(a)$ and $-2x^2y^3z = (-2)(x)(x)(y)(y)(y)(z)$.

When we have two or more terms combined by some operation, we have formed an *expression*. The expression is the next building block in algebraic thinking, this time putting together terms using addition or subtraction. Some examples of expressions are $a^2 + b^2$, $x - 2$, and $a^{\frac{1}{n}} + \sqrt[n]{b}$.

You may notice that we have covered a number of forms of combining constants and variables, all without setting them equal to each other. This is because once we place an equal sign between two expressions or variables, we have created an *equation*. An *equation* is a mathematical statement that asserts the equality of two expressions.

48. HOW CAN WE HAVE STUDENTS REALIZE THAT THE AVERAGE OF RATES IS NOT SIMPLY THE ARITHMETIC MEAN?

Begin by posing the following problem:

> On Monday, a plane makes a round-trip flight from New York City to Washington, DC with an average speed of 300 mph. The next day, Tuesday, there is a wind of constant speed (50 mph) and direction (blowing from New York City to Washington, DC). With the same speed setting as on Monday, this same plane makes the same round trip on Tuesday. What is the average velocity for the round trip on Tuesday?

This problem should be slowly and carefully posed so that students notice that the only thing that has changed is the "help and hindrance of the wind." All other controllable factors are the same: distances, speed regulation, airplane's conditions, and so on. An expected response is that the two round-trip flights ought to be the same, especially since the same wind is helping and hindering two equal legs of a round-trip flight.

One might digress to an entirely different situation, letting this problem lie unresolved for a while. More closely to "home," a question can be posed about the grade a student deserves who scored 100% on nine of 10 tests in a semester and on one test scored only 50%. Would it be fair to assume that this student's performance for the term was 75% (i.e., $\frac{100+50}{2}$)? The reaction to this suggestion will tend toward applying appropriate weight to the two scores in consideration. The 100% was achieved nine times as often as the 50% and therefore ought to get the appropriate weight. Thus, a proper calculation of the student's average ought to be $\frac{9(100)+50}{10}=95$. This clearly appears more just!

Now, how might this relate to the airplane trip? Realization that the two legs of the "wind trip" require different amounts of time should lead to the notion that the two speeds of this trip cannot be weighted equally as they were done for different lengths of time. Therefore, the time for each leg should be calculated and then appropriately apportioned to the related speeds.

We first find the times of two legs of the round trip in wind:

$$t_1 = \frac{d}{350} \text{ and } t_2 = \frac{d}{250}.$$

The total time for the wind round-trip is

$$t = \frac{d}{350} + \frac{d}{250}.$$

The "total rate of speed" or rate for the wind round-trip (which is really the average rate of speed) is

$$r = \frac{2d}{\dfrac{d}{250} + \dfrac{d}{350}} = \frac{2(350)(250)}{250 + 350} \text{, so}$$

$$r \approx 291.67,$$

which is slower than the no-wind trip, and hence took more time.

This average of rates (≈ 291.67) is called the *harmonic mean* between the two speeds of 350 mph and 250 mph. It might prove fruitful to digress to a discussion of the harmonic mean and its related series, the harmonic sequence.[1]

The harmonic mean for a and b is $\dfrac{2ab}{a + b}$, and for three numbers, a, b, and c, the harmonic mean is $\dfrac{3abc}{ab + bc + ac}$.

It is important to include as part of any good mathematics instruction program that the averaging of rates cannot be handled as though they were ordinary numbers, since they exist over varying amounts of time.

49. WHY DOES 0.99999 . . . = 1?

In mathematics, the repeating decimal 0.99999. . . (sometimes denoted as $.\overline{9}$) is a real number and can be proved to be the number 1. Various proofs have been developed; however, these proofs may have varying contextual suppositions, which include historical perspectives and cognitive levels of the student.

In order to show why 0.99999 . . . = 1, we will use the method of converting a repeating decimal into fraction form. Keep in mind that this is an intuitive approach, which informally proves the conjecture. Before we begin, let us consider the following analogous example:

To convert .2525 . . . into fraction form, we will let $x = .\overline{25}$ and then multiply both sides of the equation by 100, to get $100x = 25.252525 \ . \ . \ . = 25.\overline{25}$. By subtracting $x = .\overline{25}$ from both sides of the equation, we get $99x = 25$: thus $x = \dfrac{25}{99}$.

Using the same method as above, let us now consider $0.99999\ldots = .\overline{9}$. We let $x = .\overline{99}$, and then multiply both sides of the equation by 100 to get $100x = 99.\overline{99}$. Subtract $x = .\overline{99}$ from both sides of the equation, to get $99x = 99$; thus $x = \dfrac{99}{99}$, which is equal to 1.

We can also look at this with the following example:

Suppose we wish to find the sum $0.\overline{6} + 0.\overline{3}$.

We can do this either as decimals or as fractions:

As decimals, $0.\overline{6} + 0.\overline{3} = 0.\overline{9}$.

As fractions, $0.\overline{6} + 0.\overline{3} = \dfrac{2}{3} + \dfrac{1}{3} = \dfrac{3}{3} = 1$.

This would then imply that $0.\overline{9} = 1$.

50. IS A ROAD WITH A SLOPE OF 20% TWICE AS STEEP AS A ROAD WITH A 10% SLOPE?

This might seem like a silly question, but a thorough understanding of this problem helps to avoid basic misunderstandings later on.

What does it mean for a road to be twice as steep as another one? The answer of course depends on how you measure "steepness." In school we have two such possibilities: We could either use the grade or slope defined as the quotient of rise over run, that is, by dividing the vertical gain (measured on the y-axis) by the horizontal distance (measured on the x-axis). Or we could quantify steepness by the angle of inclination, that is, the angle of the road with the horizontal direction. Students with a knowledge of trigonometry could already convert one measure into the other by using the tangent function on their pocket calculator.

Figure 3.3 shows that twice as steep in angles is quite different from twice as steep in slope, except for very small inclination angles α, where $\tan\alpha \approx \alpha$.

Figure 3.2

Source: © Getty Images/Thinkstock

Figure 3.3

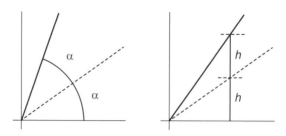

In both images of Figure 3.3, the solid line is "twice as steep" as the dashed line.

It is important to develop an early qualitative feeling for the nonlinearity of the connection between the angle of inclination and the slope of a line. This can be seen quite easily in more extreme examples. A slope of 100% = 1 means an inclination angle of 45 degrees. With "twice as steep," we could either mean twice the slope, that is, 200% (about 63 degrees), or twice the inclination angle, that is, 90 degrees.

Despite its simplicity, this problem has some aspects that may even fool an experienced teacher. The following example could well appear in a school textbook.

The Glacial Aerial Tramway Kaprun III is a famous cable car in the Austrian Alps, featuring the highest support pillar in the world. It goes from $h_1 = 2{,}452$ m to a height of $h_2 = 3{,}029$ m and covers a horizontal distance of $L = 2{,}200$ m. Compute the average angle of inclination.

Can you see why this exercise is flawed? It cannot be solved. From the given information, one could well compute the average slope $m = \dfrac{(h_2 - h_1)}{L}$ and even the angle $\alpha = \arctan(m)$ corresponding to the average slope, which is what the author of this school book probably had in mind when he wrote this exercise. However, the angle corresponding to the average slope is, in general, not the average angle of inclination (unless the slope is constant). The average angle cannot be computed, unless one has precise information about the angle as a function of the horizontal distance.

Figure 3.4 shows an example, where the average inclination angle and average slope is easily computed and compared. It is easy to see that the average slope of the two paths joining A and B is identical, but their average angle of inclination is different.

When discussing steepness, slope, and angles of inclination, you might want to add some historical remarks to stimulate your students' interest. For example, it is an interesting fact that measures of steepness were already known thousands of years ago. In ancient Egypt, one used the *seked* as a

Figure 3.4 The two paths joining the points *A* and *B* have the same average slope but different average inclination angles.

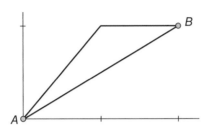

measure for the slope of pyramids. The seked was based on the *royal cubit* (about 53 cm) as a unit of length, which was divided into 28 *fingers*. The seked was then defined as the number of fingers that one has to move horizontally for a rise of one royal cubit. A seked of *n* is thus equivalent to a slope of $\dfrac{28}{n}$.

We see that a steeper pyramid has a smaller seked. For example, the seked of the Chephren pyramid on the Giza plateau near Cairo is 21; thus it is steeper than the famous Cheops pyramid next to it, which has a seked of 22. By the way, the slope $\dfrac{28}{22}$ of the Cheops pyramid is approximately equal to $\dfrac{4}{\pi}$ (here we used $\dfrac{22}{7}$ as a good approximation for π). The fact that π appears in the (approximate) proportions of the great pyramid has led to many (somewhat ill-founded) speculations about the mathematical design principles applied by Egyptian architects.

In the famous Papyrus Rhind, which is a collection of mathematical exercises dating from the Egyptian Middle Kingdom, we find, among others, the following problems:

Problem: If a pyramid is 250 cubits high and the side of its base 360 cubits long, what is its seked? (*Solution:* $\dfrac{504}{25} = 20.16$)

Problem: If you construct a pyramid with base side 140 cubits and with a seked of 21, what is its altitude? (*Solution:* $\dfrac{208}{3}$ cubits)

Perhaps your students might find some fun in solving mathematical exercises that are more than 3,500 years old.

51. IS THERE A NUMBER THAT DIFFERS FROM ITS RECIPROCAL BY 1?

Let us start by considering a positive number n and represent the reciprocal by $\frac{1}{n}$. We are told that the difference between the two numbers is 1, which leads to the equation: $n - \frac{1}{n} = 1$, which is to say also that n is greater than $\frac{1}{n}$.

We will now take this equation $n - \frac{1}{n} = 1$ and eliminate the variable in the denominator by multiplying both sides of this equation by n to get $n\left(n - \frac{1}{n}\right) = n$. This gives us $n^2 - 1 = n$, or $n^2 - n - 1 = 0$.

Using the quadratic formula, $n = \dfrac{-b \pm \sqrt{b^2 - 4ac}}{2a}$, to solve this equation, where $a = 1$, $b = -1$, and $c = -1$, we have

$$n = \frac{-(-1) \pm \sqrt{1^2 - 4(1)(-1)}}{2(1)}$$

$$= \frac{1 \pm \sqrt{5}}{2}.$$

The positive value (root) is known as the golden ratio[2] and is the only number that has the characteristic that it differs from its reciprocal by 1.

$$\phi = \frac{1 + \sqrt{5}}{2} = 1.61803398874989484820\ldots, \text{ and}$$

$$\phi - 1 = \frac{1 + \sqrt{5}}{2} - \frac{2}{2} = \frac{\sqrt{5} - 1}{2} = 0.61803398874989484820\ldots.$$

52. WHAT IS A DETERMINANT, AND HOW CAN IT BE USED TO SOLVE A SYSTEM OF LINEAR EQUATIONS?

A determinant is a square array of the coefficients and constants of the equations that permit us to solve the system of equations using only arithmetic. The determinant is useful to solve a system of linear equations, whenever the number of equations equals the number of variables. In practice, it is mainly used in the case of two or three variables. The name "determinant" actually describes what it does: the determinant is a number D that *determines* whether the system of linear equations has a unique solution. $D \neq 0$ tells us that the system has exactly one solution. From $D = 0$, we may conclude that the system has either no solution at all or more than one solution.

Consider the following system with two variables x and y in two equations:

$$ax + by = u$$

$$cx + dy = v$$

If you multiply the first equation by d and the second by $-b$, you obtain

$$adx + bdy = ud$$

$$-bcx - bdy = -vd$$

By adding these equations, we get $(ad - bc)\, x = ud - vb$.

Similarly, if you multiply the original equations by $-c$ and a, respectively, you would obtain in an analogous way $(ad - cb)y = av - cu$.

Obviously, we get a unique solution for the original system, whenever the combination $ad - bc$ is nonzero. In this case $x = \dfrac{ud - vb}{ad - bc}$, and $y = \dfrac{av - cu}{ad - bc}$.

The characteristic expression $ad - bc$ is called the determinant of the system and denoted by the symbol

$$D = \begin{vmatrix} a & b \\ c & d \end{vmatrix} = ad - bc.$$

It will be helpful to remember that the determinant is the product of the numbers along the main diagonal minus the product of the numbers along the other diagonal:

The solution of the system of equations can now be rewritten using determinants. We obtain, assuming that $D \neq 0$,

$$x = \frac{\begin{vmatrix} u & b \\ v & d \end{vmatrix}}{\begin{vmatrix} a & b \\ c & d \end{vmatrix}},$$

$$y = \frac{\begin{vmatrix} a & u \\ c & v \end{vmatrix}}{\begin{vmatrix} a & b \\ c & d \end{vmatrix}}.$$

This is known as Cramer's rule for two equations containing two variables.

The coefficients of the variable in the system of equations are often arranged in the form of a matrix as $A = \begin{pmatrix} a & b \\ c & d \end{pmatrix}$.

$D = ad - bc$ is then called the determinant of the matrix A. It is used to write the inverse of the matrix A, which exists if and only if $D \neq 0$. In order to find the inverse of a two-by-two matrix, (a) switch the elements on the main diagonal, (b) take the negative of the off-diagonal elements, (c) divide the resulting matrix by D, and you will obtain

$$A^{-1} = \frac{1}{D} \begin{pmatrix} d & -b \\ -c & a \end{pmatrix}.$$

It might be useful to mention the following properties of the determinant, which hold in any dimension and can be easily verified by students for the two-dimensional determinant defined above:

1. If all entries in any row (or any column) are 0, then the determinant is 0.

2. If the entries in one row (or column) are multiples of the entries in the other row (or column), then the determinant is 0.

3. Interchanging any two rows (or any two columns) causes the determinant to change its sign.

4. If you multiply all elements of one column (or one row) with a constant, the determinant is multiplied by the same constant.

5. If you add a multiple of one row (or column) to the other row (or column), the determinant remains unchanged.

It is a good exercise to ask your students what the items above mean for the original system of equations and its solutions.

Moreover, you might want to mention the following geometric interpretation of the determinant: *If the rows (or columns) are interpreted as vectors in the two-dimensional plane, then |D|, the absolute value of the determinant, is the area of the parallelogram spanned by these two vectors.*

This is related to the following fact about vectors in space:

$$\text{Let } \vec{s} = \begin{pmatrix} a \\ c \\ 0 \end{pmatrix} \text{ and } \vec{t} = \begin{pmatrix} b \\ d \\ 0 \end{pmatrix}; \text{ then } \vec{s} \times \vec{t} = \begin{pmatrix} 0 \\ 0 \\ D \end{pmatrix}, \text{ where } D = ad - bc.$$

53. HOW DO THE ARITHMETIC, GEOMETRIC, AND HARMONIC MEANS COMPARE IN MAGNITUDE?

The *arithmetic mean, A,* is one of the earliest taught concepts from the field of statistics. It is simply the sum of the items being averaged divided by the number of items. For two items a and b, $A = \dfrac{a+b}{2}$.

The *geometric mean, G,* may be encountered in geometry (often seen as the mean proportional) and is the nth root of the product of the n items. For two items a and b, $G = \sqrt{ab}$.

The *harmonic mean, H,* is not too popular, since there is not much that can be done with it. It usually comes up as the mean of rates over the same base, and is, for n items, n times the product of the n items divided by the sum of products of the n items taken $(n-1)$ at a time.

For two items a and b,

$$H = \frac{2ab}{a+b} = \frac{2}{\dfrac{a+b}{ab}} = \frac{2}{\dfrac{a}{ab}+\dfrac{b}{ab}} = \frac{2}{\dfrac{1}{a}+\dfrac{1}{b}} = \frac{1}{\dfrac{\dfrac{1}{a}+\dfrac{1}{b}}{2}}.$$

Thus, it is also defined to be the reciprocal of the arithmetic mean of the reciprocals.

It is furthermore possible to create a relationship between the three means as $\dfrac{2ab}{a+b} = \dfrac{ab}{\dfrac{a+b}{2}} = \dfrac{\left(\sqrt{ab}\right)^2}{\dfrac{a+b}{2}}$, so therefore $H = \dfrac{G^2}{A}$.

We shall now show how these three means may be compared in size using a geometric model.

Consider a semicircle, with center O, and radius $\overline{RO}$. A perpendicular from R meets the diameter $\overline{AB}$ at P. From P a perpendicular is drawn to $\overline{RO}$, meeting it at S.

Figure 3.5

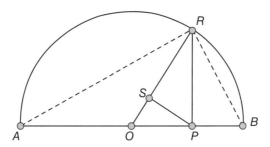

Let us begin by designating our key line segments, which will be used in our mean comparison. They are $AP = a$ and $BP = b$.

We now have to find line segments in Figure 3.5 that represent the various means in terms of a and b.

The *arithmetic mean* for a and b is RO and is found as follows:

$$RO = \frac{1}{2}AB = \frac{1}{2}(AP + BP) = \frac{1}{2}(a + b)$$

The *geometric mean* for a and b is PR and is found as follows:

$\triangle BPR \sim \triangle RPA$; therefore, $\dfrac{PB}{PR} = \dfrac{PR}{AP}$, or $(PR)^2 = (AP)(PB) = ab$; so that $PR = \sqrt{ab}$.

The *harmonic mean* for a and b is RS and is found as follows:

$\triangle RPO \sim \triangle RSP$; therefore, $\dfrac{RO}{PR} = \dfrac{PR}{RS}$, or $RS = \dfrac{(PR)^2}{RO}$, but $(PR)^2 = ab$,

and $RO = \dfrac{1}{2}(a + b)$; thus we get $RS = \dfrac{2ab}{a + b}$.

Now for the comparisons. Consider $\triangle ROP$, where, $RO > PR$. In $\triangle RSP$, $PR > RS$; therefore $RO > PR > RS$.

If, on the other hand, $\overline{RO} \perp \overline{AB}$, then $RO = PR = RS$. Therefore, $RO \geq PR \geq RS$. That is, the *arithmetic mean* is greater than or equal to the *geometric mean*, which is greater than or equal to the *harmonic mean*.

We shall now show how these three means may be compared in size using simple algebra.

For the two nonnegative numbers a and b,

$$(a - b)^2 \geq 0$$

$$a^2 - 2ab + b^2 \geq 0$$

Add $4ab$ to both sides:

$$a^2 + 2ab + b^2 \geq 4ab$$
$$(a + b)^2 \geq 4ab$$

Then take the positive square root of both sides:

$$a + b \geq 2\sqrt{ab}$$

or $\quad \dfrac{a+b}{2} \geq \sqrt{ab}$

This implies that the *arithmetic mean* is greater than or equal to the *geometric mean*. (Equality is true only if $a = b$.)

Continuing from the third step above:

$$a^2 + 2ab + b^2 \geq 4ab$$
$$\left(a + b\right)^2 \geq 4ab$$

Multiply both sides by ab:

$$ab\left(a + b\right)^2 \geq \left(4ab\right)\left(ab\right)$$
$$ab \geq \frac{4a^2 b^2}{\left(a+b\right)^2}$$

Then take the positive square root of both sides:

$$\sqrt{ab} \geq \frac{2ab}{a+b}.$$

This implies that the geometric mean is greater than or equal to the harmonic mean. (Here, equality holds whenever one of these numbers is zero or if $a = b$.)

We can then conclude that the arithmetic mean $\geq$ the geometric mean $\geq$ the harmonic mean, $A \geq G \geq H$.

54. WHAT IS A FUNCTION?

A function is a relationship between two sets in which *every* element in the first set is related to exactly one element (unique) in the second set. The sets may be distinct from each other or may be the same set; they may be finite or infinite. Let us call the first set the domain and the second set the co-domain. Expressing the relationship with diagrams often works well with finite sets.

Example 1

In Figure 3.6, we have two sets, S and T, that both have two elements. The arrows express the relationship between the elements. $x, y \in S$ and $a, b \in T$.

$$\text{Function:} \quad x \rightarrow a$$
$$y \rightarrow b$$

We have created a function between set S and set T such that x in set S relates to a in set T and y in set S relates to b in set T. Every value in set S is related to exactly one value in set T.

Figure 3.6

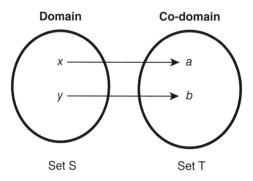

Example 2

Now, in Figure 3.7, we have set T with three elements, a, b, and c. The function still holds because there is no requirement to use all the elements of the co-domain, and each element of the domain S is related to a single element of the co-domain.

Figure 3.7

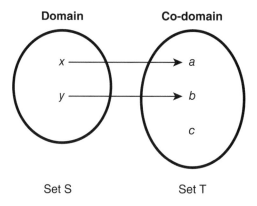

The *range* of the function is the set of those values in the co-domain that are the "images" of the values in the domain. In the above example, the range = {a, b}.

Example 3

In Figure 3.8, we have not satisfied the function definition because set S has three elements and the element z is not related to any element in set T. This violates the definition that every element in the domain must be related to exactly one value in the co-domain. $x \rightarrow a$ and $y \rightarrow b$, but z does not relate to any element in set T.

Figure 3.8

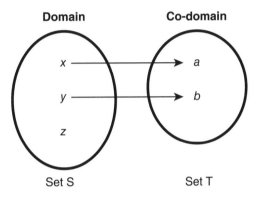

Example 4

In Figure 3.9, we see another violation of the function definition. We have element x in set S being related to two different elements in set T: $x \rightarrow a$ and $x \rightarrow b$, when the definition only permits each value in the domain to be related to a unique value in the co-domain.

Figure 3.9

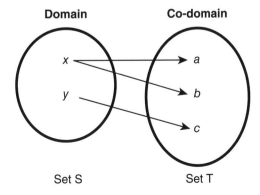

Example 5

In Figure 3.10, the function takes each value in the domain to the same value in the co-domain: $x \rightarrow a$ and $y \rightarrow a$. Each value in the domain is related to exactly one value in the co-domain. The fact that all the domain values are related to the same value makes this a valid "constant function."

Figure 3.10

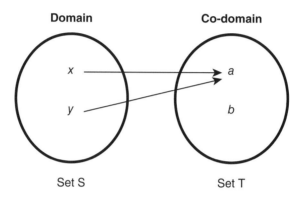

Let us look at a function between two infinite sets. Here are the three most familiar infinite sets along with their standard letter notation:

$\mathbb{R}$ is the set of all real numbers.

$\mathbb{Z}$ is the set of all integers.

$\mathbb{Q}$ is the set of all rational numbers.

As we know, $\mathbb{Z} \subset \mathbb{Q} \subset \mathbb{R}$. Since each set has an infinite number of members, we use an algebraic function notation to represent the relationship. This way the relationship will be able to work on all the values in the domain.

"$f(x)$" is read as "f of x." (You can use any letter, not only "f," to represent the words "function of.")

Example 6

Let us look at a function defined by this notation. Figure 3.11 demonstrates the function expressed by $f(x) = x + 1$. The value in parentheses is called the "argument," and it is this value that is substituted for the domain variable "*x*" in the expression *x* + 1 to get the corresponding value in the co-domain of the function when *x* is equal to a particular value.

Let this function be defined on the sets $\mathbb{Z} \rightarrow \mathbb{Z}$. The function above is known as the *successor function* and, as you can see, each integer in the domain relates to its successive integer in the co-domain.

So $f(3) = 3 + 1 = 4$, $f(55) = 55 + 1 = 56$, $f(0) = 0 + 1 = 1$, $f(-3) = -3 + 1 = -2$.

Figure 3.11

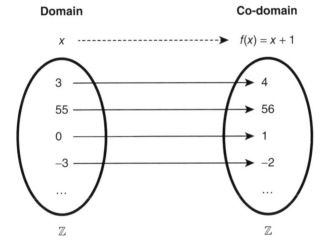

Example 7

Another familiar function is the squaring function. Example 7 demonstrates $g(x) = x^2$, using $\mathbb{R}$ as the domain and $\mathbb{R}$ as the co-domain.

$\mathbb{R} \rightarrow \mathbb{R}$

$g(2) = 4$

$g(-2) = 4$

$g(1.2) = 1.44$

$g(-.25) = .625$

$g(0) = 0$

Here you notice that none of the negative values in the co-domain will be related by the function rule to a value in the domain.

In Example 8 below, we define the square-root function. A square root of x is defined as a solution y of the equation $y^2 = x$. For any positive real number, there are two such solutions, namely, $y_1 = +\sqrt{x}$ and $y_2 = -\sqrt{x}$.

The expression $\sqrt{x}$ is called the principal square root of x and it is a nonnegative number whenever x is nonnegative. The principal square root can even be defined for negative numbers x, but in this case it is a complex number (see Question 68, "What is i?").

Example 8

$h(x) = \sqrt{x}$ with domain $\mathbb{R}^{nonneg}$ (the set of all nonnegative real numbers) and co-domain $\mathbb{R}$.

This function associates the unique positive square root to every nonnegative x; for example,

$h(4) = 2,$

$h(0) = 0.$

Notice that the range of the function h just consists of the set of nonnegative real numbers. It is not possible to extend the domain to all of $\mathbb{R}$, unless the co-domain is also changed to include complex numbers:

$h(-25) = 5i$(an imaginary value not in $\mathbb{R}$).

Associating both square roots $\pm\sqrt{x}$ with a positive number x would not define a function of x, because this relates two distinct values in the co-domain to every positive x in the domain.

55. WHAT IS MEANT BY THE INVERSE OF A FUNCTION?

When we describe inverses, we sometimes use the word "undo" in mathematics. For example, addition and subtraction are inverse operations, where one "undoes" the other, just as multiplication and division are inverse operations. This same line of thinking can be applied to inverse functions.

We denote inverse functions in two ways, and either notation may be used: $f^{-1}(x)$, or $f'(x)$. The "-1" in the first notation is not an exponent.

If we are given a function $f(x)$, we can define it operating as follows: $f(4)$ = 9. Then we would assume that the inverse function would return (relate the 9 back to the 4): $f^{-1}(9) = 4$.

More formally, we could state this as f and g are two functions, such that if $f(g(x)) = x$ and $g(f(x)) = x$, then g is the inverse of f and f is the inverse of g.

Interestingly, the graph of f^{-1} is the reflection about the line $y = x$ of the graph of f. Students might find this idea interesting, so determining and graphing inverse functions will reinforce a number of ideas and concepts. Not all functions have inverses. For example, take the simple quadratic $f(x) = x^2$. Thinking about the graph of this function (and what might happen if we try to reflect this graph over $y = x$) as well as the negative values will provide insight into why this function does not have an inverse for all values.

Upon further study of inverses, we find that f has an inverse if and only if, when its graph is reflected about the line $y = x$, the resulting graph belongs to a function. An easy test to see if a graphed figure belongs to a function is the "vertical line test" in which drawing any vertical line will intersect the graph at most once. If it intersects more than once, the graph is not the graph of a function.

As a further note, the following question can be useful to get an insight into the notion of a mathematical definition: *Why* is a function defined in such a way, that *at most one* element in the co-domain is related to *every* element in the domain? Because the function expresses the idea of the dependence of one quantity (the co-domain variable or "dependent variable") on another quantity (the domain variable or independent variable). This becomes obvious if we consider an example. When we want to describe the dependence of the temperature on the time of day, we need to have a unique temperature for every instant of time. But not every possible value of the temperature will occur during a day and it is, of course, possible that the same temperature occurs at two different times. This unsymmetric relation between time and temperature is precisely described by the statement that the temperature is a function of the time—but the time is not a function of the temperature.

56. CAN A FUNCTION BE EQUAL TO ITS INVERSE?

This is a very interesting question. But before answering this question, let us revisit functions and the inverse of functions. When learning about inverse functions, Lisa and David were comparing their graphs for the function $f(x) = 2x + 3$ and $f^{-1}(x) = f(y) = \dfrac{y-3}{2}$ using the same set of data.

Figure 3.12

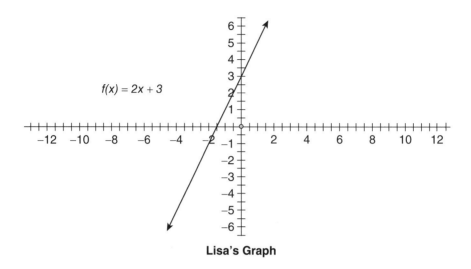

$f(x) = 2x + 3$

Lisa's Graph

Figure 3.13

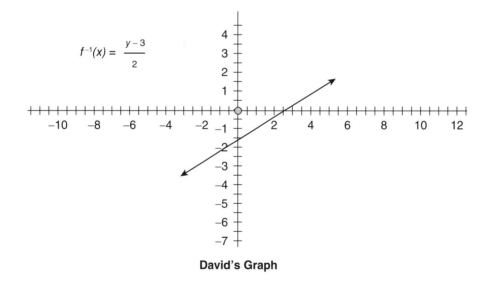

$f^{-1}(x) = \dfrac{y-3}{2}$

David's Graph

Using the graphs in Figures 3.12 and 3.13 and their corresponding table of values, let us determine which graph is correct and corresponds to the function $f(x) = 2x + 3$. The table of values that Lisa has is the correct table of values for the function $f(x) = 2x + 3$. However, David's table of values has a table of values for x and y, with the numbers in Lisa's table reversed.

Lisa's table of values
corresponds to the function $f(x) = 2x + 3$

x	−1	0	1	2
y	1	3	5	7

David's table of values corresponds
to the inverse function $f^{-1}(x) = f(y) = \dfrac{y-3}{2}$

x	1	3	5	7
y	−1	0	1	2

That is, the independent and dependent variables are reversed between Lisa's and David's table of values, respectively. The function that corresponds to David's table of values is the inverse function—denoted by $f^{-1}(x)$. One method for finding the inverse of a function is to solve for the independent variable. That is, replacing y for $f(x)$ and solving for x, we get $x = \dfrac{y-3}{2}$, so that the inverse function is $f^{-1}(x) = f(y) = \dfrac{y-3}{2}$.

Let us look at the two graphs on the same set of axes (see Figure 3.14). Notice that each ordered pair (a, b) is said to be a reflection of (b, a) about the line $y = x$. Therefore, David's function

$$f^{-1}(x) = f(y) = \frac{y-3}{2}$$

is the inverse function of Lisa's function.

Figure 3.14

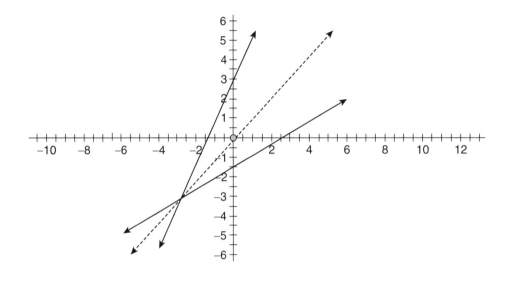

Now, let us go back to our original question: Can a function be equal to its inverse?

The answer is YES!

- One such function is known as the "identity function," which is the function $f(x) = x$.
- Also, $f(x) = -x$ for every value of x.
- Another function that is equal to its inverse is $f(x) = \dfrac{x}{x-1}$, for every nonzero number x.
- Also, $f(x) = \dfrac{1}{x}$ for every nonzero number x is its own inverse.

In general, any function that has a graph symmetric to the line $y = x$ is an inverse of itself.

57. WHAT IS A 1–1 ONTO FUNCTION?

Let us review the definition of a function: A function is a relationship between two sets in which every element in the first set corresponds to exactly one element in the second set. The relationship may be expressed using arrows in finite sets and algebraic expressions in infinite sets. The sets may be distinct from each other or may be the same set; they may be finite or infinite. Let us call the first set the *domain* and the second set the *co-domain*.

We can now examine two properties a function may additionally satisfy: namely, the property of being *one to one* and the property of being *onto*. A function that satisfies both these properties belongs to a very special group called *one-to-one correspondences (bijections)*. When a function relates the elements of the domain and the elements of the co-domain, and that function is one-to-one and onto, we are able to define an *inverse function*. This will set up a correspondence between the elements of the co-domain and the domain that somewhat "reverses" the action of the original function.

Let us take a look at the one-to-one aspect first. A function that is one-to-one has every value x in the domain set X associated with a different element y in the co-domain set Y. Suppose the function f relates every x in X to a different y in Y so that if $x_1 \neq x_2$, then $f(x_1) \neq f(x_2)$.

In finite sets the correspondence can easily be shown with diagrams. Example 1a, in Figure 3.15, displays a correspondence that is one-to-one, while Example 1b, also in Figure 3.15, shows one that is not one-to-one because the elements "1" and "2" in the domain relate to the same element, "A," in the co-domain.

Figure 3.15

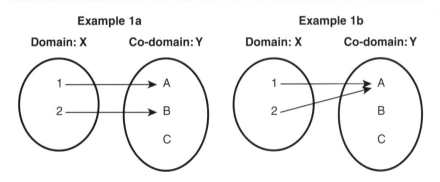

Example 1a

Domain: X   Co-domain: Y

Example 1b

Domain: X   Co-domain: Y

To demonstrate a one-to-one property on infinite sets, you need to prove that for every x_1 and x_2 in the domain, if $x_1 \neq x_2$, then $f(x_1) \neq f(x_2)$ in the co-domain.

We will use the method of proving the contrapositive, which is logically equivalent to the original statement. We shall begin with x_1 and x_2, which are elements of set X. If $f(x_1) = f(x_2)$, elements of the co-domain, then we will show that x_1 must be equal to x_2.

Let us define a function, f, on the set of real numbers such that $f: \mathbb{R} \rightarrow \mathbb{R}$ by the function rule $f(x) = 2x + 1$ for all real numbers.

Suppose x_1 and x_2 are real numbers in X, so that $f(x_1) = 2x_1 + 1$ and $f(x_2) = 2x_2 + 1$. Now, we *assume* that $f(x_1) = f(x_2)$. Hence, $2x_1 + 1 = 2x_2 + 1$. By subtracting 1 from both sides of the equation we get $2x_1 = 2x_2$, so that $x_1 = x_2$. Therefore, we have shown that if the corresponding "images" of two values in the co-domain are the same, then the two elements in the domain are the same and the correspondence is one-to-one.

Now let us consider the squaring function g on the set of real numbers such that $g: \mathbb{R} \to \mathbb{R}$ by the function rule $g(x) = x^2$ for real numbers. Is this function one-to-one? Let us analyze this before we attempt to prove it. It seems as though we get the same answer when squaring the positive of a value as we would get squaring the negative of the same value, thus violating the definition for one-to-one.

To prove that a function is not one-to-one, you need to present just one counterexample and you will have done your job. Suppose you let $x_1 = 5$ and $x_2 = -5$ and x_1, x_2 are real and distinct values in the domain.

Now $g(x_1) = (5)^2 = 25$, and $g(x_2) = (-5)^2 = 25$, and 25 is a real number and is in the co-domain. We have just shown that there exist x_1, x_2 such that $g(x_1) = g(x_2)$ while $x_1 \neq x_2$.

So now we have two elements, x_1 and x_2 of $\mathbb{R}$, that are not equal, yet correspond under the function rule to the same element in the co-domain. This proves that the function is not one-to-one.

As we saw in Figure 3.15, there may be elements in the co-domain that do not correspond to any element in the domain. However, if our function requires that each element in the co-domain corresponds to some element in the domain, we have an onto function. So we can define "onto" as having a function $f: X \to Y$, where for every element y in Y there exists an element x in X such that $f(x) = y$. Looking back at Examples 1a and 1b, we see two functions that are not onto, as there is at least one element in set Y that is not the "image" of any element in set X.

Let us draw a function between two finite sets that is onto (see Figure 3.16).

Figure 3.16

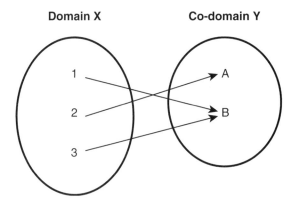

Every value in the set Y corresponds to at least one value in the set X. Obviously this function is not one-to-one since two different values in set X correspond to the same value in set Y, but it is an onto function.

Although it is fairly easy to check finite sets for the "onto" property, let us see what has to be done to prove the same in infinite sets.

We shall now show that the function f with $f(x) = 2x + 1$ is an onto function $\mathbb{R} \to \mathbb{R}$.®

Consider an element y in the co-domain. If every x in the domain is mapped to the y elements by the function, is there an "inverse" function that will map the y elements back to the x elements?

Suppose there is a y in $\mathbb{R}$ that equals $2x + 1$; let us solve for that x.

$2x + 1 = y$, which gives us $x = \dfrac{y-1}{2}$, so that if a value x exists, as the preimage of the y value, it is equal to $\dfrac{y-1}{2}$, which is a real number.

Now let us apply f to this particular value for x.

$$f(x) = f(\frac{y-1}{2}) = 2\,\frac{y-1}{2} + 1 = y - 1 + 1 = y,$$

and we have proved the function f is onto.

If we use the same function rule but work with the integers $\mathbb{Z} \to \mathbb{Z}$, would we have an onto function? The problem with the value of $x = \dfrac{y-1}{2}$ is that if y is an even integer, subtracting 1 and then dividing by 2 would give a fractional answer; thus there would be no x in the domain set of integers that would correspond to an even integer y in the co-domain. If $y = 4$ in the co-domain, then the x would have to equal $\dfrac{3}{2}$ for $f(x)$ to equal 4, which would be impossible since the domain has only integers. So this function is not onto. Here then is your counterexample to show the function is not onto.

Now a function can be both one-to-one and onto. If $f: X \to Y$ is both one-to-one and onto, then there is a function, f, that maps any given element x in X to one element y in Y such that $y = f(x)$ and given any y in Y there is a function, f^{-1}, that maps every element in Y to one element x in X such that $f^{-1}(y) = x$. The functions f and f^{-1} are inverses of each other. This is called a *one-to-one correspondence* between the sets and establishes unique pairs of elements (x, y). The co-domain then equals the *range* of the function.

An example of a function that is both one-to-one and onto is the successor function working on the integers: $f(x) = x + 1: \mathbb{Z} \to \mathbb{Z}$. The inverse function would be $f^{-1}(x) = x - 1: \mathbb{Z} \leftarrow \mathbb{Z}$ (see Figures 3.17 and 3.18).

Figure 3.17

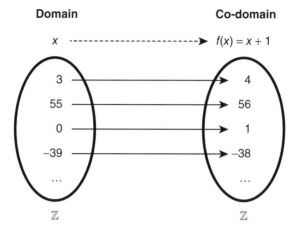

Figure 3.18

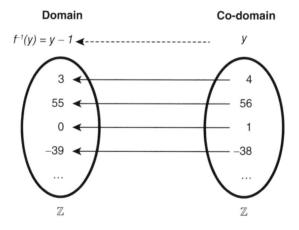

58. WHERE DOES THE QUADRATIC FORMULA COME FROM?

Before answering this question, it is important to consider the origins of the quadratic formula and the many mathematicians who worked on this topic.

In 1545, Gerolamo Cardano (1501–1576) was an Italian Renaissance mathematician who accumulated works related to quadratic equations. The quadratic formula covering all cases was first obtained by Simon Stevin

(1548–1620), who was a Flemish mathematician and military engineer. In 1637, René Descartes (1596–1650), a French mathematician, published *La Géométrie*, which contained the quadratic formula in the form we know today. The first appearance of the general solution in recent mathematical works emerged in a paper by Henry Heaton in 1896.

In general, students are familiar with the quadratic formula, which is used as a tool to find the roots of any quadratic equation. But from where does this formula come, and how is it derived? First we look at the quadratic equation in standard form with a, b, and c representing the coefficients of the terms all on one side and set equal to zero: $ax^2 + bx + c = 0$. Its solution is given by a formula involving only the three coefficients a, b, and c.

The solution to this quadratic equation will be that $x = \dfrac{-b \pm \sqrt{b^2 - 4ac}}{2a}$.

Let us derive the above quadratic formula using a technique known as *completing the square*.

Divide the above equation by a to get the following equation: $x^2 + \dfrac{b}{a}x + \dfrac{c}{a} = 0$.

Isolate the terms containing x by subtracting $\dfrac{c}{a}$ from both sides to get the following: $x^2 + \dfrac{b}{a}x = -\dfrac{c}{a}$.

We now take $\dfrac{1}{2}$ of the coefficient of the x term and square it to get $\left(\dfrac{b}{2a}\right)^2$, which we then add to both sides of the equation to get the following:

$$x^2 + \frac{b}{a}x + \left(\frac{b}{2a}\right)^2 = -\frac{c}{a} + \left(\frac{b}{2a}\right)^2.$$

Factor the left-hand side of the equation as follows:

$$\left(x + \frac{b}{2a}\right)^2 = -\frac{c}{a} + \left(\frac{b}{2a}\right)^2.$$

Taking the square root of both sides of the equation results in

$$x + \frac{b}{2a} = \pm\sqrt{-\frac{c}{a} + \left(\frac{b}{2a}\right)^2}.$$

Subtracting $\dfrac{b}{2a}$ from both sides of the equation, we get

$$x = -\frac{b}{2a} \pm \sqrt{-\frac{c}{a} + \left(\frac{b}{2a}\right)^2}.$$

Simplifying, we get

$$x = -\frac{b}{2a} \pm \sqrt{\frac{-4ac + b^2}{4a^2}} = -\frac{b}{2a} \pm \frac{\sqrt{-4ac + b^2}}{2a} = \frac{-b \pm \sqrt{b^2 - 4ac}}{2a},$$ which is the

quadratic formula that we sought to develop.

59. WHAT IS A PARABOLA?

Figure 3.19

The *parabola* is one of the four conic sections, and its shape is formed by the intersection of a plane and a nappe of a right circular cone. The plane is parallel to a line on the surface of the cone (see Figure 3.19). The other three shapes occur when the "cutting" plane assumes other directions.

From an analytical point of view (see Figure 3.20), we consider the path of point P moving in the plane so that it is always an equidistant from a fixed point called the *focus*, F, and a fixed line called a *directrix*. This path is the *locus* of all points that meet this condition and forms the parabolic curve. The turning point of the parabola as it reverses direction is called the *vertex point*.

Examining the parabola in the Cartesian *xy*-plane, we can see the path developing as the point moves on so it is equidistant from the focus point F and the directrix line. Remember that the distance from the point P to the line is always measured along perpendiculars.

Figure 3.20

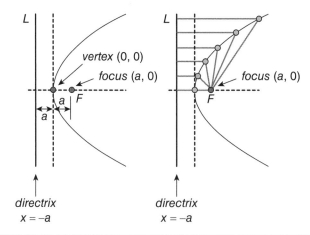

All conic sections can be defined in analytic geometry as second-degree equations. The general equation of a conic section is given as

$$Ax^2 + Bxy + Cy^2 + Dx + Ey + F = 0.$$

The parabola has only one square term, so either A or C must equal zero and the equation has either an x-squared term or a y-squared term. As shown in Figure 3.21, the equation of this simple parabola would be $x^2 = 4ay$, where a is the distance from the vertex point, assumed to be $(0, 0)$, to the focus point, F, or to the directrix line, L. Extending the line from the vertex point to the directrix and beyond forms a vertical axis of symmetry for the parabola, and if the vertex point is at the origin, the axis of symmetry is the y-axis. This is also the case if the vertex point lies on the y-axis and is $(0, y)$. If the equation of the parabola is $y^2 = 4ax$, where the square term is "y," the shape has symmetry with a horizontal axis formed by the line from its vertex to the focus point and perpendicular to its directrix line. Analogously, if the vertex point is the origin, the axis of symmetry will be the x-axis. This will also be true if the vertex point lies on the x-axis and is $(x, 0)$.

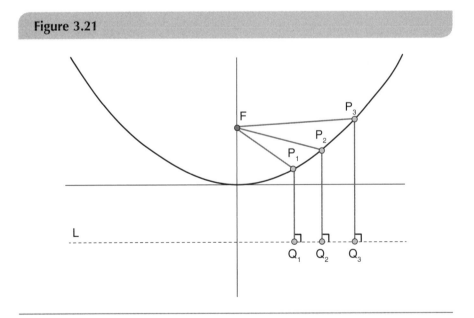

Figure 3.21

Parabolic shapes are popular and have many uses. A few examples of parabolic paths include when a ball is thrown between two people or when a flying fish jumps out of the water. In car headlights, the light is at the focus point, reflected onto a parabolic surface and then distributed out along parallel lines (see Figure 3.22).

Figure 3.22

  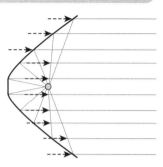

Source: Wikimedia Commons   *Source:* Wikimedia Commons

The opposite principle operates in flashlights, mirrors, and satellite dishes in which the light or waves reflect off the parabolic surface and from there come to the focus point.

60. HOW CAN YOU FIND THE TURNING POINT OF A PARABOLA?

A parabola was named (though not discovered) by the wealthy Greek philosopher Apollonius from the first century BC and is defined as the set of all points in the plane equidistant from a given line (called the directrix) and a given point not on the line (called the focus) (see Figure 3.23).

Figure 3.23

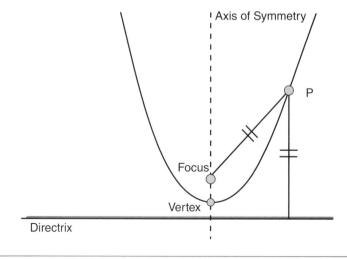

This definition is not always shared in early algebraic thinking, where the parabola is described as the graph of a quadratic function. A number of well-known mathematicians contributed to our understanding of the parabola, including Pappus, Galileo, Gregory, and Newton.

The parabola can be expressed in more than one way; the most common expressions follow:

Standard form: $y = ax^2 + bx + c$ where $x = \dfrac{-b}{2a}$ is the axis of symmetry

Vertex form: $y = a(x - h)^2 + k$ where (h, k) is the turning point

Intercept form: $y = (x - p)(x - q)$ where p and q are x-intercepts of the parabola

There are different procedures for finding the turning point, which is also known as the vertex of the parabola.

Standard Form	Vertex Form	Intercept Form
$y = ax^2 + bx + c$	$y = a(x - h)^2 + k$	$y = (x - p)(x - q)$
1. Find the axis of symmetry: $x = \dfrac{-b}{2a}$ 2. Substitute this value, $\dfrac{-b}{2a}$, into the original equation and solve for y.		1. Find the average of p and q: $x = \dfrac{p + q}{2}$ 2. Substitute this x-value into the original equation to find the y-value.
Vertex = $\left(\dfrac{-b}{2a},\ a\left(\dfrac{-b}{2a}\right)^2 + b\left(\dfrac{-b}{2a}\right) + c \right)$	Vertex = (h, k)	Vertex = $\left(\dfrac{p + q}{2},\ \left(\dfrac{p + q}{2} - p\right)\left(\dfrac{p + q}{2} - q\right) \right)$

61. WHAT IS AN ELLIPSE?

The *ellipse* is one of the four conic sections, and its shape is formed by the intersection of a plane and a nappe of a right circular cone. If the "cutting" plane is perpendicular to the vertical axis of the cone, the curve formed is a *circle*. The center of the circle will lie on the vertical height line of the cone, and the diameter will be determined by how far from the apex point the cut is made. The further from the apex point the cut is made, the larger the diameter of the circle. This cut will be in only one nappe of the cones (see Figure 3.24). The circle is often considered a special case of the ellipse. Tilting the "cutting" plane so that it is not perpendicular to the axis of the cone nor parallel to a straight line on the surface of the cone and making a cut entirely in one nappe will yield an ellipse (a slightly "compressed" circle; see Figure 3.25).

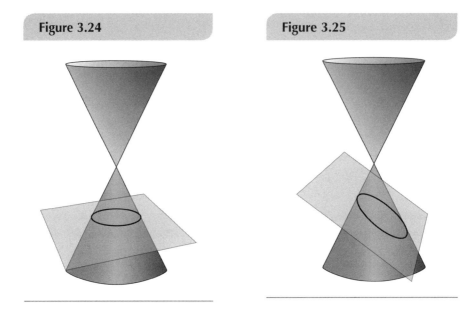

Figure 3.24

Figure 3.25

From an analytical point of view, we consider two fixed points in the plane, F_1 and F_2, and the path of a point X moving in the plane so the sum of its distances from these two points has a constant value. The path is the locus of all points that meet this condition and forms the ellipse (see Figure 3.26). If the two focus points become one point such that $F_1 = F_2$, then the ellipse

Figure 3.26

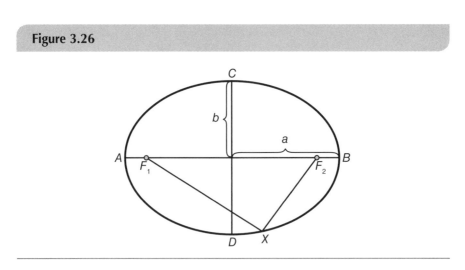

becomes a circle, the F point becomes the center of the circle, and the constant sum becomes the diameter of the circle.

All conic sections can be defined in analytic geometry as second-degree equations. The general equation of a conic section is given as

$$Ax^2 + Bxy + Cy^2 + Dx + Ey + F = 0.$$

The ellipse has both an x^2 and y^2 term so the A and C are never zero. If $A = C$ and A and C have the same sign, the equation represents a circle. If $A \neq C$ but they still have the same sign, it is the equation of an ellipse.

In Figure 3.26, an ellipse with a *semi-major* axis a and *semi-minor* axis b, centered at the point $(0, 0)$ and having its major axis on the x-axis, may be specified by the equation $\dfrac{x^2}{a^2} + \dfrac{y^2}{b^2} = 1$.

If the center of the ellipse is not at the origin but at some point (j, k), then the equation becomes $\dfrac{(x - j)^2}{a^2} + \dfrac{(y - k)^2}{b^2} = 1$.

It is sometimes easier to work with the "discriminant" of the general equation, $B^2 - 4AC$, to confirm the shape of the conic section. For an ellipse, the value of the discriminant must be less than zero, as the B coefficient is always zero.

There are two degenerate cases that can occur. If the equation reduces to a form $Ax^2 + Cy^2 = 0$, the only solution is the point $(0, 0)$, and if it reduces to a form such that $Ax^2 + Cy^2 < 0$, then there is no real solution.

Elliptic shapes appear all around us. In an elliptical trainer, the oval foot pedal path is smoother and more like natural motion. Planetary movements were described in the 17th century by German scholar Johannes Kepler as elliptical orbits with the sun at one of the two foci. Many shapes of pills, eyeglass lenses, soaps, watch faces, gems, cameos, architectural windows, and roofs can be viewed as elliptical or circular (see Figures 3.27 and 3.28).

Figure 3.27

Source: Polka Dot/Thinkstock

Figure 3.28

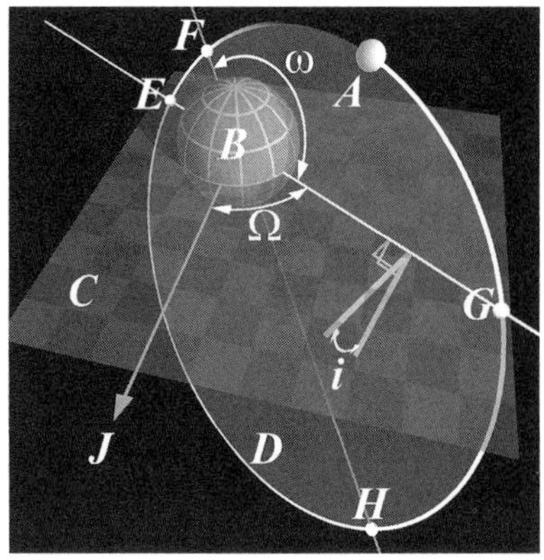

Source: Wikimedia Commons

Elliptical shapes that enhance and improve performance are used in electronics, optics, calculations in statistics and finance, engineering, gear mechanics, and harmonic oscillators to name a few. Elliptical, or spherical geometry (non-Euclidean), is conducted on the surface of a sphere in which all lines are great circles of the sphere, and there are no parallel lines. This geometry was the basic hypothesis in Einstein's general relativity theory and became the foundation of new branches of mathematics.

A mirror in an elliptical shape having a light source at one of its foci will have all the rays reflected to the second focus. Sound waves can be reflected in a similar manner as have been shown in the elliptical-shaped whisper section of the United States Capitol building, where John Quincy Adams was known to eavesdrop on his political foes by standing at one focus in the room while they spoke "political secrets" standing at the other focus.

You can draw your own ellipse. Establish two fixed points (foci) on a horizontal line on a board. Then take a length of string (greater than the distance between the foci) and tie one end to one point and the other end to the other point. Hold a pencil, marker, or piece of chalk vertically and pull the string taut (forming a triangle) as you draw; then move the pencil about the two foci to create the locus path. You should see an ellipse shape emerging.

62. WHAT IS A HYPERBOLA?

The *hyperbola* is one of four conic sections, and its shape is formed by the intersection of a plane and the two nappes of the right circular cone. When a plane is parallel to the vertical axis or makes an angle less than a line on the surface of the cone makes with the axis, it will produce a shape called a hyperbola. This cut will be two branches or two arcs of the hyperbola, one in each nappe (see Figure 3.29).

Figure 3.29

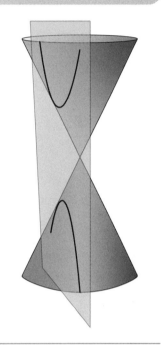

From an analytical point of view, we consider two fixed points in the plane, F_1 and F_2 (foci), determining a line, and the path of point P moving in the plane so the absolute value difference of its distances from the foci is a constant: $\left|P_1F_2 - P_1F_1\right| = \left|P_2F_2 - P_2F_1\right| = \left|P_3F_2 - P_3F_1\right|$ (see Figure 3.30). The path is the *locus* of all points that meet this condition and it forms two disconnected branches (bows), one in each nappe, called a hyperbola. The two arcs that are formed extend outward, approaching a pair of intersecting straight lines (called *asymptotes*) as they widen but never cross, all moving to infinity. In these horizontal arcs, the line joining the rightmost point of the left branch with the leftmost point of the right branch (the *vertices*) is called the *transverse axis,* and the line perpendicular to and bisecting the segment between the vertices is called the *conjugate axis.*

Figure 3.30

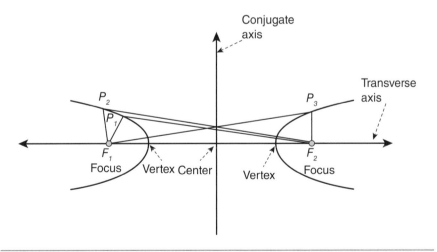

Source: Polka Dot/Thinkstock

All conic sections can be defined in analytic geometry as second-degree equations, with the general equation of a conic section as $Ax^2 + Bxy + Cy^2 + Dx + Ey + F = 0.$.

It is sometimes easier to work with the "discriminant" of the general equation, $B^2 - 4AC$, to confirm the shape of the conic section. For a hyperbola, the value of the discriminant must be greater than zero.

There is a degenerate hyperbolic shape that can occur, when coefficients A and C have opposite signs and $F = 0$, such as $x^2 - y^2 = 0$. In that case, the hyperbola becomes two straight lines intersecting at the axis point (see Figure 3.31).

Figure 3.31

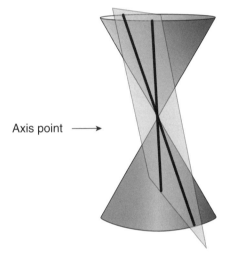

Axis point $\longrightarrow$

In October 1947, Chuck Yeager, an ace pilot from World War II, was dropped into an experimental rocket-propelled Bell X-1 jet from a B-29 bomber at an altitude of 45,000 feet. He flew the plane faster than the speed of sound (approximately 768 mph) and produced a sonic boom over the Mojave Desert. The shape of that sound wave was a cone, and it intersected the ground at an angle forming part of the hyperbolic curve. He repeated his flight 65 years later at the age of 89!

In a less dramatic manner, we can find hyperbolas in ordinary light reflections, aircraft design, architectural design, and orbital paths of spaceships and other galactic and intergalactic bodies (see Figure 3.32).

Figure 3.32

Source: Comstock/Thinkstock

63. WHEN DOES ONE USE THE LAW OF SINES?

When a teacher presented an example for solving problems involving oblique triangles in a mathematics class, she was promptly asked by a confused student: How could you know in advance that the Law of Sines would help you to solve this problem? Fortunately, there is a better answer than the one the teacher gave: "Because in the textbook the problem appears in the chapter about the Law of Sines."

The Law of Sines states that in a triangle with sides a, b, and c and opposite angles α, β, and γ, respectively, we have the relationship as follows: $\dfrac{\sin\alpha}{a} = \dfrac{\sin\beta}{b} = \dfrac{\sin\gamma}{c} = 2R$, where R is the radius of the circumscribed circle of the triangle.

Therefore, one could try to use the Law of Sines for determining missing parts of any triangle where we are given the measures of sides and opposite angles and asked to find another side opposite a given angle or an angle opposite a known side.

An arbitrary triangle can be determined or all parts determined, if some information about the length of its sides and the measures of its angles is given. Quite generally, one can seek to have one of the following cases:

SSS: all three sides are known.

SAS: two sides and the included angle are known.

SSA: two sides and the angle opposite one of them are known.

SAA or ASA: one side and two angles are known.

It is clear that the first two cases (SSS and SAS) just do not provide the right kind of information for an application of the Law of Sines (these cases will be considered in the section about the Law of Cosines). Only SSA, SAA, and ASA triangles are of interest in the context of the Law of Sines. These situations are depicted in Figure 3.33.

Figure 3.33

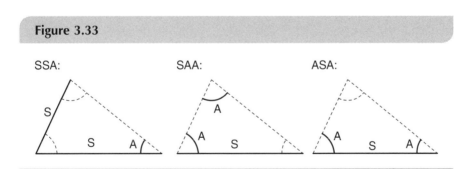

The SSA and SAA triangles clearly contain information about a side and its opposite angle. In the ASA triangle, this information is immediately obtained using the angle-sum rule. Knowing two angles, α and β, the third angle is simply given by $\gamma = 180° - \alpha - \beta$.

Once you know a side and its opposite angle, say c and γ, and another side or angle, you compute $\dfrac{\sin\gamma}{c}$ and use the Law of Sines to obtain missing information. In the cases SAA and ASA, we still know another angle, for example α, and you may compute a from $a = c\dfrac{\sin\alpha}{\sin\gamma}$, and in an analogous way you would compute b from $\beta = 180° - \alpha - \gamma$.

Perhaps the most difficult case is SSA, which is ambiguous, because the given data do not necessarily define a unique solution. This is immediately clear if you remember how to construct a SSA triangle. Assume that the lengths of the sides b and c and the angle β are known. You would start by drawing the angle β with the side c, as in Figure 3.34. Then you would draw a circle with radius b centered at the other endpoint of c. This circle will intersect the opposite leg of the angle β at two points (as in Figure 3.34a), whenever $b > h_a = c\sin\beta$. This gives either two triangles, if $b < c$ (as in Figure 3.34a), or a unique triangle, if $b > c$ (Figure 3.34b). For $b = h_a$ (h_a represents the length of the altitude from vertex A to side a), we would obtain a unique triangle with $\gamma = 90°$, and we would obtain no triangle at all if $b < h_a$ (see Figure 3.34c).

Figure 3.34

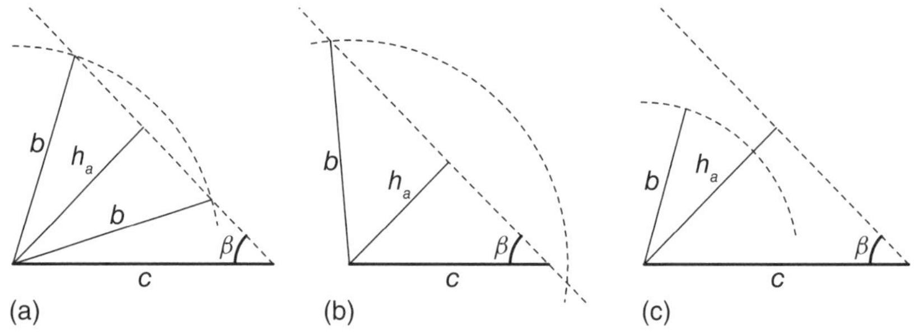

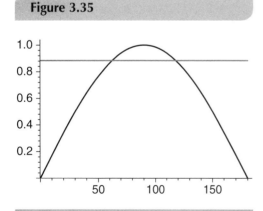

(a) (b) (c)

Figure 3.35

Let us now consider an explicit example. Find all triangles with $b = 4$, $c = 5$, and $\beta = 45$. From the Law of Sines, $\dfrac{\sin\beta}{b} = \dfrac{\sin\gamma}{c}$, and inserting the numbers gives us $\sin\gamma = \dfrac{c}{b}\sin\beta = \dfrac{5}{4\sqrt{2}} \approx 0.88$.

We can draw $\sin\gamma$ for γ between 0 and π together with the constant at 0.88 and obtain the image in Figure 3.35.

We see that there are two possible solutions, one at $\gamma = 62°$ and another at $\gamma = 118°$. Notice in Figure 3.34a that $h_a = c\sin\beta = b\sin\gamma$ is the height of the triangle on the base a. It can be computed in two different ways, using either the sine of β or the sine of γ. This obviously proves $\dfrac{\sin\gamma}{c} = \dfrac{\sin\beta}{b}$. Repeating this argument with the other two heights proves the Law of Sines.

64. WHEN DOES ONE USE THE LAW OF COSINES?

A typical application of the Law of Cosines arises when navigating a ship. It is the problem of finding the way home (see Figure 3.36). Assume that a ship sails from port A to island B, which is 140 miles away. Then the captain changes the direction of the ship by exactly 60 degrees and travels another 90 miles to reach island C. After that he wants to go home again, but port A and the shore are now out of sight. Through what angle should the captain turn the ship to head directly back to port A? And what is the distance between island C and port A?

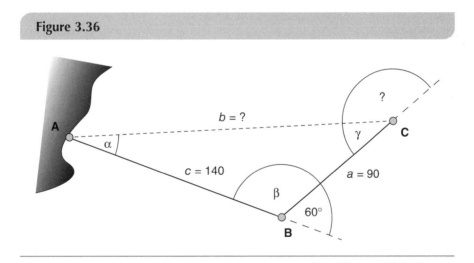

Figure 3.36

The captain has to determine the measures of the parts of a triangle, where the measures of two adjacent sides (a and c) are given and the angle β between them is easily determined: $\beta = 180° - 60° = 120°$. This is a situation where the Law of Cosines helps to determine the length of side b, that is, the distance between A and C.

The law of cosines is usually stated as follows: $c^2 = a^2 + b^2 - 2ab\cos\gamma$. In this form, it refers to an arbitrary triangle where the length of side c

can be determined from the length of sides a and b and the measure of the included angle γ (which is opposite side c). By simply exchanging the notation, we can use it to solve any problem involving a side of an SAS triangle, where two other adjacent sides and the included angle are given:

$$a^2 = b^2 + c^2 - 2bc\cos\alpha$$
$$b^2 = a^2 + c^2 - 2ac\cos\beta$$

To solve the navigational problem in Figure 3.36, we would use the last version of the Law of Cosines and compute side b from $b^2 = 90^2 + 140^2 - 2 \cdot 90 \cdot 140 \cdot \cos 120° = 40300$. Therefore, $b = 200.749$.

Hence, the distance to port A would be about 201 miles. To determine the angle γ, one could now proceed in two different ways. Either one could use the Law of Sines, or one could use the Law of Cosines again. Using the first form of the Law of Cosines, we easily obtain $\cos\gamma = \dfrac{(a^2 + b^2 - c^2)}{2ab}$.

Inserting the known values for the sides, we find that $\cos\gamma = 0.797017$. A calculator now tells us that $\gamma = \arccos(0.797017) = 37.1538°$. Hence, we find that at island C the captain has to turn his ship through an angle of $180° - \gamma \approx 143°$ to head directly toward port A.

Stated in words, the Law of Cosines reads as follows: *The square of one side of a triangle equals the sum of the squares of the other sides minus twice their product times the cosine of their included angle.*

Whenever the triangle is a right triangle, for example, if $\gamma = 90°$, we find that the Law of Cosines specializes to $c^2 = a^2 + b^2$, because $\cos 90° = 0$. This is the familiar Pythagorean theorem. Hence, the Law of Cosines is a generalization of the Pythagorean theorem!

The Law of Cosines will be useful in solving triangles in the following cases:

SSS: all three sides are known.

SAS: two sides and the included angle are known.

It therefore covers the situations that cannot be solved using the Law of Sines alone. For an SSS triangle, use the formula for $\cos\gamma$ given above to determine γ. The remaining angles can then be determined either by the Law of Sines or by the Law of Cosines (with analogous formulas for $\cos\alpha$ and $\cos\beta$). In case of an SAS triangle, the Law of Cosines allows you to determine the length of the side opposite the given angle, and again you can use the Law of Sines or the Law of Cosines to obtain the measures of the remaining angles.

65. WHAT IS THE DIFFERENCE
BETWEEN $y = \arccos x$ AND $y = \cos^{-1} x$?

Inverse functions are extremely important for calculus, and trigonometric functions may serve well to illustrate that concept. Unfortunately, due to historic reasons, the topic of trigonometric functions abounds with unusual notations.

For a function f that is 1–1 (one-to-one), the equation $y = f(x)$ has a unique solution x for every given y in the range of f. Hence we can define a function mapping y to the solution x of $y = f(x)$. This new function is called the inverse function of f and is usually denoted by f^{-1} (see Question 55, "What is meant by the inverse of a function?"). Hence we have $x = f^{-1}(y)$, or $f^{-1}(f(x)) = x$, and $f(f^{-1}(y)) = y$.

Unfortunately, the superscript "–1" is also used for the multiplicative inverse, $a^{-1} = \dfrac{1}{a}$ for any nonzero number a. Therefore, $f^{-1}(x)$ could easily be interpreted as $\dfrac{1}{f(x)}$, which would be *wrong* in most cases.

But for trigonometric functions, it is indeed quite customary to write powers as a superscript to the name of the function—as an example, consider the well-known formula $\sin^2 x + \cos^2 x = 1$. Here we mean, of course, $\cos^2 x = (\cos x)^2$. By analogy, $\cos^{-1} x$ would be $\dfrac{1}{\cos x} = \sec x$.

Thus, our mathematical notation for inverse functions is in a logical conflict with common ways of writing expressions involving powers. It would be better to avoid the notation $\cos^{-1} x$ completely and use exclusively the more common notation "arccos" for the compositional inverse and "$\dfrac{1}{\cos x}$" or "$\sec x$" for the multiplicative inverse.

The notation $\cos^{-1}$ for the compositional inverse is pedagogically inappropriate for yet another reason. It suggests that the function cos (which is usually defined as a mapping from the real numbers onto the interval $[-1, 1]$) has an inverse—which is clearly not the case, because the cosine function is not 1–1. A function would be 1–1 ("one-to-one") if any horizontal line intersects the graph of the function in at most one point. But a horizontal line with y in $[-1, 1]$ would intersect the graph the of cosine in infinitely many points. Hence the angle x, for which $\cos x$ has a certain value, is not unique. Instead, the equation $y = \cos x$ has infinitely many solutions x for any given y in $[-1, 1]$. For example, $0 = \cos x$, for $x = \pm\dfrac{\pi}{2}, \pm\dfrac{3\pi}{2}, \pm\dfrac{5\pi}{2}, \pm\dfrac{7\pi}{2}, \ldots$. As a consequence, the definition of the cosine function has to be changed before we can attempt to define an inverse. This change is made by altering its domain of definition.

Figure 3.37

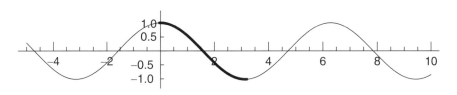

If we restrict the cosine function to the interval $[0, \pi]$, there is precisely one angle x for each value y in $[-1, 1]$ (see Figure 3.37). This unique x is called arccos y. The function arccos is, strictly speaking, not the inverse of the cosine function (and because of this the notation $\cos^{-1}$ would be inappropriate). Instead, the function arccos is the inverse of the function that is obtained from the cosine function after restricting its domain to the interval $[0, \pi]$.

$$\cos|_{[0, \pi]}: \qquad [0, \pi] \qquad \rightarrow \qquad [-1, 1]$$

$$\text{arccos:} \qquad [-1, 1] \qquad \rightarrow \qquad [0, \pi]$$

$$y = \cos x, \text{ for } x \in [0, \pi] \qquad \Leftrightarrow \qquad x = \arccos y, \text{ for } y \in [-1, 1]$$

In the formula $x = \arccos y$, we may exchange y and x, if we prefer to denote the independent variable by x and the dependent variable by y. Then we obtain $y = \arccos x$, for $x \in [-1, 1]$.

The graph of this function (the thick solid line in Figure 3.38) can be found by reflecting the graph of the restricted cosine function (the thin line) at the axis $y = x$ (the dashed line). This reflection corresponds to the exchange of y and x mentioned above.

Figure 3.38

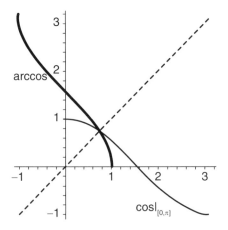

66. WHAT IS A VECTOR?

To a mathematician, vectors are mathematical objects—elements of a vector space—with some axiomatically defined operations (addition, multiplication by a scalar). The most important applications of vectors are in physics, so it is helpful to use some examples from physics to prepare the groundwork leading to a mathematical treatment. One usually starts with the following intuitive observation: There exist quantities that have not only a magnitude (size), but also a direction. The mathematical objects used to describe this type of quantity are called *vectors,* and they are best visualized by arrows. An arrow always points in some direction, and it has a length representing a magnitude. Quantities characterized by direction and magnitude are, for example,

- *Position in space* (more generally, in *n*-dimensional space), described with respect to a coordinate system—an arrow with the coordinate origin as an initial point and the given position in space as a terminal point.
- *Translation in space*—an arrow indicating a direction and a distance (usually without specified initial point).
- *Velocity of an object*—an arrow, usually drawn at the momentary position of the object showing the direction of the motion and the length of the arrow indicating the speed.
- *Force applied to an object*—an arrow, drawn at the point where the force is applied, indicating the direction and the magnitude of the force.

Vectors should be distinguished from scalars that have magnitude only. Physical examples of scalars include temperature, speed, volume, mass, and energy.

One sometimes distinguishes between free vectors (arrows, drawn without any fixed position, which can be translated freely) and localized vectors, which are attached to a fixed point (which is often the coordinate origin). Mathematically, free vectors are more difficult to define (as elements of an affine space), and they are sometimes convenient but hardly ever needed. The overwhelming number of applications use localized vectors. Thus, it is probably wise not to overemphasize the aspect that sometimes vectors with different initial points may be identified and thus can be shifted around freely in Euclidean space.

Therefore, one would usually start to describe a vector as an object that can be represented by an arrow with a certain initial point, a certain direction, and a certain length representing magnitude. Hence, two vectors are equal only if they have the same direction, the same magnitude, and the same initial point. Likewise, it is better not to explain vector addition by shifting one arrow onto the top of the other but simply by drawing a parallelogram as an auxiliary construction (which is applicable as long as the arrows do not point in the same direction). Consider the example of a tightrope walker (see Figure 3.39).

Figure 3.39

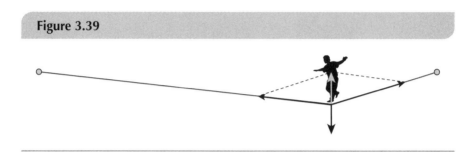

We have a vertical force, the weight of the tightrope walker, that pushes the rope down at a certain point. This has to be compensated by elastic forces that point along the ropes toward the mounting points. The combined effect of the two forces in the direction of the rope—the sum of these vectors—is the gray arrow pointing upward. This sum must compensate the weight of the tightrope walker. The sum is obtained as an arrow along the diagonal of the parallelogram spanned by the two forces but without shifting one arrow to the top of the other (which would create a force on a different point of the rope). You can also use this example to explain that the sum of two vectors can be much smaller in magnitude than the individual summands—something that is bound to surprise your students.

Algebraically, n-dimensional vectors should be represented by n-tuples of numbers with respect to a coordinate system. For example, a vector v in two dimensions can be represented by two numbers (v_1, v_2) with the following meaning: v_1 tells you how far to go from the initial point in the direction of the first coordinate axis (and the sign of v_1 tells you whether to go in the positive or negative direction), and v_2 tells you how far to go in the direction of the second coordinate axis. You end up at a certain terminal point and can draw an arrow from the initial point to that point. The basic operations to be performed with vectors are vector addition and multiplication by a scalar (that is, a number). Addition is done component-wise, and the connection with the parallelogram rule is easily established. Multiplication by a scalar is done by multiplying each component with the same number, which amounts to changing the length of the arrow representing the vector.

Figure 3.40

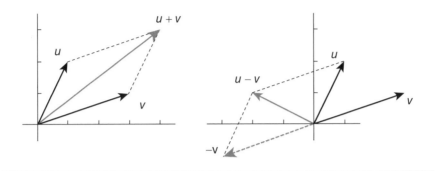

Using free vectors is sometimes convenient for dealing with geometric problems in Euclidean space (normal vectors to a plane, describing a straight line by a position vector, with a free vector describing the direction, etc.), and sometimes the difference $u - v$ is drawn as an arrow from the tip of v to the tip of u. Even here, it is perhaps easier for a beginner to picture the difference vector as the sum of u and the negative of v, as in Figure 3.40.

67. WHY CAN A VECTOR NOT BE DIVIDED BY A VECTOR?

This question probably occurs to everybody who has to learn about vectors. Only very few students are able to give a correct answer. Even for mathematics students at universities, it is a common mistake to place a vector in the denominator of an algebraic expression. Therefore, it should be made very clear: vectors can't be divided by vectors. It is well worth discussing the reasons (and possible exceptions) in some detail.

Division is the inverse operation to multiplication. To perform a division, one would need to find a multiplicative inverse to a given element v. Let us denote the multiplication by the symbol "$*$". Given v, we need another element, usually denoted by v^{-1}, such that $v^{-1} * v = 1$, where 1 is the neutral element for multiplication. (The neutral, or identity, element is defined by the property $1 * u = u$ for all u). Hence, given one factor v and the result of the product, $v * u = w$, we can determine the other factor: $u = v^{-1} * w$.

In school, we typically learn about two types of "products" that apply to vectors: the scalar product and the cross product. Both operations do not have an inverse. The scalar product is defined as

$$v \cdot u = v_1 u_1 + v_2 u_2 + v_3 u_3.$$

Geometrically, it can be interpreted as the length of the projection of the vector v in the direction of u, multiplied by the length of u. The scalar product of two vectors clearly results in a scalar, not a vector. Thus, the scalar product is not a product in the usual sense, and the question of division is meaningless, because there is not even a neutral element. Moreover, given one factor v and the result $v \cdot u$ of the scalar product, the other factor would not be unique: if we add to u any vector w that is orthogonal to v, then the product $v \cdot (u + w)$ would have the same value as $v \cdot u$ (because $v \cdot w = 0$). Hence, there is no way to "invert" the multiplication by vector v.

The cross product (in three dimensions) is defined as

$$v \times u = (v_2 u_3 - v_3 u_2, \; v_3 u_1 - v_1 u_3, \; v_1 u_2 - v_2 u_1).$$

It is a vector orthogonal to the plane spanned by v and u, and its length is equal to the area of the parallelogram spanned by v and u. The cross product is not a product in the usual sense because it does not admit a neutral element: for any $u \neq 0$, the equation $n \times u = u$ has no solution n (because $n \times u$ is always orthogonal to u). The cross product is not associative: $w \times (v \times u) \neq (w \times v) \times u$.

Moreover, given one factor v and the result of the product $v \times u = w,$ the second factor is not unique, because adding to u any multiple of v does not change the value of $v \times u$. Hence, $v \times u = v \times (u + \lambda v)$, because $v \times v = 0$. For example, $(1, 0, 0) \times (\lambda, 1, 0) = (0, 0, 1)$ for all real numbers λ. Hence, there is no possible way to invert the multiplication by v to determine the second factor of $v \times u$.

There are, however, other possible definitions of a product between vectors. For example, the Hadamard product of two vectors is the element-wise product $v \circ u = (v_1 u_1, \; v_2 u_2, \; v_3 u_3)$, and hence results in a vector. Hadamard multiplication is associative and commutative, the neutral element is $(1, 1, 1)$, and a multiplicative inverse of a vector v can be defined, whenever all components of v are nonzero: $((v_1)^{-1}, (v_2)^{-1}, (v_3)^{-1})$. However, the Hadamard product is regarded to be of very limited use and is therefore not taught in school.

There are some special cases where one can define a division of vectors. For example, a two-dimensional vector (x, y) could be interpreted as a complex number $z = x + iy$. The multiplication of complex numbers then also defines a multiplication of two-dimensional vectors, and this sort of product is commutative and associative. The "complex-number" division of two-dimensional vectors $u = (a, b)$ and $v = (c, d) \neq (0, 0)$ is then defined as follows: $\dfrac{u}{v} = \left(\dfrac{(ac + bd)}{(c^2 + d^2)}, \; \dfrac{(bc - ad)}{(c^2 + d^2)} \right)$

The result of this division corresponds exactly to the quotient $\dfrac{(a+ib)}{(c+id)}$ of the corresponding complex numbers. The multiplicative inverse of $v = (c, d)$ would be the vector $v^{-1} = \dfrac{c}{(c^2+d^2)}, \dfrac{-d}{(c^2+d^2)}$ and the neutral element would be (1, 0). In fact, the set of two-dimensional real vectors with this multiplication and division is just the complex plane.

In a quite similar way, a product (and an associated division) can be defined for three-dimensional vectors with the help of the theory of quaternions. The resulting product, however, would not be commutative.

68. WHAT IS *i*?

The usual answer, namely that *i* is an imaginary quantity representing the square root of −1, usually leaves students with an uneasy feeling. If it is imaginary, does it really exist? If not, why bother? To this, the answer is quite often that with the help of imaginary numbers we can solve the equation $x^2 = -1$. Actually, this explanation is not very satisfactory, because why would we want to solve an equation like this? Having learned that for any number x, its square is nonnegative, it seems perfectly okay that this equation should have no solution at all. So, the question remains: Why should we deal with imagined, "nonexisting" solutions?

Whenever you encounter this discussion, it helps to refer to history. The actual reason for the introduction of imaginary numbers in the 16th century was the cubic equation. Even if one is not interested in imaginary numbers at all, to obtain all real solutions of the cubic equation, one has to compute intermediate results that involve imaginary numbers.

A general cubic equation (with real coefficients) can always be reduced to the form $x^3 = bx + c$, where b and c are real numbers. Here a formula by Scipione del Ferro and Tartaglia (which was published first by Gerolamo Cardano in 1545 and is therefore widely called Cardano's formula) gives a solution:

$$x = \sqrt[3]{\frac{c}{2} + w} + \sqrt[3]{\frac{c}{2} - w}, \quad \text{where } w = \sqrt{\frac{c^2}{4} - \frac{b^3}{27}}.$$

Now, there is a special case that occurs whenever the cubic equation has three real solutions. This was called the irreducible case. It is characterized by w becoming the square root of a negative number. A simple example is provided by the equation $x^3 = 15x + 4$, which was solved by Rafael Bombelli (1526–1572). Bombelli, just for fun, considered the expression $2 \pm \sqrt{-1}$ and computed its powers using $\sqrt{-1} \cdot \sqrt{-1} = -1$. In that way he found that $(2 \pm \sqrt{-1})^3 = 2 \pm 11\sqrt{-1}$. He also noted that Cardano's formula, if applied to the equation $x^3 = 15x + 4$, leads to the expression $x = \sqrt[3]{2 + \sqrt{-121}} + \sqrt[3]{2 - \sqrt{-121}}$. Now he used his earlier result to write $2 \pm \sqrt{-121} = 2 \pm 11\sqrt{-1} = (2 \pm \sqrt{-1})^3$, and hence $\sqrt[3]{2 \pm \sqrt{-121}} = 2 \pm \sqrt{-1}$.

Bombelli was now able to compute x:

$$x = 2 + \sqrt{-1} + 2 - \sqrt{-1} = 4.$$

Indeed, $x = 4$ is one of the solutions of the cubic equation $x^3 = 15x + 4$, and with its help we can reduce this equation to a quadratic equation for which the remaining roots can be found in an elementary way. Bombelli had thus shown that by using the symbol $\sqrt{-1}$ just like an ordinary number, one could solve a cubic equation even for the irreducible case—a very important result that justifies calculations with the strange square root of -1.

The symbol i with the property $i^2 = -1$ was finally introduced by Leonhard Euler (1707–1783). He showed that the set of complex numbers $x + iy$ is closed with respect to elementary arithmetic and that roots and logarithms can be defined for these numbers. Hence, with complex numbers we can perform addition, subtraction, multiplication, and division quite in the usual way; we just have to remember that we can replace i^2, wherever it occurs, by -1.

In 1799, Carl Friedrich Gauss finally proved the fundamental theorem of algebra: for every polynomial of degree n with complex coefficients a_k there exist complex numbers $x_1, \ldots, x_n$, such that

$$x^n + a_1 x^{n-1} + \ldots + a_{n-1} x + a_n = (x - x_1)(x - x_2) \ldots (x - x_n)$$

(and hence these numbers are the unique roots of the polynomial). Only for n up to 4 do there exist general formulas for the explicit computation of these roots. Galois Theory allows no such formula for $n \geq 5$.

In modern mathematics, numbers are abstract objects (members of a set), for which certain operations (like "+" or "·") are defined. In that sense, the complex numbers do exist in the same way as the natural or real numbers exist. Perhaps this discussion about whether complex numbers really exist can be avoided altogether by introducing them as pairs of real numbers in an early stage. According to Gauss, complex numbers may be considered as elements (points) of a two-dimensional plane, denoted by $\mathbb{C}$ (the complex plane, or Gaussian plane; see Figure 3.41). The points of the complex plane are henceforth called complex numbers. They are described, as usual, by pairs of real numbers or coordinates (x, y).

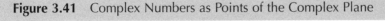

Figure 3.41   Complex Numbers as Points of the Complex Plane

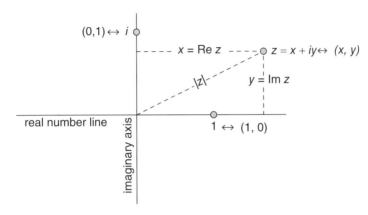

The horizontal axis of the complex plane is identified with the real number line. The points $(x, 0)$ are simply called real numbers. The points on the vertical axis $(0, y)$, with real numbers y, are called "imaginary numbers." In particular, $(0, 1)$ corresponds to i.

The elements (x, y) of the Gaussian plane differ from two-dimensional vectors (x, y) *only* in a new kind of multiplication, which is introduced for elements of the complex plane as follows:

$$(x, y)\,(u, v) = (xu - yv, xv + yu).$$

This rule looks strange at first sight, but it describes precisely the result for the multiplication of two complex numbers. In particular, $(0, 1)(0, 1) = (-1, 0)$, which corresponds to $i^2 = -1$.

Moreover, $(x, y) = (x, 0) + (0, 1)(y, 0)$, and this clearly corresponds to $x + iy$. Using the notation $x + iy$ instead of (x, y) clearly holds some convenience: when we compute the product

$$(x + iy)\,(u + iv) = xu - yv + i\,(xv + yu),$$

we only have to remember the rule $i^2 = -1$, and not the complicated rule given above for the product of the pairs (x, y) and (u, v).

Introducing complex numbers as two-dimensional objects might have some advantages. It is conceptually simpler, because it does not start with mysterious, unexplained objects like i. The complex plane appears as an essential part of the definition and need not be introduced as an additional concept. The most difficult element of this approach would be the rule for multiplication. One might wish to point out that unlike the scalar product $(x, y)(u, v) = xu + yv$, the defined product has an inverse operation, namely the division of complex numbers.

69. WHAT IS e?

The value of e is equal (approximately) to 2.71828182845904523536028747135266249775724709369995 . . .

The number e is an irrational number, because the decimal portion of the number it represents does not repeat or cease, so no fraction or decimal can appropriately approximate or represent the actual value. Above is an approximation of e to 50 decimal places. Yet this number is so very important to mathematics that it has been simply referred to as "e" so that we might use and apply the number as needed.

Jacob Bernoulli was examining the problem of compound interest in the late 17th century and attempted to find $\lim_{n \to \infty} \left(1 + \dfrac{1}{n}\right)^n$. In trying to see what would happen when interest was compounded continuously, he began by using the binomial theorem to approximate this limit to be between 2 and 3. Although the number was used before his time by numerous mathematicians, it was Leonhard Euler who first used the letter e in his 1731 letter to Christian Goldbach, which appeared in *Mechanica,* that ensured that the letter "e" would become familiar in the mathematical society of the time and begin to appear in common usage.

Interestingly enough, there are many ways to define and apply e, also known as Euler's constant. The base of the natural logarithm is called e. The natural logarithm function ln(x) is defined as $\ln(x) = \log_e(x)$.

We can calculate e by finding the sum of this infinite series:

$$e = \lim_{n \to \infty} \left(1 + \frac{1}{n}\right)^n$$

In expanded form, we see $e = 1 + \dfrac{1}{1} + \dfrac{1}{1 \cdot 2} + \dfrac{1}{1 \cdot 2 \cdot 3} + \dfrac{1}{1 \cdot 2 \cdot 3 \cdot 4} + \cdots$ (see Figure 3.42).

Figure 3.42

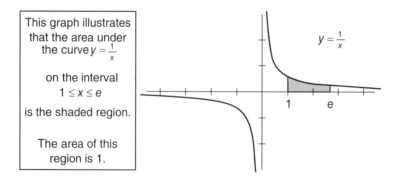

This graph illustrates that the area under the curve $y = \frac{1}{x}$

on the interval $1 \le x \le e$

is the shaded region.

The area of this region is 1.

$y = \frac{1}{x}$

1   e

One nickname for this very special number is "The Banker's Number," and there is a reason why this number is so important to finance. We can begin by considering the calculation of simple interest. Let us say that you have lent a very good friend $100 and the friend returns the money to you with 8% interest. Your friend will give you $108 upon paying you back. On the other hand, when we pay interest on a loan to a bank, or the bank pays us interest on money we deposit in our account, we see from our statements that the interest is not calculated just once annually, but rather daily, so we are getting or giving interest and the amount is rarely a whole number.

This is because banks compute interest based not only on the amount of money you have deposited, but also on the interest earned. *Simple interest* may be paid at intervals (again on the principal only and not the interest), but *compound interest* includes the total money you have in your account (principal and accrued interest).

Let us say that you put P dollars into an account and the compound interest rate is r per year. At the end of the first year, you will have $P + Pr$ dollars in your account. At the end of the second year, you will have $(P + Pr) + (P + Pr)r$. At the end of n years, we can use the distributive property to find our interest to be $P(1 + r)^n$

If the interest is not paid yearly but semiannually, we can divide the interest rate in half and use this formula to find the total T after t years. We multiply t by 2 in the exponent because we will now be making the calculations twice per year:

$$T = P\left(1 + \frac{r}{2}\right)^{2t}$$

Exploring this formula even further, we can compound interest quarterly and will divide our rate in quarters, but be sure to calculate four times by also updating our exponent:

$$T = P\left(1 + \frac{r}{4}\right)^{4t}$$

We can generalize that money in an account for t years, with t referring to "time," would have a principal P, and interest compounded n times per year:

$$T = P\left(1 + \frac{r}{n}\right)^{nt}$$

We can consider that banks might pay interest monthly, weekly, daily, hourly, or even each minute! Now, think about interest being compounded every second. Or half-second. Or millisecond! We are coming closer to seeing why "e" is so critical to these calculations. Let us start with a simplified problem. If 100% interest on just one dollar for just one year is paid n times, the amount is obtained by the formula $\left(1+\dfrac{1}{n}\right)^n$.

As we compound interest more and more often, n gets larger and larger. Although we can approximate this value—a number of mathematicians have expanded the decimal to hundreds of digits—this number is irrational but very important. So, for any x when x approaches infinity in the expression $\left(1+\dfrac{1}{x}\right)^x$, we call the value e. The calculation on a deposit of A dollars with interest compounded continuously with the yearly interest rate of r% per year and in the bank for t years is Ae^{tr}.

On the other hand, we may consider depreciation, or the decrease in value of something. In this case, we would have a negative rate, and we could use the formula Ae^{-tr}. This e constant is also essential in the calculation of motion, suspension bridges, and barometric pressure, as well as mathematical topics such as logarithms, calculus, and number theory. Google even used the digits from e as its valuation for its initial public offering when the company went public!

NOTES

1. Additional information can be found in Posamentier, A. S., Smith, B., & Stepelman, J. (2014). *Teaching secondary mathematics: Techniques and enrichment units* (9th ed.). Boston, MA: Pearson/Allyn & Bacon.

2. For more about this unique number, see Posamentier, A. S., & Lehmann, I. (2012). *The glorious golden ratio.* Amherst, NY: Prometheus Books.

4 Geometry Questions

70. WHY IS THE DIAGONAL OF A SQUARE LONGER THAN ITS SIDE?

To determine if it is always true that the diagonal of a square is longer than its side, let us explore the properties of a square. We know that each square has four congruent sides and four congruent angles. Let us call each side s. Since the sum of interior angles in a quadrilateral is 360°, each of the four angles is 90°, or a right angle. Although this may seem like elementary information, we will be using this information in our proof, so it is useful to make plain all of the ideas in this problem.

Now, let us look at the figures formed when we add in a diagonal of the square (see Figures 4.1 and 4.2):

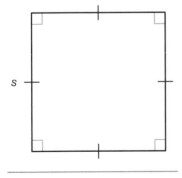

Figure 4.1

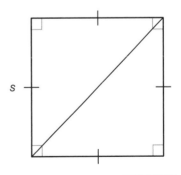

Figure 4.2

We notice that two right triangles are formed. Using the Pythagorean theorem to determine the length of the diagonal, which we will call d, notice:

Pythagorean theorem:	$a^2 + b^2 = c^2$
Substitute s for the sides and d for the hypotenuse	$s^2 + s^2 = d^2$
Combine like terms	$2s^2 = d^2$
Take the square root of both sides	$s\sqrt{2} = d$

We find that the length of the diagonal will always be equal to $\sqrt{2}$ multiplied by the length of the side. Since $\sqrt{2} \approx 1.4$, the length of the diagonal will always be about 1.4 times the length of the side in any given square, or about one and one-half times as large.

71. HOW CAN YOU DEMONSTRATE THAT THE CIRCUMFERENCE OF A CIRCLE IS $2\pi r$?

More than a thousand years ago, an Arab mathematician, Mohammed Ibn Musa al-Khwārizmī, wrote: "*The best method to obtain the circumference of a circle is to multiply the diameter by $3\frac{1}{7}$. This is the quickest and easiest method. God knows of a better one.*"

The measure of the length of the perimeter of a circle, or the circumference, has puzzled mathematicians for centuries. Civilizations have weighed in their approximations for this very important number π, which is the ratio of the circumference to the diameter of a circle. Hundreds of years BC, the Indian text *Shatapatha Brahmana* notes π to be $\frac{339}{108}$. Thousands of years prior, the Babylonians used $\frac{25}{8}$ and the Egyptians used $\frac{256}{81}$. Archimedes, in Greece, proved geometrically that π must be between the fractions $\frac{223}{71}$ and $\frac{22}{7}$. On the other hand, Zu Chongzhi of China approximated π to be between $\frac{355}{71}$ and $\frac{22}{7}$ in the fifth century. There are books of the Old Testament

(Chronicles and Kings) that imply that the approximate length of the circumference of a circle is about three times the length of the diameter (actually, recent revelations put this approximation at 3.1416).[1] A motivational activity for students might be to find the relative error of each of the approximations of π so that they might discover which group came closest in approximating this irrational number. In any case, clearly the measure of the circumference of a circle has been so important that it has always been studied and applied.

How did all of these civilizations come to these approximations? How did they know that this "3.14 . . ." was important? When constructing circles, or the locus of points equidistant from a given point, something notable happened. No matter the size of the circle, the ratio of the distance around the circle to the length of the diameter always stayed the same (and approximated to around 3 or 3.1). If we were to unravel the circles, the ratio of circumference to the diameter would always result in the same number, and that number would be π.

We begin with the notion that π is the ratio of the circumference to the diameter:

$$\pi = \frac{\text{length of circumference}}{\text{length of diameter}}$$

We can abbreviate this as follows: $\pi = \dfrac{C}{d}$

Solving for C, we have the following: $C = \pi d$

Since the diameter is twice the radius, we can substitute $2r$ for d: $C = 2\pi r$

This is the familiar formula for the circumference of a circle.

72. HOW CAN YOU DEMONSTRATE THAT THE AREA OF A CIRCLE IS EQUAL TO πr^2?

In elementary school, students learn that the area of a circle is the number of square units inside that circle. If each square in the circle in Figure 4.3 has an area of 1 in^2, you could count the total number of squares to get an approximation of the area of the circle. Thus, if there were a sum of approximately 50 squares inside the circle, the area of this circle would be approximately 50 in^2.

Figure 4.3

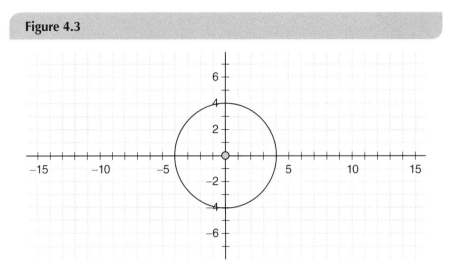

However, in middle school mathematics, most students are taught how to find the area of a circle by using the formula $A = \pi r^2$, where A represents the area of a circle, r represents the radius of the circle, and π is approximated to 3.14. But rarely are students given the opportunity to informally demonstrate and prove that the area of a circle is equal to πr^2.

First, the standard definition of π is the ratio of the circumference of a circle to its diameter; therefore, the circumference of a circle is π times the diameter, or 2π times the radius r. Figure 4.4 shows that a circle can be cut, rearranged, and positioned to bear a resemblance to a parallelogram whose height is r and whose base is half the circumference, or about π times r. The area of the parallelogram would then be equal to the product of the base (πr) times the height (r), or πr^2, which is then the area of the circle.

Figure 4.4

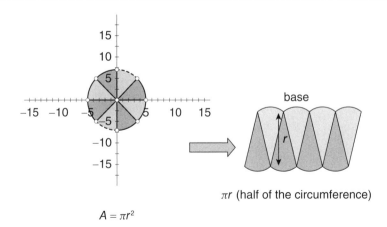

$A = \pi r^2$

base

πr (half of the circumference)

By separating the circle into more than eight sectors, the approximation found would be even more accurate, that is, the successive parallelograms (made up of increasingly smaller circle sectors) would approximate the area of the circle to a closer degree. This offers a demonstration and geometric justification that the area of a circle is πr^2.

Another method is to divide a circle into concentric rings that can be opened and stacked to look like a triangle (with height r and base $2\pi r$). By separating the circle into smaller additional rings and unfolding, the result appears more like a triangle, so the approximation becomes improved. Taking more and more rings, the triangle of area πr^2 approximates the area of the circle. This gives a geometric demonstration that the area of a circle really is πr^2. See Figure 4.5, which illustrates the "unfolding" process.

$$\text{Area of triangle (A)} = \frac{1}{2}b \cdot h$$

$$A = \frac{1}{2}(2\pi r)(r)$$

$$A = \pi r^2$$

Figure 4.5

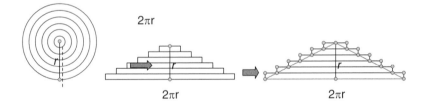

---

73. CAN A TRIANGLE CONTAIN TWO RIGHT ANGLES?

In order to answer the question of whether a triangle can contain two right angles, we will explore several basic definitions and theorems pertaining to triangles.

First, the definition of a triangle:

A triangle is a polygon in a plane containing three angles and three sides.

Second, let us consider the following theorem pertaining to the angles of any triangle:

Theorem: The sum of the measures of the interior angles of any triangle is equal to 180°.

Third, the definition of a right angle: A right angle is an angle that contains 90°.

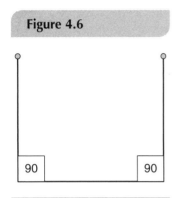

Figure 4.6

90   90

Hence, using the three facts above, a triangle cannot possibly contain two right angles because the sum of the measures of the two right angles is equal to 180°, which means that there is no angle measurement left for the third angle, and by definition a triangle is a polygon containing three angles and the sum of the measures of the three angles is equal to 180° and not two angles whose sum is equal to 180°.

Figure 4.6 shows two right angles. As you can see, the two vertical line segments will never meet to form a triangle.

It should be noted that this is true in Euclidean geometry, but if you venture off to spherical geometry, then you will find that a triangle can have three right angles!

74. WHY MUST THE SUM OF ANY TWO SIDES OF A TRIANGLE BE GREATER THAN THE THIRD SIDE?

Let us consider the notion that the sum of two sides of a triangle might be equal in length to the third side. If we were to attempt to construct a triangle using sides of length 2, 8, and 10, let us see what might happen (see Figure 4.7).

Figure 4.7

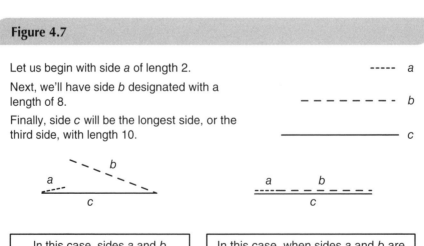

Let us begin with side a of length 2.

Next, we'll have side b designated with a length of 8.

Finally, side c will be the longest side, or the third side, with length 10.

----- a

– – – – – – – · b

———————— c

b
a
c

a   b
c

In this case, sides a and b are not able to connect when they are at any angle above side c.

In this case, when sides a and b are connected, they do not form angles and simply sit directly on side c.

Euclid proved the triangle inequality as Proposition 20 in his book, *Elements*, Book 1.

With any given triangle *ABC*, which has been shaded gray in Figure 4.8, an adjacent isosceles triangle can be constructed. We have constructed line segment *AD* passing through point *B*, creating $BD \cong BC$. Constructing line segment *CD* creates the base of our isosceles triangle. Since the base angles of an isosceles triangle are congruent, $\angle BCD \cong \angle CDB$.

We have identified the measures of these angles as α. $\overline{CD}$ is the base of our isosceles triangle.

We have designated the sum of $\angle ACB$ and $\angle BCD$ as β.

We have $\beta > \alpha$, because the whole must be greater than a part. The side opposite the greater angle in a triangle is longer; therefore, *AD* is longer than *AC*. And $AD = AB + BD$, and $BD = BC$. Thus, $AB + BC > AC$.

Figure 4.8

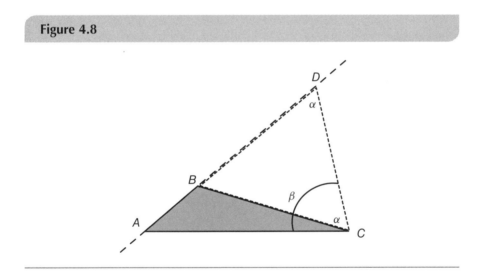

This proof can be repeated for the remaining two sides, and the conclusions would state:

$$AC + BC > AB \text{ as well as } AB + AC > BC.$$

75. HOW DO THE TERMS "ACUTE ANGLE" AND "OBTUSE ANGLE" RELATE TO THE ENGLISH LANGUAGE?

Whenever a new word or term is introduced in mathematics, it should be related back to common English usage. This may require having a good dictionary at ready reference. The time it takes to tie mathematical terms back to ordinary English will help strengthen the mathematical understanding as well as enlarge a student's regular vocabulary. It is time well spent!

Many words have a specific mathematical meaning and a more general English meaning. Sometimes these meanings are very similar, and sometimes they are very distinct.

Before we discuss the terms "acute angle" and "obtuse angle" and how they relate to the English language, let us first consider their important mathematical definitions. We will begin with the term "acute angle."

An *acute angle* is an angle with a measure between 0° and 90°, inclusively.

In the English language, *acute* means sharp, as in an acute pain, or acute may be considered a "sharp" point if it is used as an arrowhead. Hence, we can see that the mathematical term *acute angle* does relate to some degree to the English definition of the word *acute,* because an acute angle is "pointed."

An *obtuse angle* is an angle measuring between 90° and 180°, inclusively.

In the English language, obtuse means "dull witted," "blunt," or "insensitive."

Hence, we can see that the mathematical term *obtuse angle* does relate in some degree to the English definition of the word *obtuse,* which is used to describe a person who is not very sharp and to the point.

You might want to refer to Question 2 for more math word origins.

76. CAN TRIGONOMETRY BE USED TO PROVE THE PYTHAGOREAN THEOREM?

In his book *The Pythagorean Proposition* (NCTM, 1967), originally published in 1940, Elisha Loomis provided 370 proofs of the Pythagorean theorem and stated that none of the proofs used trigonometry. Today there are more than 400 proofs of this famous theorem, but still none uses trigonometry. This is very simply explained. Since trigonometry is based on the Pythagorean theorem (often seen in the form of $\sin^2 x + \cos^2 x = 1$), it would be circular reasoning to use this branch of mathematics to prove a theorem on which it is based.

77. HOW IS THE DISTANCE FORMULA DERIVED?

The distance formula is used to calculate the oblique linear distance between two points on the Cartesian plane. It is derived by using our familiar Pythagorean theorem.

First we draw the oblique line segment on the plane that connects the two points and use it as a hypotenuse of a right triangle by extending vertical and horizontal lines as shown in Figures 4.9 and 4.10. We can then find the length of the sides of this triangle by counting the boxes on the plane since the sides are vertical and horizontal lines. With these values, we can use the Pythagorean theorem to find the length of the hypotenuse. The hypotenuse of the triangle will be the distance between the two points.

Figures 4.9 and 4.10 show a coordinate plane and a diagonal line segment with endpoints. Using the Pythagorean theorem, we will compute the distance between these two points and simultaneously show the process of how the distance formula is derived.

Figure 4.9

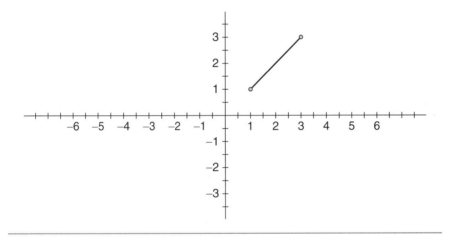

Step 1: Construct vertical and horizontal line segments to form a right triangle (see Figure 4.10).

Figure 4.10

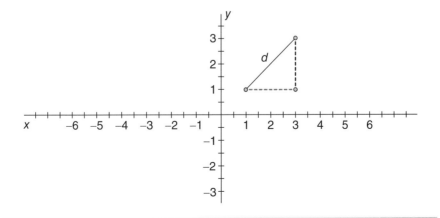

Step 2: Label two points on the *x*-axis as x_1 and x_2 that correspond with the endpoints of the line segment.

Label two points on the *y*-axis as y_1 and y_2 that correspond with the endpoints of the line segment (see Figure 4.11).

Figure 4.11

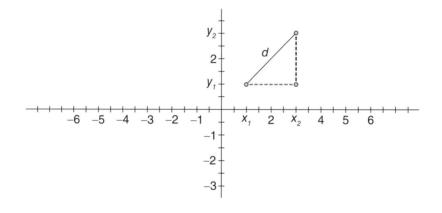

Step 3: x_1 and y_1 are the *x, y* coordinates for the first point.

x_2 and y_2 are the *x, y* coordinates for the second point.

d is the distance between the two points (see Figure 4.12).

Figure 4.12

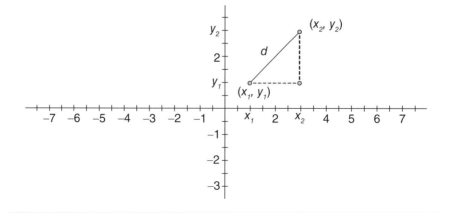

Step 4:   Let $x_2 - x_1$ represent the distance of the horizontal line segment.

Let $y_2 - y_1$ represent the distance of the vertical line segment (see Figure 4.13).

Figure 4.13

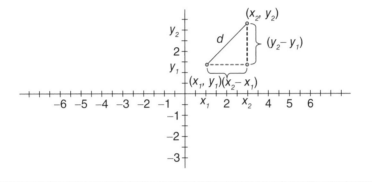

Step 5:   Use the Pythagorean theorem to solve for d as follows:

$$\sqrt{(x_2 - x_1)^2 + (y_2 - y_1)^2} = \sqrt{d^2}, \text{ so}$$

$(x_2 - x_1)^2 + (y_2 - y_1)^2 = d$, which is our familiar distance formula.

Example: Find the distance between (6, 8) and (2, 5) (see Figure 4.14).

Figure 4.14

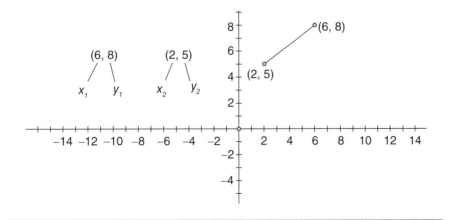

$$d = \sqrt{\left(x_2 - x_1\right)^2 + \left(y_2 - y_1\right)^2}$$

$$d = \sqrt{\left(2 - 6\right)^2 + \left(5 - 8\right)^2}$$

$$d = \sqrt{\left(-4\right)^2 + \left(-3\right)^2}$$

$$d = \sqrt{16 + 9} = \sqrt{25}$$

$$d = 5$$

78. HOW CAN THE PYTHAGOREAN THEOREM BE USED TO DETERMINE IF AN ANGLE OF A TRIANGLE IS ACUTE OR OBTUSE?

The Pythagorean theorem states that in a right triangle, the square of the length of the hypotenuse is equal to the sum of the squares of the lengths of the other two sides. We know that the angle opposite the hypotenuse is 90°, a right angle.

The converse of the Pythagorean theorem can be used to establish a right angle in a triangle. If the "hypotenuse" is lengthened, and the other two sides remain the same, then the angle opposite the hypotenuse becomes enlarged, thus becoming an obtuse angle. On the other hand, were the "hypotenuse" to be reduced in length, with the other two sides remaining the same length, then the angle becomes less than 90°, or an acute angle. Therefore, we can use a Pythagorean theorem extension to determine whether an angle in the triangle is acute or obtuse, as follows:

For a triangle with sides a, b, and c, with c the longest side, then:

If $c^2 < a^2 + b^2$, then the angle opposite side c is an acute angle. Since c is the longest side, all the angles in the triangle are acute (see Figure 4.15).

Figure 4.15

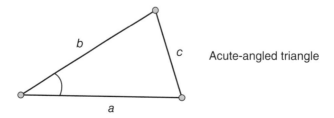

Acute-angled triangle

If $c^2 = a^2 + b^2$, then the angle opposite side c is a right angle and we have a right triangle (see Figure 4.16).

Figure 4.16

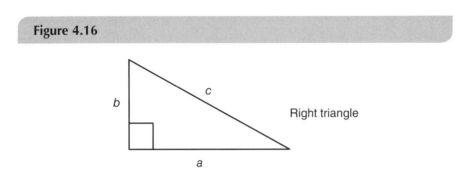

Right triangle

If $c^2 > a^2 + b^2$, then it is an obtuse triangle; that is, the angle opposite side c is an obtuse angle (see Figure 4.17).

Figure 4.17

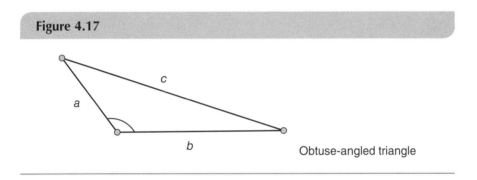

Obtuse-angled triangle

79. WHAT IS A PLATONIC SOLID?

In geometry it is important for students to become familiar with and explore the properties and relevant characteristics of geometric solids, which include the number of vertices, edges, and shapes of faces. It would also be valuable for students to recognize and appreciate the multitude of geometric solids in the world around them; these include a rectangular prism, square pyramid, sphere, cone, cylinder, and so on.

Platonic solids are three-dimensional shapes, also known as regular polyhedra, that contain congruent sides, angles, and faces. There are only five Platonic solids. They are the tetrahedron (four-sided), cube (hexahedron, or six-sided), octahedron (eight-sided), dodecahedron (12-sided), and icosahedron (20-sided). These shapes are named after the ancient Greek philosopher Plato, who speculated that these five solids were the shapes representing the basic components of the physical universe.

To a great extent, the ancient Greeks studied the Platonic solids; in fact, Pythagoras is actually credited with their discovery. Other sources submit that Pythagoras may have only been aware of the tetrahedron, cube, and dodecahedron, and that the other Platonic solids, such as the octahedron and icosahedron, were discovered by Theaetetus, a contemporary of Plato. Theaetetus provided a mathematical description of all five Platonic solids and is responsible for first proving that there are no other convex regular polyhedra than the five named above.

The illustrations in Figures 4.18 through 4.22 show different perspectives of the five Platonic solids.

The tetrahedron, shown in Figure 4.18 from two different perspectives, is a four-sided polyhedron with four equilateral triangles for faces. It appears like a three-sided pyramid (where the fourth side is a triangular base).

Figure 4.18

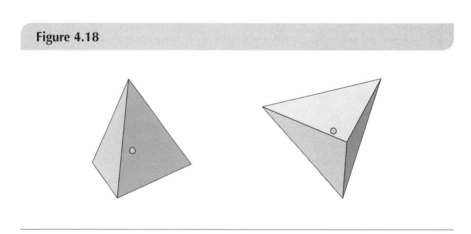

The cube, shown in Figure 4.19 from two different perspectives, is a six-sided polyhedron with six squares for faces.

Figure 4.19

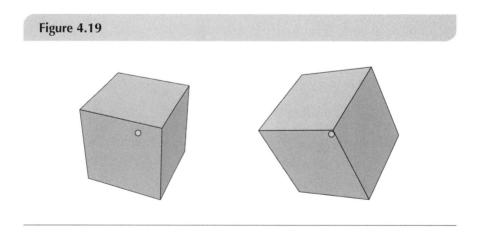

The octahedron is an eight-sided polyhedron with eight equilateral triangles for faces (see Figure 4.20).

Figure 4.20

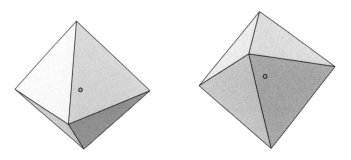

The dodecahedron is a 12-sided polyhedron with twelve regular pentagons for faces (see Figure 4.21).

Figure 4.21

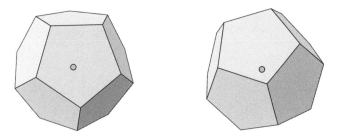

The icosahedron is a 20-sided polyhedron with 20 equilateral triangles for faces (see Figure 4.22).

Figure 4.22

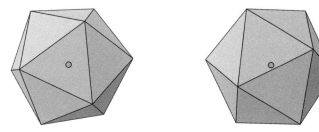

The table on the next page shows the images, properties, and relevant characteristics of the five Platonic solids.

Platonic Solids

Platonic Solid	Icon	Number of Faces	Shape of Faces	Number of Faces at Each Vertex	Number of Vertices	Number of Edges	Platonic Solid Unfolded "Net"
Tetrahedron		4	Equilateral triangle (three-sided)	3	4	6	
Cube		6	Square (four-sided)	3	8	12	
Octahedron		8	Equilateral triangle (three-sided)	4	6	12	
Dodecahedron		12	Regular pentagon (five-sided)	3	20	30	
Icosahedron		20	Equilateral triangle (three-sided)	5	12	30	

The relationship of the vertices (V), faces (F), and edges (E) of these polyhedra, as well as any other polyhedra, can be expressed in the formula developed by the Swiss mathematician Leonhard Euler (1707–1783), namely: $V + F = E + 2$.

It is easy to see that there are no other convex regular polyhedra than the five Platonic solids shown above. We just have to look at one of the vertices, which is also the common vertex of at least three faces. For example, we can have five equilateral triangles meeting at some point in the plane, as in Figure 4.23.

Figure 4.23

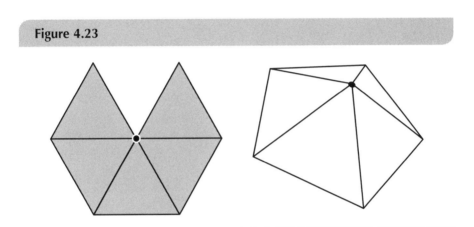

In three-dimensional space, we can pull the point in the center out of the plane to form the vertex of a solid, and thereby close the remaining gap. In that way, five equilateral triangles would form the vertex and a part of the surface of an icosahedron. In a similar way, we obtain the vertex of a tetrahedron (three equilateral triangles meeting at a point) or the vertex of an octahedron (four triangles). Could we have a solid where six equilateral triangles meet at a point? Obviously not, because six equilateral triangles would have a combined angle of 360° at their meeting point, with no space left between them to form a three-dimensional vertex.

In a regular polyhedron, at least three identical regular polygons must meet at a vertex. We have seen that the sum of all the angles at the vertex must be less than 360°. Each polygon must therefore have an angle less than $\frac{360°}{3} = 120°$ between adjacent sides. This leaves triangles (angle 60°), squares (90°), and regular pentagons (108°) as the only possibilities. Three hexagons meeting at a point would already form a flat figure, not a vertex in space, as seen in Figure 4.24. Three hexagons cannot meet at a point without overlapping; hence, they cannot be the faces of a regular solid in space.

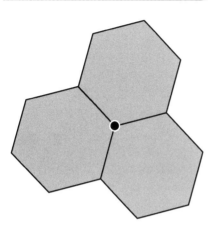

Figure 4.24

How many squares or pentagons could meet at one vertex of a regular polyhedron? Remember that the sum of the angles at that vertex has to be strictly less than 360°. Hence, we can have three squares (sum of angles 270°, forming a part of a cube), or three pentagons (sum of angles 324° < 360°, dodecahedron). In that way, we have shown that at most five different regular polyhedra can exist, because a vertex of a solid in space can only be a common vertex of three, four, or five identical triangles, or of three squares, or of three pentagons.

Note that we have only shown that at most five regular polyhedra can exist in three-dimensional space. The proof that all these polyhedra actually exist is more difficult and can be done by explicit constructions.

80. WHAT IS A GOLDEN RECTANGLE?

Your students might already have an intuitive idea of rectangle proportions even before they learn about this in school. For example, it is usually well known that modern TV sets are characterized by the length to width proportion 16:9, which describes the shape of the rectangle in a way independent of its actual size. The proportion 16:9 means that the length L of the longer side divided by the length S of the shorter side is $\frac{L}{S} = \frac{16}{9}$, which is approximately 1.77778. Other famous rectangles of everyday life have the proportions 4:3 (old TV sets, or the images of many digital cameras) or 2:3 (the most common image format in photography), or 1:1 (which is simply a square).

The "golden rectangle" is one in which the ratio of the longer side to the shorter side was found by the Greeks to be the most pleasing to the eye. It was and still is used in art as well as in architecture.[2] To find this ratio, we form a proportion of the ratio $L{:}S$ and set it equal to the ratio of $L + S{:}L$ so that $\frac{L}{S} = \frac{L+S}{L}$. Denoting $\frac{L}{S} = \phi$, and substituting in the equation above, we obtain $\phi = 1 + \frac{S}{L} = 1 + \frac{1}{\phi}$, and multiplying this by ϕ, we get the quadratic equation $\phi^2 = \phi + 1$. The unique positive solution of this equation is $\phi = \frac{1+\sqrt{5}}{2} \approx 1.618$,[3] which is commonly known as the golden ratio, or golden section. Many people believe that the rectangle with proportion $L{:}S = \phi$ is, of all rectangles, the most pleasing to the eye. In any case, it is full of mathematical wonders waiting to be discovered by your students.

A nice approach to the golden rectangle (as well as Fibonacci numbers and the golden ratio) is the following method of covering a rectangular region with squares. Start with two squares with side 1 and put them next to each other to obtain a rectangle. On its long side you can put a square with side 2 to obtain a new, larger rectangle. On its longer side fits a square with side 3. Continue to create larger and larger rectangles by attaching, in each step, a square to the longer side of the rectangle obtained in the previous step (see Figure 4.25).

Figure 4.25

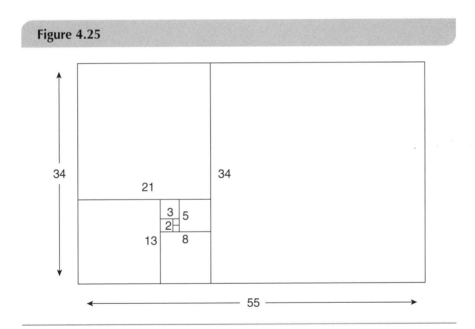

One finds that the side lengths of the squares used in this construction form the Fibonacci sequence $(1, 1, 2, 3, 5, 8, 13, 21, \ldots)$, characterized by the property that every number in this sequence is the sum of the two preceding numbers: $F_{n+1} = F_n + F_{n-1}$. The proportions of the rectangles created by this method are the ratios $F_{n+1}{:}F_n$, which approach the golden ratio $\phi = \frac{\sqrt{5}+1}{2} \approx 1.618$, as n becomes larger and larger. The rectangle in Figure 4.25 has the proportion $55{:}34 \approx 1.61765$ and is, to the naked eye, already indistinguishable from a golden rectangle.

When you cut off a square from a golden rectangle (with sides, say, $L = \phi$ and $S = 1$), you are left with a smaller rectangle, as in Figure 4.26. The smaller rectangle has sides 1 and $\phi - 1$. It follows from the equation $\phi = 1 + \frac{1}{\phi}$ stated above that $\phi - 1 = \frac{1}{\phi}$. The proportion of the smaller rectangle is therefore $\frac{1}{\phi - 1} = \frac{1}{\frac{1}{\phi}} = \phi$.

Hence, it is again a golden rectangle! Whenever we cut off a square from a golden rectangle, we are left with a new golden rectangle. We may thus continue this process to obtain an infinite sequence of golden rectangles, as indicated in Figure 4.26.

Figure 4.26

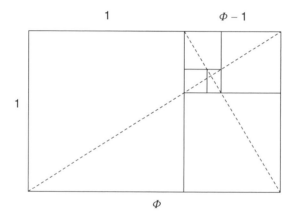

Figure 4.27

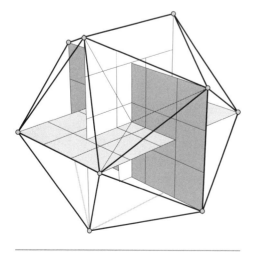

The large rectangle in Figure 4.26 has the sides ϕ and 1, and the smaller rectangle has sides 1 and $\frac{1}{\phi}$. Hence, the smaller rectangle is obtained from the larger one through a scaling transformation by the factor $\frac{1}{\phi}$. The same is then true for the diagonals. Thus, the two diagonals in Figure 4.26 also represent the golden ratio. Moreover, the two diagonals are, in fact, perpendicular.

Here is an interesting observation about golden rectangles in three-dimensional space: Put three golden rectangles perpendicular to each other in the coordinate planes with center at the coordinate origin and sides parallel to the axes, as indicated in Figure 4.27. Then the 12 corners of the three rectangles will be the corners of an icosahedron.

81. WHAT IS A GOLDEN TRIANGLE?

The golden triangle,[4] like the golden rectangle, is a geometric figure that can be used to demonstrate the mathematical beauty of the golden ratio.

Consider a regular decagon, as in Figure 4.28. It is made of 10 congruent triangles. Each of these triangles is isosceles with a vertex angle of $\frac{360°}{10} = 36°$. We will call an isosceles triangle with a vertex angle of 36° a *golden triangle* for reasons soon to be revealed.

Figure 4.28

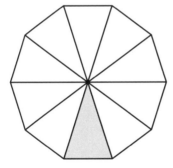
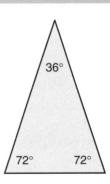

As the sum of all angles in any triangle is 180°, we find that the base angles are each 72°. Because 72° = 2 · 36°, we can draw an angle bisector at one of the base angles to obtain a new golden triangle, as shown in Figure 4.29(a). Here the shaded triangle also has the angles 72°, 72°, and 36°. It is therefore similar to the original triangle and has the same proportions: $\frac{a}{c} = \frac{c}{x}$. Since $x = a - c$, we find that $\frac{a}{c} = \frac{c}{a-c} = \frac{1}{\frac{a}{c}-1}$, or

$$\left(\frac{a}{c}\right)^2 - \left(\frac{a}{c}\right) - 1 = 0.$$

We see that $\frac{a}{c}$ is the unique positive solution of the equation $x^2 - x - 1 = 0$, which is the equation defining the *golden ratio* ϕ. $\frac{a}{c} = \phi = \frac{\sqrt{5}+1}{2} \approx 1.618$.

The appearance of the golden ratio as the ratio of side to base is, of course, the reason for the name "golden triangle."

Figure 4.29

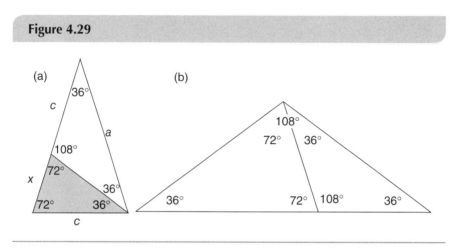

The angle bisector in Figure 4.29(a) divides the original triangle into two triangles. The second triangle is an obtuse isosceles triangle with side $c = a - x$, and base a. Here the ratio $\frac{a}{c}$ of base to side is the golden ratio ϕ, which makes this triangle another sort of golden triangle, often called the golden gnomon. It has the angles 36°, 36°, and 108° (which is three times 36°; see Figure 4.29[b]).

The area of the original golden triangle in Figure 4.29(a) can be written as $A = a \cdot \frac{h_a}{2}$, where h_a is the height of the triangle on the side a. Notice that the golden gnomon also has h_a as height; its area is $A' = c \cdot \frac{h_a}{2}$. Finally, the area of the shaded golden triangle in Figure 4.29(a) is $A'' = (a - c) \cdot \frac{h_a}{2}$. Hence, the areas of the three golden triangles in Figure 4.29(b) are in the proportion $A:A' = a:c = \phi$, and $A':A'' = c:(a - c) = \phi$, or $A:A':A'' = \phi^2:\phi:1$. (Note: $h_c = h_{a-c}$, and because of the symmetry, $h_c = h_a$).

We note that, as with the golden rectangle, the process of generating new golden figures can be continued indefinitely, as indicated in Figure 4.30(a).

Figure 4.30(b) shows the appearance of the golden triangle (and the golden gnomon) in the regular pentagon. Moreover, we find golden triangles in the pentagram, which is formed by the diagonals of a regular pentagon, as shown in Figure 4.30(c).

Figure 4.30

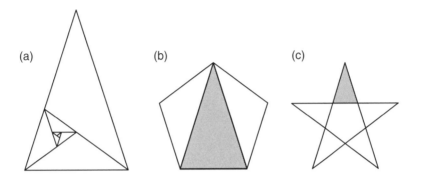

(a)   (b)   (c)

82. FROM WHICH POINT IN A TRIANGLE IS THE SUM OF THE DISTANCES TO THE THREE VERTICES SMALLEST?

The point O of intersection of the perpendicular bisectors of the sides of a triangle gives us the center of the circumscribed circle (with radius R) of a triangle. This point O has the property that its distance is the same to all three vertices ($OA = OB = OC = R$). Is the sum of the distances to the three vertices from this point the minimum distance? No! One reason is that this point could well lie far outside of the given triangle. We then must seek the point, P, from which the sum of the distances to the three vertices is smallest. Consider the triangle ABC, where the three angles formed are equal—that is, in Figure 4.31, we have

$$\angle APB = \angle BPC = \angle CPA = 120°.$$

The point P is determined by constructing equilateral triangles on the sides of the given triangle and getting the point of intersection of the lines joining each vertex of the given triangle, with the remote vertex on the opposite side of the indicated vertex as shown in Figure 4.31.

Figure 4.31

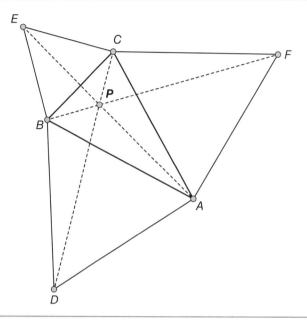

This point P, unexpectedly, is also the very same point in a triangle from which the sum of the distances to the vertices is the smallest. That is, $AP + BP + CP$ is smaller than the sum of the distances from any other point in the triangle to the vertices. The point we are looking for is called the *Fermat point*, P, named after the French mathematician Pierre de Fermat (1607/08–1665). This point P is also called the *equiangular point* of $\triangle ABC$ since $\angle APB = \angle APC = \angle BPC = 120°$ (see Figure 4.32).[2]

Figure 4.32

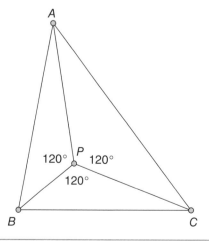

In other words, this point now has *two* important properties: the *minimum-distance point* from the three vertices of triangle *ABC* and the *equiangular point* of this triangle.

We begin by considering Δ*ABC* with no angle measuring greater than 120° (Figure 4.33). To show that the sum of the distances from point *F* to each of the three vertices of triangle *ABC* is less than that from any other point to the vertices, we need to take any other randomly selected point *D* and show that the sum of the distances from this point is greater than the sum of the distances from point *F* to the vertices of the triangle.

Figure 4.33

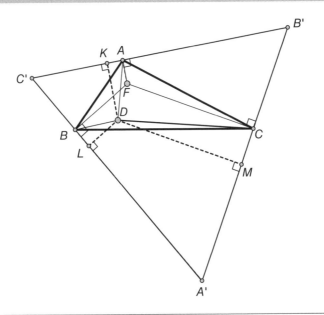

Let *F* be the equiangular point in the interior of Δ*ABC*, that is, where ∠*AFB* = ∠*BFC* = ∠*AFC* = 120°. We draw lines through *A*, *B*, and *C*, which are perpendicular to *AF*, *BF*, and *CF*, respectively. These lines meet to form yet another equilateral triangle, *A'B'C'*. (To prove Δ *A'B'C'* is equilateral, notice that each angle has measure 60°. This can be shown by considering, for example, quadrilateral *AFBC'*. Since ∠*C'AF* = ∠*C'BF* = 90°, and ∠*AFB* = 120°, it follows that ∠ *AC'B* = 60°.) Let *D* be *any other* point in the interior of Δ*ABC*. We must then show that the sum of the distances from *F* to the vertices of triangle *ABC* is less than the sum of the distances from the randomly selected point *D* to the vertices of triangle *ABC*.

We can easily show that the sum of the distances from any point in the interior of an equilateral triangle to the sides is a constant, namely, the length of the altitude (see Viviani's theorem in the next question).

Now using this constant relationship, we have (Figure 4.33) $FA + FB + FC = DK + DL + DM$ (where DK, DL, and DM are the perpendiculars to $B'KC'$, $A'LC'$, and $A'MB'$, respectively).

But $DK + DL + DM < DA + DB + DC$. (The shortest distance from an external point to a line is the length of the perpendicular segment from that point to the line.) By substitution, $FA + FB + FC < DA + DB + DC$.

You may wonder why we chose to restrict our discussion to triangles with angles of measure less than $120°$. If you try to construct the point F in a triangle with one angle of measure of $150°$, you will find that the equiangular point is outside of triangle ABC. When $\angle BAC = 120°$, the equiangular point is on vertex A. Therefore, the equiangular point *in* a triangle (with no angle of measure greater than $120°$) is the minimum-distance point (i.e., the point at which the sides of the triangle subtend congruent angles).

A further relationship involving the distances form a point within a triangle to the vertices was discovered in 1902 by the Dutch mathematician J. N. Visschers, who showed that with the assumption that AB is the shortest side of triangle ABC, we have: $PA + PB + PC < AC + BC$.

83. WHAT IS THE SUM OF THE DISTANCES FROM A POINT IN A TRIANGLE TO ITS THREE SIDES?

The concurrency point of the angle bisectors of a triangle gives us the center I of the inscribed circle (with radius r) of the triangle. This point I has the property that it is equidistant from the sides of the triangle ($II_a = II_b = II_c = r$). We can easily find a point in the triangle where the sum of the distances to the sides is greater than the sum of the distances from the center of the inscribed circle to the sides. That is, $PD + PE + PF > II_a + II_b + II_c = 3r$ (see Figure 4.34).

Figure 4.34

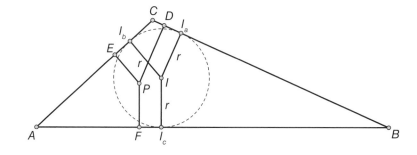

We will consider a theorem developed by Vincenzo Viviani (1622–1703):

In an equilateral triangle, the sum, $PD + PE + PF$, of the distances from this randomly chosen point to the three sides is always the same. That sum is equal to the altitude of the equilateral triangle. This is shown in Figure 4.35, where the altitude is CH_c.

Figure 4.35

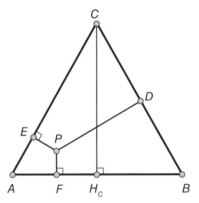

This surprising property can be proved true by using the formula for the area of a triangle (i.e., the area of a triangle one-half the product of the base and the altitude drawn to that base). We begin with equilateral triangle ABC, where $PF \perp AB$, $PD \perp BC$, $PE \perp AC$, and $CH_c \perp AB$. We then draw PA, PB, and PC, as shown in Figure 4.36.

Figure 4.36

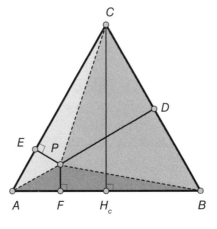

The $Area\triangle ABC = Area\triangle APB + Area\triangle BPC + Area\triangle CPA =$

$\frac{1}{2}AB \cdot PF + \frac{1}{2}BC \cdot PD + \frac{1}{2}AC \cdot PE.$

Since $AB = BC = AC$, the $Area\triangle ABC = \frac{1}{2}AB \cdot (PF + PD + PE).$

However, the $Area\triangle ABC = \frac{1}{2}AB \cdot CH_c.$ Therefore, $PD + PE + PF = CH_c,$

which is then a constant. This is what we wanted to prove for the given equilateral triangle.

We return to the randomly selected point in an arbitrary triangle, and we will consider the perpendicular distances to the three sides of the triangle. In Figure 4.37, we get the following relationship:

$$PD + PE + PF \leq \frac{PA + PB + PC}{2},$$

which was posed by Paul Erdös (1913–1996) and later solved by Louis Joel Mordell (1888–1972) and is known as the *Erdös-Mordell inequality*. We should note that the equality here only holds when point P is the centroid of an equilateral triangle.[6]

Figure 4.37

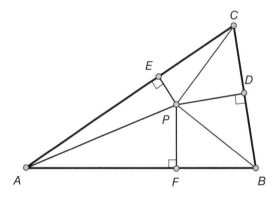

84. WHAT IS PRESIDENT JAMES A. GARFIELD'S PROOF OF THE PYTHAGOREAN THEOREM?[7]

The United States is one of the few countries in the world that presents high school students with a year's course in deductive geometry. This has a long history going back to one of the first English adaptations of Euclid's *Elements* by Robert Simson, whose book, *The Elements of Euclid,* was published throughout the 18th and 19th centuries in England, and to Adrien-Marie

Legendre, whose 1794 geometry textbook paved the way for Charles Davies to write the first American model textbooks in the 19th century. He set the course for today's high school geometry course.

There are historical perspectives that can enliven the geometry course as well as other mathematics courses. We owe it to our students to make our mathematics courses come alive. It is important to use these motivational techniques so students can begin to appreciate mathematics. Enriching our mathematics instruction with some unexpected historical anecdote can prove to be very effective. For example, the fact that President James A. Garfield (1831–1881), the 20th president of the United States, contributed to our knowledge of geometry can be fascinating.

You can begin by asking your class what the following three men have in common: Pythagoras, Euclid, and President James A. Garfield.

After some moments of perplexity, you can relieve the class of its frustration by telling them that all three fellows proved the Pythagorean theorem. The first two world-renowned mathematicians bring no surprise, but President Garfield? He wasn't a mathematician, nor did he ever study mathematics. As a matter of fact, his only study of geometry,[8] some 25 years before he published his proof of the Pythagorean theorem, was informal and alone.

Although a member of the House of Representatives, Garfield, who enjoyed "playing" with elementary mathematics, came upon a cute proof of this famous theorem. It was subsequently published in the *New England Journal of Education* after being encouraged by two professors (Quimby and Parker) at Dartmouth College, where he went to give a lecture on March 7, 1876. The text begins with the following:

> In a personal interview with General James A. Garfield, Member of Congress from Ohio, we were shown the following demonstration of the pons asinorum,[9] which he had hit upon in some mathematical amusements and discussions with other M.C.'s. We do not remember to have seen it before, and we think it something on which the members of both houses can unite without distinction of party.

By this time, the students are probably motivated to see what a nonmathematician U.S. president could possibly have done with this famous theorem. Garfield's proof is actually quite simple and therefore can be considered "beautiful." We begin the proof by placing two congruent right triangles ($\triangle ABE \cong \triangle DCE$) so that points *B, C,* and *E* are collinear and connect point *A* to point *D* forming a trapezoid as shown in Figure 4.38, and then a trapezoid is formed. Notice also that since $\angle AEB + \angle CED = 90°$, $\angle AED = 90°$, making $\triangle AED$ a right triangle.

Figure 4.38

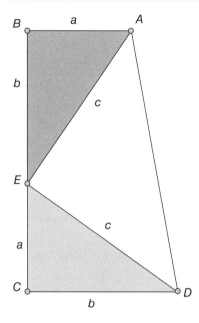

The area of the trapezoid $= \dfrac{1}{2}$(sum of bases)(altitude)

$$= \frac{1}{2}(a+b)(a+b)$$

$$= \frac{1}{2}a^2 + ab + \frac{1}{2}b^2.$$

The sum of the three triangles (also the area of the trapezoid) is

$$\frac{1}{2}ab + \frac{1}{2}ab + \frac{1}{2}c^2$$

$$= ab + \frac{1}{2}c^2.$$

We now equate the two expressions of the area of the trapezoid:

$$\frac{1}{2}a^2 + ab + \frac{1}{2}b^2 = ab + \frac{1}{2}c^2$$

$$\frac{1}{2}a^2 + \frac{1}{2}b^2 = \frac{1}{2}c^2,$$

which is the familiar $a^2 + b^2 = c^2$, the *Pythagorean theorem*.

There are more than 400 proofs[10] of the Pythagorean theorem available today; many are ingenious, yet some are a bit cumbersome. However, none will ever use trigonometry. Why is this? An astute student will tell you that there can be no proof of the Pythagorean theorem using trigonometry, since trigonometry depends (or is based) on the Pythagorean theorem. Thus, using trigonometry to prove the very theorem on which it depends would be circular reasoning. We indicated this in Question 76. Encourage your students to discover a new proof of this most famous theorem.

85. WHAT IS THE NINE-POINT CIRCLE?

Perhaps one of the true joys in geometry is to observe how some seemingly unrelated points are truly related to each other. We begin with the very important notion that any three noncollinear points determine a circle. When a fourth point also emerges on the same circle, it is quite noteworthy. Yet when nine points all end up being on the same circle, that is phenomenal! Moreover, these nine points, for any given triangle, are

- the midpoints of the three sides,
- the feet of the three altitudes, and
- the midpoints of the segments from the orthocenter (the point of intersection of the altitudes) to the vertices.

Have your students do the necessary construction to locate each of these nine points. Careful construction will allow them to be on the same circle. This circle is called the *nine-point circle* of the triangle. Using an unmarked straightedge and compasses or the *Geometer's Sketchpad* computer program would be fine for this activity.

In 1765 Leonhard Euler showed that six of these points, the midpoints of the sides and the feet of the altitudes, determine a unique circle. Yet not until 1820, when a paper[11] published by Brianchon and Poncelet appeared, were the remaining three points (the midpoints of the segments from the orthocenter to the vertices) found to be on this circle. The paper contains the first complete proof of the theorem and uses the name "the nine-point circle" for the first time.

Theorem: In any triangle, the midpoints of the sides, the feet of the altitudes, and the midpoints of the segments from the orthocenter to the vertices lie on a circle.

Figure 4.39

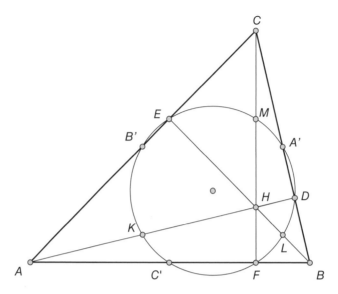

Proof: In order to simplify the discussion of this proof, we shall consider each part with a separate diagram. Bear in mind, though, that each of the figures from Figure 4.40 to Figure 4.43 is merely an extraction from Figure 4.39, which is the complete diagram.

Figure 4.40

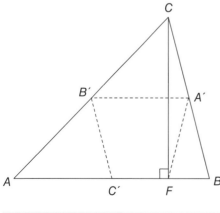

In Figure 4.40, points A', B', and C' are the midpoints of the three sides of $\triangle ABC$ opposite the respective vertex. $\overline{CF}$ is an altitude of $\triangle ABC$. Since $\overline{A'B'}$ is a midline of $\triangle ABC$, $\overline{A'B'} \parallel \overline{AB}$. Therefore quadrilateral $A'B'C'F$ is a trapezoid. $\overline{B'C'}$ is also a midline of $\triangle ABC$, so that $B'C' = \frac{1}{2}BC$.

Since $\overline{A'F}$ is the median to the hypotenuse of right $\triangle BCF$, $A'F = \frac{1}{2}BC$. Therefore $B'C' = A'F$ and trapezoid $A'B'C'F$ is isosceles.

You will recall that when the opposite angles of a quadrilateral are supplementary, as in the case of an isosceles trapezoid, the quadrilateral is cyclic. Therefore quadrilateral $A'B'C'F$ is cyclic.[12]

So far we have four of the nine points on one circle.

To avoid any confusion, we redraw $\triangle ABC$ (see Figure 4.41) and include altitude $\overline{AD}$. Using the same argument as before, we find that quadrilateral $A'B'C'D$ is an isosceles trapezoid and therefore cyclic. So we now have five of the nine points on one circle (i.e., points A', B', C', F, and D).

By repeating the same argument for altitude $\overline{BE}$, we can then state that points D, F, and E lie on the same circle as points A', B', and C'. These six points are as far as Euler got with this configuration.

With H as the orthocenter (the point of intersection of the altitudes), M is the midpoint of $\overline{CH}$ (see Figure 4.42). Therefore, $\overline{B'M}$, a midline of $\triangle ACH$, is parallel to $\overline{AH}$, or altitude $\overline{AD}$. Since $\overline{B'C'}$ is a midline of $\triangle ABC$, $\overline{B'C'} \parallel \overline{BC}$. Therefore, since $\angle ADC$ is a right angle, $\angle MB'C'$ is also a right angle. Thus quadrilateral $MB'C'F$ is cyclic (opposite angles are supplementary). This places point M on the circle determined by points B', C', and F. We now have a seven-point circle.

We repeat this procedure with point L, the midpoint of $\overline{BH}$ (see Figure 4.43). As before, $\angle B'A'L$ is a right angle, as is $\angle B'EL$. Therefore points B', E, A', and L are concyclic (opposite angles supplementary). We now have L as an additional point on our circle, making it an eight-point circle.

To locate our final point on the circle, consider point K, the midpoint of $\overline{AH}$. As we did earlier, we find $\angle A'B'K$ to be a right angle, as is $\angle A'DK$. Therefore, quadrilateral $A'DKB'$ is cyclic and point K is on the same circle as points B', A', and D. We have therefore proved that *nine specific points* lie on this circle. This is not to be taken lightly; it is quite spectacular![13]

Figure 4.41

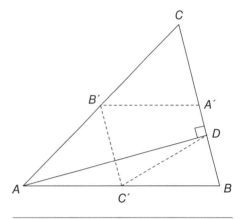

Figure 4.42

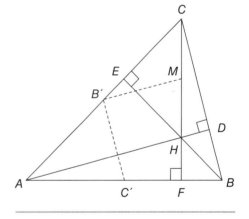

Figure 4.43

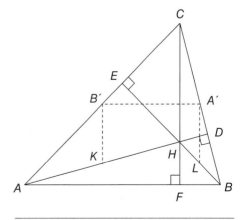

86. HOW CAN THE PYTHAGOREAN THEOREM BE PROVED BY PAPER FOLDING?

After all the struggles students go through to prove the Pythagorean theorem, imagine we will now prove this famous theorem by simply folding paper. Your first thought might be why didn't my teachers ever show me this when I was in school? A good question, but perhaps that is one of the reasons many adults need to be convinced in later life that mathematics is beautiful and holds many delights as yet unexposed. So here is an opportunity to show your students a beauty they are not likely to forget.

We can extend from the statement of the Pythagorean theorem: *The sum of the squares on the legs of a right triangle is equal to the square on the hypotenuse of the triangle.*

By replacing the word "square" with "areas of similar polygons," we read: *The sum of the areas of similar polygons on the legs of a right triangle is equal to the area of the similar polygon on the hypotenuse of the triangle.*

This replacement can be shown to be correct and holds true for any similar polygons appropriately (correspondingly) placed on the right triangle's sides.

Consider the following right triangle with altitude $\overline{CD}$. Figure 4.44 shows this with three triangular flaps folded over the $\triangle ABC$. The flaps are $\triangle ABC$, $\triangle ADC$, and $\triangle BDC$. Each student should be working along with you as you develop this demonstration.

Figure 4.44

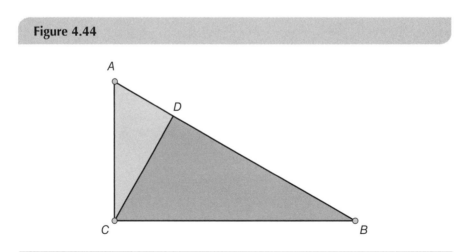

Notice that $\triangle ADC \sim \triangle CDB \sim \triangle ACB$. In the above figure, $\triangle ADC$ and $\triangle CDB$ are folded over $\triangle ACB$. So clearly, $Area \triangle ADC + Area \triangle CDB = Area \triangle ACB$. If we unfold the triangles (including $\triangle ACB$ itself), we get the result in Figure 4.45, which shows that the relationship of the similar polygons (here right triangles) is an extension of the Pythagorean theorem: *The sum of the areas of similar right triangles on the legs of a right triangle is equal to the area of the similar right triangle on the hypotenuse of the triangle.*

This essentially "proves" the Pythagorean theorem by paper folding!

Figure 4.45

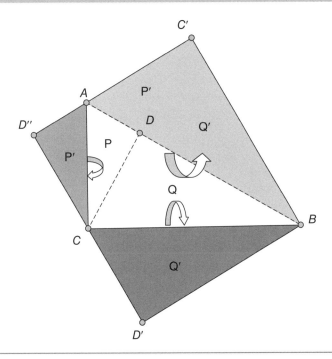

87. HOW CAN WE PROVE THAT THE SUM OF THE MEASURES OF THE ANGLES OF ANY TRIANGLE IS 180° USING PAPER FOLDING?

Students are often "told" that the sum of the (measures of) angles of a triangle is 180°. This by no means ensures that they know what that really means, and consequently it doesn't etch a lasting mark in their memory. This basis for Euclidean geometry ought to be genuinely understood by all. Most people know that when they make one complete revolution, that represents 360°. There is nothing sacrosanct about this measure, other than it is generally accepted and so used.

So how does the angle sum of a triangle relate to this? The simplest and perhaps the most convincing way to demonstrate this angle sum is to tear the three vertices from a paper triangle and place them together to form a straight line. The straight line represents one-half of a complete revolution, hence, the 180°.

It is perhaps more elegant to use a folding procedure. Students should be told to cut a conveniently large scalene triangle from a piece of paper. They should then fold one vertex so that it touches the opposite side and so that the crease is parallel to that side (see Figure 4.46).

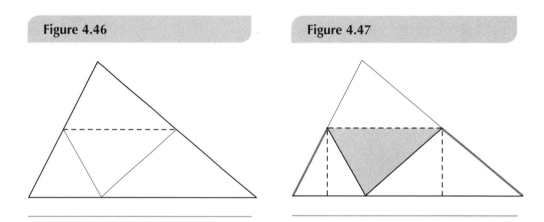

Figure 4.46   **Figure 4.47**

They should then fold the remaining two vertices to meet the first vertex at a common point (Figure 4.47). Students will notice that the three angles of the triangle together form a straight line, and hence have an angle sum of 180° (Figure 4.48). (Note: Points *D* and *E* are the midpoints of the sides of the triangle, as shown in Figure 4.48.)

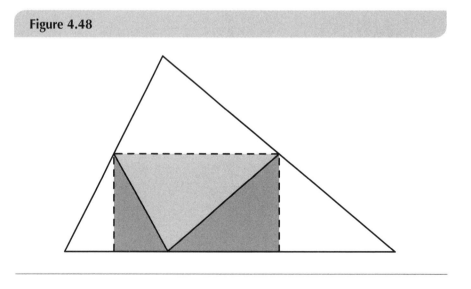

Figure 4.48

Figure 4.49

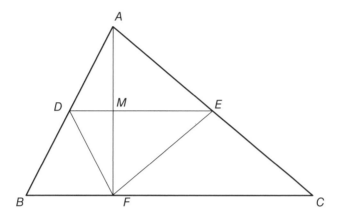

However, it is also nice to show why this folding procedure has the vertices meet at a point on the side of the triangle. Establishing this phenomenon is tantamount to proving the theorem of the angle sum of a triangle.

The proof of this theorem follows directly from the paper-folding exercise. By folding the top vertex along a parallel crease (i.e., $\overline{DE} \parallel \overline{BC}$), $\overline{AF} \perp \overline{ED}$ at M. Since $\overline{MF} \cong \overline{AM}$, or M is the midpoint of $\overline{AF}$, D and E are midpoints of $\overline{AB}$ and $\overline{AC}$, respectively, since a line parallel to one side of a triangle (either $\triangle BAF$ or $\triangle CAF$) and bisecting a second side $\left(\overline{AF}\right)$ of the triangle also bisects the third side. It is then easy to show that since $\overline{AD} \cong \overline{DF}$, $\overline{DB} \cong \overline{DF}$, and similarly $\overline{EF} \cong \overline{EC}$, the folding over of vertices B and C would fit at F, forming a straight line along $\overline{BFC}$ (see Figure 4.49).

The most important part of this unit is to convince your students that a paper-folding exercise can be quite valid in *demonstrating* a property.

Remember though to mention the difference between a paper-folding demonstration and a proof.

88. WHAT FIGURE IS CREATED BY JOINING THE MIDPOINTS OF ANY QUADRILATERAL?

Have each of your students draw an ugly (i.e., any shaped) quadrilateral. Then, have them (very carefully) locate the midpoints of the four sides of the quadrilateral. Now have them join these points consecutively. Everyone's drawing should have resulted in a parallelogram. Wow! How did this happen? Everyone began (most likely) with a differently shaped quadrilateral. Yet everyone ended up with a parallelogram, the so-called Varignon[14] parallelogram.

Figure 4.50 shows a few possible results.

Figure 4.50

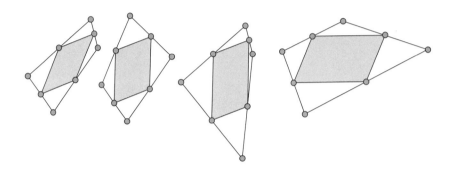

A question that ought to be asked at this point is how might the original quadrilateral have been shaped for the parallelogram to be a rectangle, rhombus, or square?

Either through guess and check or by an analysis of the situation, students should discover the following:

When the diagonals of the original quadrilateral are perpendicular, the parallelogram is a *rectangle* (see Figure 4.51).

Figure 4.51

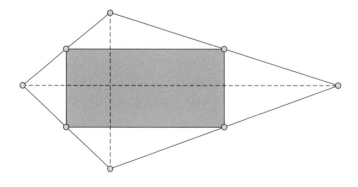

When the diagonals of the original quadrilateral are congruent, then the parallelogram is a *rhombus* (Figure 4.52).

Figure 4.52

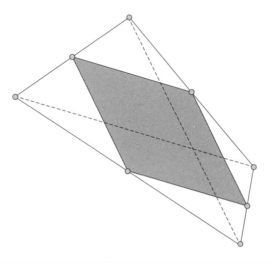

When the diagonals of the original quadrilateral are congruent and perpendicular, then the parallelogram is a *square* (Figure 4.53).

Figure 4.53

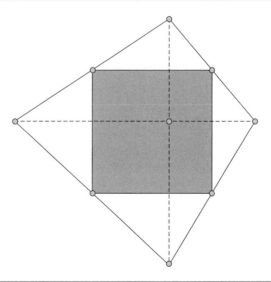

For the teacher who wishes to demonstrate this for the class, *Geometer's Sketchpad* software is highly recommended. For the teacher who wishes to prove that all of the above is "really true," a short proof outline is provided, one that should be in easy reach for a high school geometry student.

Proof Outline

The proof is based on a simple theorem that states that a line segment joining the midpoints of two sides of a triangle is parallel to and half the length of the third side of the triangle. This is precisely what happens here.

Consider Figure 4.54. In $\triangle ADB$, the midpoints of sides $\overline{AD}$ and $\overline{AB}$ are F and G, respectively. Therefore, $\overline{FG} \parallel \overline{DB}$ and $FG = \frac{1}{2}BD$, and $\overline{EH} \parallel \overline{DB}$ and $EH = \frac{1}{2}BD$. Therefore, $\overline{FG} \parallel \overline{EH}$ and $FG = EH$. This establishes *FGHE* as a parallelogram.

Figure 4.54

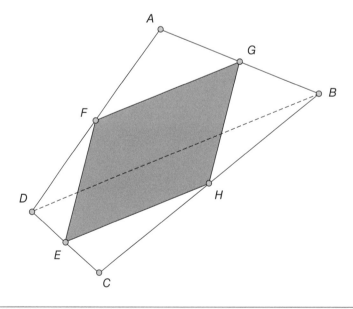

Furthermore, if the diagonals, $\overline{DB}$ and $\overline{AC}$, are congruent, then the sides of the parallelogram must also be congruent, since they are each one-half the length of the diagonals of the original quadrilateral. This results in a rhombus.

Similarly, if the diagonals of the original quadrilateral are perpendicular and congruent, then since the sides of the parallelogram are, in pairs, parallel to the diagonals and half their length, the sides of the parallelogram must be perpendicular and congruent to each other, making it a square.

89. HOW CAN THE CONCURRENCY OF THE MEDIANS OF A TRIANGLE BE PROVED IN ONE STEP?

The topic of concurrency of lines in a triangle deserves more attention than it usually gets in an elementary geometry course. To prove that the medians of a triangle are concurrent, we must establish an extremely useful relationship. This will be done with the help of the famous theorem first published[15] by the Italian mathematician Giovanni Ceva (1647–1734), and which now bears his name.

In simple terms, the relationship that Ceva established says that if you have three concurrent line segments (*AL, BM,* and *CN*) joining a vertex of a triangle with a point on the opposite side, then the product of the alternate segments along the sides are equal. In Figure 4.55, you can see this, noting that the products of the alternate segments along the sides of the triangle are equal: $AN \cdot BL \cdot CM = NB \cdot LC \cdot MA$.

Figure 4.55

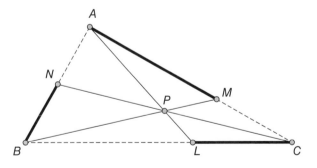

This can be more formally stated as follows:

Ceva's Theorem: The three lines containing the vertices A, B, and C of ΔABC and intersecting the opposite sides at points L, M, and N, respectively, are concurrent if and only if $\dfrac{AN}{NB} \cdot \dfrac{BL}{LC} \cdot \dfrac{CM}{MA} = 1$, or $AN \cdot BL \cdot CM = NB \cdot LC \cdot MA$.

Figure 4.56

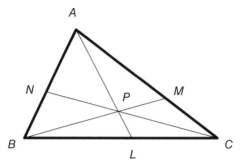

Figure 4.57

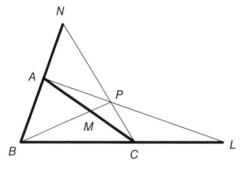

To prove this theorem, we must note that there are two possible situations in which the three lines drawn from the vertices may intersect the sides and still be concurrent. These are shown in Figures 4.56 and 4.57. It is perhaps easier to follow the proof with Figure 4.56 and verify the validity of the statements with Figure 4.57. In any case, the statements made in the proof hold true for *both* figures.

Ceva's theorem is an equivalence (or biconditional) and therefore requires two proofs (one the converse of the other). We shall first prove that *if the three lines containing the vertices of $\triangle ABC$ and intersecting the opposite sides in points L, M, and N, respectively, are concurrent, then*

$$\frac{AN}{NB} \cdot \frac{BL}{LC} \cdot \frac{CM}{MA} = 1.$$

Proof I: In the figure, $\overline{AL}$, $\overline{BM}$, and $\overline{CN}$ meet in point P. Since $\triangle ABL$ and $\triangle ACL$ share the same altitude (i.e., from point A),

$$\frac{Area\,\triangle ABL}{Area\,\triangle ACL} = \frac{BL}{LC} . \tag{I}$$

Similarly,

$$\frac{Area\,\triangle PBL}{Area\,\triangle PCL} = \frac{BL}{LC} . \tag{II}$$

From (I) and (II):

$$\frac{Area\,\triangle ABL}{Area\,\triangle ACL} = \frac{Area\,\triangle PBL}{Area\,\triangle PCL} .$$

A basic property of proportions $\left(\dfrac{w}{x} = \dfrac{y}{z} = \dfrac{w-y}{x-z} \right)$ provides that

$$\frac{BL}{LC} = \frac{Area\,\triangle ABL - Area\,\triangle PBL}{Area\,\triangle ACL - Area\,\triangle PCL} = \frac{Area\,\triangle ABP}{Area\,\triangle ACP} . \tag{III}$$

We now repeat the same process as above using $\overline{BM}$ instead of $\overline{AL}$ (used above).

Here

$$\frac{CM}{MA} = \frac{Area\,\triangle BMC}{Area\,\triangle BMA} = \frac{Area\,\triangle PMC}{Area\,\triangle PMA} .$$

It follows that:

$$\frac{CM}{MA} = \frac{Area\,\triangle BMC - Area\,\triangle PMC}{Area\,\triangle BMA - Area\,\triangle PMA} = \frac{Area\,\triangle BCP}{Area\,\triangle BAP} . \tag{IV}$$

Once again, we repeat the process using $\overline{CN}$ where $\overline{AL}$ was used earlier.

Now $\dfrac{AN}{NB} = \dfrac{Area\,\triangle ACN}{Area\,\triangle BCN} = \dfrac{Area\,\triangle APN}{Area\,\triangle BPN} .$

This permits us to get

$$\frac{AN}{NB} = \frac{Area\triangle ACN - Area\triangle APN}{Area\triangle BCN - Area\triangle BPN} = \frac{Area\triangle ACP}{Area\triangle BCP} \qquad (V)$$

We now simply multiply (III), (IV), and (V) to get the desired result:

$$\frac{BL}{LC} \cdot \frac{CM}{MA} \cdot \frac{AN}{NB} = \frac{Area\triangle ABP}{Area\triangle ACP} \cdot \frac{Area\triangle BCP}{Area\triangle BAP} \cdot \frac{Area\triangle ACP}{Area\triangle BCP} = 1$$

By introducing an auxiliary line, we can produce a simpler proof.

Figure 4.58

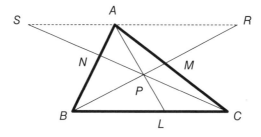

Figure 4.59

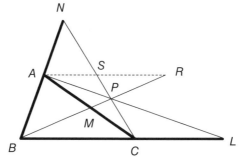

Proof II: Consider Figures 4.58 and 4.59 with a line containing A and parallel to $\overline{BC}$ intersecting $\overrightarrow{CP}$ at S and $\overrightarrow{BP}$ at R.

The parallel lines enable us to establish the following pairs of similar triangles:

$$\triangle AMR \sim \triangle CMB, \text{ therefore } \frac{AM}{MC} = \frac{AR}{CB} \qquad \text{(I)}$$

$$\triangle BNC \sim \triangle ANS, \text{ therefore } \frac{BN}{NA} = \frac{CB}{SA} \qquad \text{(II)}$$

$$\triangle CLP \sim \triangle SAP, \text{ therefore } \frac{CL}{SA} = \frac{LP}{AP} \qquad \text{(III)}$$

$$\triangle BLP \sim \triangle RAP, \text{ therefore } \frac{BL}{RA} = \frac{LP}{AP} \qquad \text{(IV)}$$

From (III) and (IV) we get $\dfrac{CL}{SA} = \dfrac{BL}{RA}$.

This can be rewritten as $\dfrac{CL}{BL} = \dfrac{SA}{RA}$. $\qquad \text{(V)}$

Now by multiplying (I), (II), and (V), we obtain our desired result:

$$\frac{AM}{MC} \cdot \frac{BN}{NA} \cdot \frac{CL}{BL} = \frac{AR}{CB} \cdot \frac{CB}{SA} \cdot \frac{SA}{RA} = 1$$

We rearrange the terms and invert the fractions to get

$$\frac{AN}{NB} \cdot \frac{BL}{LC} \cdot \frac{CM}{MA} = 1.$$

We are now ready to answer the original question by proving that the medians of a triangle are concurrent. Normally (i.e., without the help of Ceva's theorem) this would be a very difficult proof to do. Now observe how simple it is to prove this concurrency (see Figure 4.60).

Proof: In $\triangle ABC$, $\overline{AL}$, $\overline{BM}$, and $\overline{CN}$ are medians. Therefore, $AN = NB$, $BL = LC$ and $CM = MA$. Multiplying these equalities gives us,

$$(AN)(BL)(CM) = (NB)(LC)(MA) \text{ or } \frac{AN}{NB} \cdot \frac{BL}{LC} \cdot \frac{CM}{MA} = 1 .$$

Thus by Ceva's theorem, $\overline{AL}$, $\overline{BM}$, and $\overline{CN}$ are concurrent.

Figure 4.60

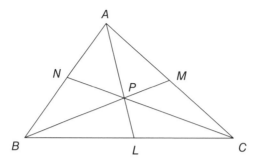

NOTES

1. See Posamentier, A. S., & Lehmann, I. (2004). *π: A biography of the world's most mysterious number.* Amherst, NY: Prometheus Books.

2. For more on the golden rectangle, see Posamentier, A. S., & Lehmann, I. (2012). *The glorious golden ratio.* Amherst, NY: Prometheus Books.

3. The negative solution of this equation is $\frac{1-\sqrt{5}}{2} \approx -0.618$.

4. For more on the golden triangle, see Posamentier, A. S., & Lehmann, I. (2012). *The glorious golden ratio.* Amherst, NY: Prometheus Books.

5. For more on this point and a proof, see Posamentier, A. S., & Lehmann, I. (2012). *The secrets of triangles: A mathematical journey.* Amherst, NY: Prometheus Books (pp. 65–69, 75–78).

6. For a proof, see Posamentier, A. S., & Lehmann, I. (2012). *The secrets of triangles: A mathematical journey.* Amherst, NY: Prometheus Books (pp. 356–357).

7. See Posamentier, A. S. (2010). *The Pythagorean theorem: The story of its power and beauty.* Amherst, NY: Prometheus Books.

8. In October 1851, he noted in his diary that "I have today commenced the study of geometry alone without class or teacher."

9. This would appear to be a wrong reference, since we usually consider the proof that the base angles of an isosceles triangle are congruent as the pons asinorum, or "bridge of fools."

10. A classic source for 370 proofs of the Pythagorean theorem is Elisha S. Loomis's *The Pythagorean Proposition* (Reston, VA: NCTM, 1968).

11. *Recherches sur la determination d'une hyperbole équilatère moyen de quartes conditions données* (Paris, 1820).

12. A cyclic quadrilateral is one whose four vertices lie on the same circle.

13. There are actually four more points on this circle. See Posamentier, A. S., & Lehmann, I. (2012). *The secrets of triangles: A mathematical journey.* Amherst, NY: Prometheus Books (pp. 146–148, 349–350).

14. Pierre Varignon (1654–1722), a French mathematician.

15. *De lineis se invicem secantibus statica constructio* (Milan, 1678).

5 Probability Questions

90. WHAT IS THE FUNDAMENTAL PRINCIPLE OF COUNTING?

Suppose an event, E_1, can occur in n_1 different ways, a second event, E_2, can occur in n_2 different ways, and so on, and a kth event, E_k, can occur in n_k different ways. Then the fundamental principle of counting states that the number of different ways for these k events to occur in succession is given by $n_1 \times n_2 \times \ldots \times n_k$.

Let us say you have gone shopping and were able to find items of clothing that you could easily match with each other. You found 5 shirts, 3 pants, 2 pairs of shoes, and 2 hats. How many outfit combinations can you make given these options? Using the fundamental principle of counting, you would multiply $5 \times 3 \times 2 \times 2$ for a total of 60 possible outfits.

Suppose it is after class and you are hungry and decide to go to McDonalds for a snack. They have a daily special: Big Mac or Fried Fish sandwich + french fries or salad + soda, juice, or water for only $3.99. How many different "snacks" can you create? Using a tree diagram approach, you can draw all the possibilities.

You can see that you would have 12 different $3.99 snack meals possible, which agrees with the fundamental principle of counting because $2 \times 2 \times 3$ also gives you 12.

Let's roll a pair of dice. How many combinations are possible? There are six possibilities for the first die and six possibilities for the second die. Using the fundamental rule, we would have $6 \times 6 = 36$ different combinations. This can also be demonstrated using a tree diagram as in Figure 5.1 or creating **a sample space** as shown in Figure 5.2, in which each roll is represented as a pair of numbers in parentheses.

Figure 5.1

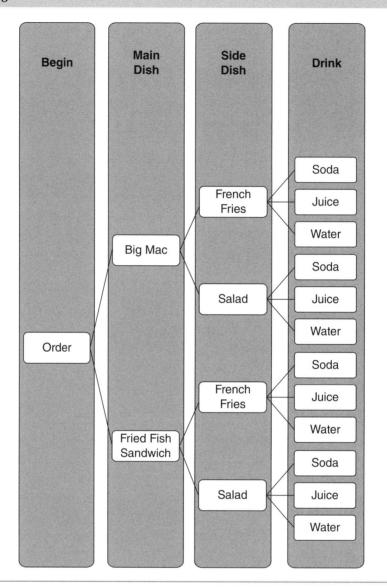

Figure 5.2

(1, 1) (2, 1) (3, 1) (4, 1) (5, 1) (6, 1)
(1, 2) (2, 2) (3, 2) (4, 2) (5, 2) (6, 2)
(1, 3) (2, 3) (3, 3) (4, 3) (5, 3) (6, 3)
(1, 4) (2, 4) (3, 4) (4, 4) (5, 4) (6, 4)
(1, 5) (2, 5) (3, 5) (4, 5) (5, 5) (6, 5)
(1, 6) (2, 6) (3, 6) (4, 6) (5, 6) (6, 6)

91. WHAT DOES IT MEAN WHEN THE PROBABILITY OF AN EVENT IS 1? IS 0?

Probability opens the door to a topic that really interests students—the science of uncertainty. Beginning with basic definitions and calculations along with their interpretations you will lay the foundation needed for more sophisticated topics in the field and will enable them to understand expected values, sports statistics, odds, and inferences in daily news and apply what they learn in class to real-life situations. In general, probability is the likelihood (or chance), expressed in numerical terms, that an event, E, will occur. The probability of an event, symbolically P(E), can be expressed as a fraction, decimal, or percentage. It can never be negative or greater than 1: $0 \leq P(E) \leq 1$. If an event will never happen, its probability is zero: P(Thanksgiving will fall on Friday) = 0. If an event will most definitely happen, its probability is one: P(Thanksgiving will fall on Thursday) = 1. In real life, it is very rare that the probability of an event is either 0 or 1, and most probabilities fall between 0 and 1 and are represented as three-place decimals, percentages, or fractions.

To calculate the probability of an event, you form a fraction:

P(E) = number of successful outcomes/number of all possible outcomes

P(January 1 will fall on a Monday) = $\dfrac{1}{7}$

P(Guessing correctly on a true/false question) = $\dfrac{1}{2}$

P(Rolling an even digit on a die) = $\dfrac{3}{6}$

P(Rolling a 7 on a die) = $\dfrac{0}{6} = 0$

Using the sample space of possible outcomes from rolling two dice (see Figure 5.2), P(roll a 6) = $\dfrac{5}{36}$, P(roll a 10) = $\dfrac{3}{36}$, P(roll an 11) = $\dfrac{6}{36}$ while P(roll a 7) = $\dfrac{6}{36}$. You can see that the probability of rolling a 7 is better than rolling any other combination. In the game of "craps," once you complete your first roll, that value becomes your "point," and you must match that point in a successive roll to win your bet. However, if you happen to roll a 7 before you roll a match to your point, you lose and the casino takes your money. The probability that the house will take your money is *always* highest.

Suppose students in a math class began a unit on probability. Their teacher had her students conduct a probability experiment tossing a fair coin. Each student tosses the coin 4 times. There are 25 students in the class, so together there are 100 tosses. The students know there are two possible outcomes for the coin toss, either heads or tails. Selecting heads as the "successful" outcome for a single coin toss, we get P(E = heads) = $\dfrac{1}{2}$, since the total number of possible outcomes is two and the outcome of heads is the one we have labeled as successful. This probability can also be expressed as 0.500, or 50%. A probability of 0.5 means that the likelihood of the event occurring is equal to the likelihood of it not occurring. In this case, a fair coin has a 0.5 probability of turning up heads and a 0.5 probability of turning up tails.

The students in the class gather their data into one chart to see if they get 50 heads out of 100 tosses in the class experiment. They will probably get a bit less or a bit more, and this is a good time to explain that probability of .5 is what is expected. If we repeat this experiment many, many times and take the average results of all our trials, we would find our results would get closer and closer to .500.

92. WHAT ARE MUTUALLY EXCLUSIVE EVENTS?

Mutually exclusive events are events that cannot happen at the same time. If we let the first event be A and the second event be B, then P(A and B) = 0. They are called "disjoint" events and are often represented by a Venn diagram (Figure 5.3).

Figure 5.3

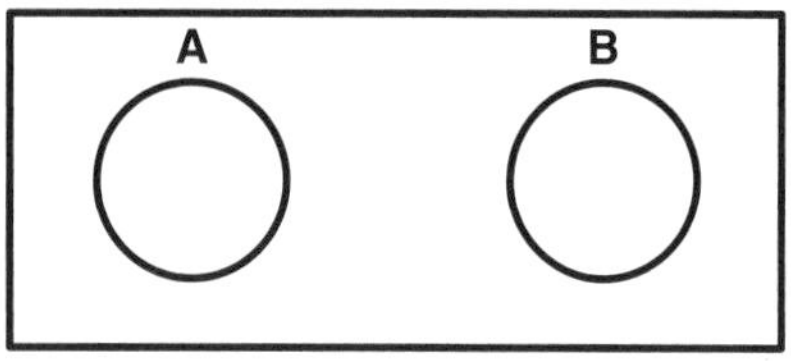

Let S, representing a sample space of all possible events, be a rectangle and place a circle representing event A and another circle representing event B inside of S; A and B appear as disjoint sets and don't touch each other.

This relationship can also be represented by the set notation $A \cap B = \phi$. The intersection of A and B is empty, and this is represented by the Greek letter phi, ϕ, which is the empty set.

For example, when drawing one card from a regular deck of 52 cards, if A = draw a king and B = draw a 7, there are no elements (cards) that belong to both sets. No card will have both a king and a 7 on it.

P(A and B) = 0: The probability of both A and B happening is zero.

Let's look at an experiment involving flipping a coin. P(heads and tails) = 0, since the coin will land on one side or the other and not on both.

93. WHAT IS THE PROBABILITY OF EITHER OR BOTH OF TWO EVENTS HAPPENING?

Select a card from a regular deck of 52 cards where you have four 13-card suits, hearts, spades, clubs, and diamonds, in which each suit runs from ace high, king, queen, jack, 10 down to 2.

Suppose you are asked to select one card. What is the possibility that you select an ace or a king?

The Addition Rule states that if the two events, selecting an ace or a king, cannot happen at the same time (of course one card can't be both), the events are considered "mutually exclusive" and P(A or B) = P(A) + P(B). So P(selecting an ace or selecting a king) = P(selecting an ace) + P(selecting a king) $= \frac{4}{52} + \frac{4}{52} = \frac{8}{52}$, or 0.154. The mutually exclusive events are shown as circles that do not intersect in the Venn diagram in Figure 5.4.

Figure 5.4

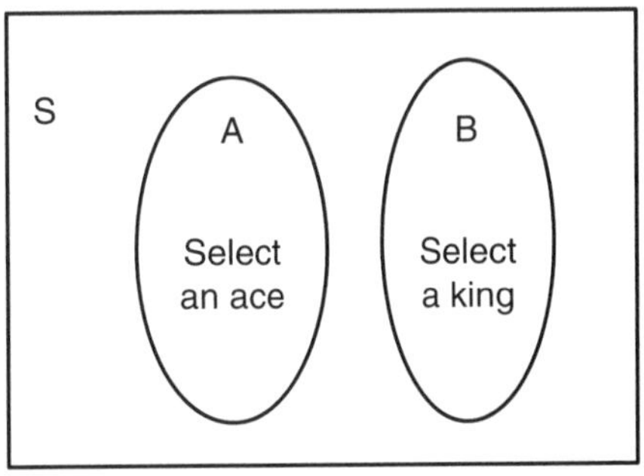

S

A

Select an ace

B

Select a king

If we change the problem a bit and ask, "What is the probability of selecting an ace or a heart?" we have introduced two events that are *not mutually exclusive,* and you can select one card that is *both* an ace and a heart. Now the Addition Rule changes and states that if the two events are NOT mutually exclusive, P(A or B) = P(A) + P(B) – P(A and B). We have to subtract the occasion when both events can occur as we are counting it twice; once as a pick that is an ace (event A) and a second time as a pick that is a heart (event B). The Addition Rule for this selection is, P(selecting an ace or selecting a heart) = P(selecting an ace) + P(selecting a heart) – P(selecting a card that is the ace of hearts) $= \frac{4}{52} + \frac{13}{52} - \frac{1}{52} = \frac{16}{52} = 0.308$. The Venn diagram in Figure 5.5 shows the intersection of the two events, which are *not* mutually exclusive.

Figure 5.5

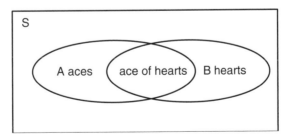

Now let us consider multiple events, and we want to find the probability of all of the events occurring. What would be the probability of a situation like that? To find the probability of several events occurring in succession involves multiplying the probabilities of the individual events. Let's look at the Multiplication Rule for Independent Events first.

P(event A and event B and event C) = P(event A) · P(event B) · P(event C), where Independent Events means that the occurrence of one event does *not* affect the probabilities of the other event(s).

Let us return to our standard deck of cards. Suppose this time we are going to select *two* cards and we will replace the first card selection before we make our second card selection. These are independent events. What is the probability that we will select a card (hopefully it will be an ace) as the first card, replace that card into the deck, maybe shuffle the deck, and then select our second card, hopefully a king?

$$\text{P(selecting an ace and selecting a king)} = \left(\frac{4}{52}\right)\left(\frac{4}{52}\right) = 0.00592.$$

Now let us *not* replace the first card we select before we select the second card. We have just made these two events dependent, as we have changed the probability of the second event.

P(selecting an ace and selecting a king) without replacement $= \left(\frac{4}{52}\right)\left(\frac{4}{51}\right) = 0.00603.$ We have improved our probability slightly and have used the Multiplication Rule for Dependent Events, where the probability of event B has changed:

P(event A and event B) = P(event A) · P(event B with smaller deck)

However, if you know that your first event definitely did occur, then you are working with a slightly different probability called conditional probability. In a general sense, the probability of event B occurring if event A has already occurred is noted as $P(B|A)$ and read as "the probability of B given A has happened." For two events, it is given by the following formula:

$$P(B|A) = \frac{P(A \cap B)}{P(A)} , P(A) \neq 0,$$

and in higher mathematics as it is expanded to include several events, it becomes beyond the scope of our book and is known as Bayes's theorem.

Let us focus on only two events. Suppose in our example above I know that I have definitely selected and not replaced an ace from our deck. Then the probability of selecting a king as my second card is $\frac{4}{51} = 0.0784.$ Using the formula, you would get the same answer:

$$\text{P(king|ace has been selected)} = \frac{\frac{4}{52} \cdot \frac{4}{51}}{\frac{4}{52}} = \frac{4}{51}$$

Here is an example that should clarify when you use conditional probability. Suppose you are the Quality Control Officer at ABC TECH and you receive a box of six flash drives of which you are told two are defective. You need to use two of the perfect drives immediately. You select one drive and then, without replacing it, select a second drive. What is the probability that both drives you selected are good?

Numbering the good drives g_1, g_2, g_3, g_4 and the defective ones d_1 and d_2, we have 30 possible outcomes—six choices for the first drive and five choices for the second selection. Filling all possible 30 pairs in the sample space in Figure 5.6 would help the students see all the possible outcomes in this problem.

Figure 5.6

$$g_1g_2 \quad g_1g_3 \quad g_1g_4 \quad g_1d_1 \quad g_1d_2$$
$$g_2g_1 \quad g_2g_3 \quad g_2g_4 \quad g_2d_1 \quad g_2d_2$$
$$g_3g_1 \quad g_3g_2 \quad g_3g_4 \quad g_3d_1 \quad g_3d_2$$
$$g_4g_1 \quad g_4g_2 \quad g_4g_3 \quad g_4d_1 \quad g_4d_2$$
$$d_1g_1 \quad d_1g_2 \quad d_1g_3 \quad d_1g_4 \quad d_1d_2$$
$$d_2g_1 \quad d_2g_2 \quad d_2g_3 \quad d_2g_4 \quad d_2d_1$$

Of those 30 outcomes, 12 would be what we want, two good drives, so the probability, using the Multiplication Rule for Dependent Events, would be $\left(\dfrac{4}{6}\right)\left(\dfrac{3}{5}\right) = \dfrac{12}{30} = \dfrac{2}{5}$ or 40% or 0.400.

However, suppose we *know for sure* that the first drive we selected was good; then the probability becomes *conditional*. We cut out the last two rows and have only 20 possible outcomes in our sample space, and the probability becomes $\dfrac{12}{20} = \dfrac{3}{5}$ or 60% or 0.600.

Conditional probability is used by actuaries. They are mathematicians who are able to predict results based on numerous factors found in varied situations. For example, if you are applying for car insurance, your rate will be based on your age, gender, and previous history, as well as the make, model, year, and color of your car. All of these conditions influence your "risk," and therefore dictate the cost of your car insurance policy. Actuaries also help calculate probabilities that determine the cost of health care contracts and life expectancies that dictate the cost of life insurance policies as well as pension and annuity payouts.

94. WHAT IS THE DIFFERENCE BETWEEN COMBINATIONS AND PERMUTATIONS?

The short answer is *order!* The central question to ask to find the difference between combinations and permutations will always be "Does order matter?"

Let's start with this question: How many ways can we arrange 6 books on a shelf? We can use the concept of permutations to answer it. We can have 6 choices for the first place on the shelf; once that book is selected, we have 5 choices for the second place on the shelf, and then we will have 4 choices for the third place on the shelf, and then 3 choices, 2 choices, and 1 book left for the last position on the bookshelf. We would then multiply 6(5)(4)(3)(2)(1), which looks like, and is, the same as 6!. Six factorial gives us 720 different arrangements of 6 books on a shelf. Here, order is important! If we name the books A, B, C, D, E, an F, and arrangement of ABCDEF is quite different from ABCDFE and ABCEFD and so on. This also would be true if we only had room on that shelf for 3 books. We would have to limit our choices to 6 for the first place, 5 for the second, and 4 for the third, giving us only 6(5)(4) = 120 different arrangement sequences for the 3 books. There is a formula we can use when calculating a permutation. Let us use n = number of objects we are working with and r = number we are taking from the n for our arrangements. In the first example above, $n = r$ and just using the factorial works fine. However, in the second example where we do not have room for all 6 books, we need a formula for the number of arrangements (permutations) of r items selected from a group of n when $n > r$:

$$_nP_r = \frac{n!}{(n-r)!}$$

Let us select 3 students from a group of 20 for the prom council's president, treasurer, and secretary. Let the first pick be the president, the second pick be the treasurer, and the third pick be the secretary. Does the arrangement (order) of the students matter? Would an arrangement of the committee officers of Alice, Bob, and Chaz be the same officers as when Bob, Chaz, and Alice were picked or Chaz, Alice, and Bob? Yes, they would be different, so we have $_{20}P_3 = \frac{20!}{17!} = 20(19)(18) = 6{,}840$ different arrangements of 3 people selected from a group of 20.

However, suppose we now want to select 3 students from that group of 20, but we want them to form a decorating committee from our group of 20. Here we must think about whether the order of choosing the 3 people is important. We could have the same three people chosen in a different order, but they would constitute the same committee. When order is not important, we have a combination! Again, working with n items and selecting r at a time in no particular order, we have

$$_nC_r = \frac{n!}{(n-r)!r!} \text{ or } _nC_r = \frac{_nP_r}{r!},$$

and for our problem, $_{20}C_3 = \frac{20!}{[17!][3!]} = 1{,}140$ different combinations for our three-student decorating committee. Combinations do not concern themselves with the order of selection and therefore give a smaller numerical solution than permutations with the same n and r, but they do take into consideration different combinations regardless of order. Remember that when working with permutations and combinations, your answers will always be whole numbers.

Below is a table highlighting differences between factorials, combinations, and permutations.

	Meaning	Formula	Reminder	Example
Factorial	The product of an integer and all the positive integers less than it	$n! = (n)(n-1)$ $(n-2)\ldots$ $(3)(2)(1)$	**All objects used in arrangement**	Arranging all items on a shelf
Combination	The number of different groups of items	$_nC_r = \dfrac{n!}{(n-r)!r!}$	**Order does not matter**	Selecting team members from a larger group
Permutation	The number of arrangements of a group of items where their order distinguishes each arrangement	$_nP_r = \dfrac{n!}{(n-r)!}$	**Order matters**	Choosing a slate of officers (president, vice president, secretary, etc.)

Based on these definitions, you can ask your students: Are combination locks appropriately named? Should they be called "permutation locks"?

Students will enjoy determining the validity of the following statement: "You are more likely to be struck by lightning than to win the lottery."

Let us define the probability of an event occurring as the fraction where the numerator is the number of favorable outcomes of the event and the denominator is the number of all possible outcomes.

In our lottery, we have to select 6 numbers from 1 to 49. If our selection matches the 6 numbers we see selected by chance (on TV), we win. Order does not count!

To determine our probability of winning this lottery, we need one combination out of the total number of all possible

Figure 5.7

Source: Comstock/Thinkstock

combinations of 6 numbers drawn from 49 balls. In our formula, there are 49 numbered balls, so $n = 49$, and $r = 6$ of them are chosen in combinations. Our formula reads: $_{49}C6 = \dfrac{49!}{6!(49 - 6)!}$. This yields 13,983,816 total possible combinations of 6 numbers from 1 to 49 in any given lottery drawing. Our chance of winning becomes 1 in 13,983,816, which is a probability of .0000000715112384201851626194166617037867...

Now let us look at your chances of being hit by lightning: As reported by the National Lightning Safety Institute, approximately 1,000 people per year are struck by lightning in the United States (source: http://www.lightningsafety.com/nlsi_pls/probability.html), and as reported by the U.S. Census Bureau, the population of the United States is about 312,000,000 (source: http://www.census.gov/main/www/popclock.html). Using these two figures, the probability of a person being struck by lightning in a given year is about 1 in 312,000, or .000003205.

As you can see, your chance of being struck by lightning is about .000003205 while your chance of winning this lottery is .0000000715, making it almost 50 times more likely you will be struck down by lightning than win this lottery this year!

95. WHAT IS THE DIFFERENCE BETWEEN CORRELATION AND CAUSATION?

"Massachusetts Has the Lowest Divorce Rate"

"Swedish Children Who Live in Homes With Vinyl Floors Are More Likely to Have Autism"

"Avid Sports Fans 52% More Likely to Own a Tablet"

"Test Scores Plunge for Students With Heightened Math Anxiety"

Headlines like the ones above make the reader consider the connections between two trends. Sometimes the two trends are connected in a way that makes sense, where one of the actions might cause the other. Other times, the two trends are correlated, but there might be a third lurking factor that would cause the trends to coincide. And in other cases, it may just be coincidence.

For further interpretation, we can review the definitions of each term. Correlation is a relationship between two or more phenomena, especially noted when the relation exists between two occurrences not expected based on chance. On the other hand, we know that to "cause" something would be to act on something and to produce an effect; causation is the act or process of causing something to happen. We might say that it's Monday and it's raining, two events that have happened to coincide. However, it's not raining because it is Monday—so the relationship is not causal.

We can study these patterns and their relationships, and students can become astute in discerning headlines and data. Given two events that have been compared, let us call them A and B, there are a number of relationships that may have occurred. For example:

- A caused B
- B caused A
- A and B were caused by C
- A and B have no connection; they coincidentally occurred together

Determining correlation generally produces headlines and discussions, making for interesting conversation. However, causation is much more difficult to prove. One way to determine causation is to study the laws of science and nature. For example, "smoking causes lung cancer" has been confirmed by numerous statistically significant studies as well as by the study of cells and autopsies of humans who smoked during their lifetimes. Controlled studies can be used to seek proof of causation.

We know that living in Massachusetts does not cause you to stay married longer, even though this state has the lowest divorce rate. Students can think of a number of reasons that might impact each headline. For example, we may consider that students with math anxiety are not as confident, didn't study as much, do not have support in doing their homework, did not sleep well—all factors that impact test performance.

96. WHAT IS THE PASCAL TRIANGLE?

The Pascal triangle is the triangular array of integers shown in Figure 5.8, named after the French mathematician Blaise Pascal (1623–1662). It can be continued indefinitely. Let your students guess the arithmetic law underlying its construction: Every number inside the Pascal triangle is the sum of the two numbers on either side of it in the row above it. The Pascal triangle contains many surprising mathematical relations and helps to solve several

Figure 5.8

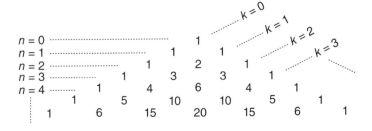

interesting problems. Hence, it has become an important part of mathematics instruction by providing many opportunities to convince students of the beauty of mathematics.

In the following, we denote the number of the horizontal rows in the Pascal triangle by n and the vertical place in each row by k, as indicated in Figure 5.8. Note that we start counting from zero. So, for example, the number 6 has the "coordinates" $n = 4$ and $k = 2$.

The entry at place k in the nth row of the Pascal triangle is the binomial coefficient

$$_n C_k = \frac{n!}{k!(n-k)!},$$

where n is an arbitrary nonnegative integer, $0 \leq k \leq n$, and $n! = 1 \cdot 2 \cdot 3 \cdot 4 \cdot \ldots \cdot (n-1)(n)$ denotes the *factorial* of n. The Pascal triangle may therefore serve as a mnemonic device for formulas involving binomial coefficients; for example, using the numbers in row number 4, we obtain:

$$(a + b)^4 = \mathbf{1} \ a^4 b^0 + \mathbf{4} \ a^3 b^1 + \mathbf{6} \ a^2 b^2 + \mathbf{4} \ a^1 b^3 + \mathbf{1} \ a^0 b^4,$$

or, more generally, we have the binomial formula:

$$(a + b)^n = \sum_{k=0}^{n} {_n C_k} \cdot a^{n-k} b^k.$$

The Pascal triangle helps in counting problems, and thus is important in combinatorics. A prototypical case is the problem of a frog descending a cubic stairway. This is illustrated in Figure 5.9. A frog jumping down the cubic stairway has, on each platform, the choice of jumping either to the left ("L") or to the right ("R"). The problem consists in finding the number of paths that lead from the top platform ($n = 0$, $k = 0$) to a position (n, k), which is n steps down and k steps to the right of the left border. Any such path can be described as a "word" made of the letters L and R that describes the sequence of jumps. To describe a path to position (n, k), the word must have length n and contain the letter R precisely k times.

In Figure 5.9, the frog has reached a position three steps down by jumping LRR, as shown. He would have reached the same position by using one of the sequences RRL or RLR. Obviously, there are three possible paths leading to the same position ($n = 3$, and $k = 2$). Interestingly, 3 is just the number at the corresponding position in the Pascal triangle. Indeed, we can show that the Pascal triangle gives the general solution for the problem of the frog on a cubic stairway.

Figure 5.9

Denote the number of paths starting at the top and ending at position (n, k) by $p(n, k)$. The position (n, k) can only be reached from two platforms in the row above, either from $(n – 1, k – 1)$ by jumping to the right, or from $(n – 1, k)$ by jumping to the left. Hence, $p(n, k)$ can be obtained as the number of paths ending at $(n – 1, k – 1)$ plus the number of paths ending at (n, k). Hence $p(n,k) = p(n – 1, k – 1) + p(n – 1, k)$.

And, of course, there is only one possible path leading to a position at the border, hence $p(n, 0) = p(n, n) = 1$ for all n. We see that the numbers $p(n, k)$ are computed by the same rule as (and are therefore identical with) the numbers of the Pascal triangle.

The following problems are, as it is not too difficult to see, equivalent with the problem of the frog on a cubic stairway:

- What is the number of strings of length n consisting of two symbols (L and R, or 0 and 1), such that one of the symbols occurs exactly k times (and the other $n – k$ times)?
- What is the number of ways to choose k objects from among n objects (disregarding order)?
- What is the number of k-element subsets of an n-element set?

In every case, the answer is $_nC_k$, the number at position (n, k) in Pascal's triangle!

Pascal's triangle was known long before Pascal. Perhaps its first occurrence was in ancient India, more than two thousand years ago, when Pingala classified the metric patterns of verses in the Vedas. (Given that any verse pattern in Sanskrit is a sequence of long and short syllables, there are $_nC_k$ distinct verse patterns of total length n that contain precisely k short syllables and $n - k$ long syllables.) In the 10th century, the Pascal triangle was known in India as the "staircase of Mount Meru" (the mystical mountain at the center of the Hindu universe).

97. WHAT IS BINOMIAL PROBABILITY?

When considering the etymology of the word *binomial,* we immediately notice the prefix "bi," which in literary Latin means "two," and we see "nomial," which reminds us of "name" from the Latin root *nomus*. Binomial translates to "having two names" using its roots. However, since the 16th century we have used this term in algebra to denote expressions with two terms.

In probability, then, we use the term "binomial experiment" for an event that has only two results: success or failure. You can consider flipping a penny as a binomial experiment. There are only two possible results: heads or tails. We can also use a "true-false" test in this case. Rolling a cubic die for a numeric result would not be considered a binomial experiment, since the die has six faces numbered 1 through 6, allowing for six unique outcomes. However, we can determine the probability of rolling a "3" since this would be considered a success and all other outcomes would be failures. Sometimes, binomial experiments are also referred to as Bernoulli trials after mathematician Jacob Bernoulli from Switzerland.

Binomial probability can be calculated when we know the probability of success. If we call p the probability of success, then we know that the probability of failure is $1 - p$, since we have two mutually exclusive events whose probabilities must have a sum of 1. We can find the number of ways to select exactly r successes in n trials by the following formula: $_nC_r \cdot p^r \cdot q^{n-r}$.

This formula can assist in determining the fairness of a die. When rolling a die 100 times, what is the probability of rolling a "3" exactly 25 times? Consider each variable in our problem:

The total number of rolls:	$n = 100$
The number of rolls we seek to be successful:	$r = 25$
The nonsuccessful rolls:	$n - r = 75$
The probability of "success," or rolling a 3:	$p = \dfrac{1}{6}$
The probability of "failure," or not rolling a 3:	$q = 1 - p = \dfrac{5}{6}$

Entering each of these into our equation, we get the following:

Probability of rolling a 3 = $_{100}C_{25} \cdot \left(\dfrac{1}{6}\right)^{25} \cdot \left(\dfrac{5}{6}\right)^{75} \approx .0010$.

98. WHAT IS THE BIRTHDAY PROBLEM?

The birthday problem presents one of the most surprising results in mathematics. It is best that you present it to your class with as much "drama" as you can. This unit will win converts to probability as no other example can because it combats the students' intuition quite dramatically.

Let us suppose you have a class with about 35 students. Begin by asking the class what they think the chances (or probability) are of two classmates having the same birth date (month and day only) in their class of about 30-plus students. Students usually begin to think about the likelihood of 2 people having the same date out of a selection of 365 days (assuming no leap year). Perhaps 2 out of 365?

Ask them to consider the "randomly" selected group of the first 35 presidents of the United States. They may be astonished that there are two with the same birth date:

the 11th president, James K. Polk (November 2, 1795), and

the 29th president, Warren G. Harding (November 2, 1865).

The class will probably be surprised to learn that for a group of 35, the probability that two members will have the same birth date is greater than 8 out of 10, or $\dfrac{8}{10} = 80\%$.

Students may wish to try their own experiment by visiting 10 nearby classrooms to check on date matches. For groups of 30, the probability that there will be a match is greater than 7 out of 10, so it is very likely to find a match in 7 of these 10 rooms. What causes this incredible and unanticipated result? Can this be true? It seems to go against our intuition.

To relieve students of their curiosity, guide them as follows:

First ask what the probability is that one selected student matches his own birth date. Clearly *certainty*, or 1.

This can be written as $\dfrac{365}{365}$.

The probability that another student does *not* match the first student is

$\dfrac{365-1}{365} = \dfrac{364}{365}$.

The probability that a third student does *not* match the first and second students is $\dfrac{365-2}{365} = \dfrac{363}{365}$.

The probability of all 35 students *not* having the same birth date is the product of these probabilities:

$$p = \frac{365}{365} \cdot \frac{365-1}{365} \cdot \frac{365-2}{365} \cdot \ldots \cdot \frac{365-34}{365}.$$

Since the probability (q) that two students in the group <u>have</u> the same birth date and the probability (p) that two students in the group <u>not</u> have the same birth date is a certainty, the sum of those probabilities must be 1. Thus, $p + q = 1$.

In this case, $q = 1 - \dfrac{365}{365} \cdot \dfrac{365-1}{365} \cdot \dfrac{365-2}{365} \cdot \ldots \cdot \dfrac{365-33}{365} \cdot \dfrac{365-34}{365}$

$\approx .8143832388747152$. In other words, the probability that there will be a birth date match in a randomly selected group of 35 people is somewhat greater than $\dfrac{8}{10}$. This is quite unexpected when one considers there were 365 dates from which to choose. Students may want to investigate the nature of the probability function. Here are a few values to serve as a guide:

Number of people in group	Probability of a birth-date match
10	.1169481777110776
15	.2529013197636863
20	.4114383835805799
25	.5686997039694639
30	.7063162427192686
35	.8143832388747152
40	.891231809817949
45	.9409758994657749
50	.9703735795779884
55	.9862622888164461
60	.994122660865348
65	.9976831073124921
70	.9991595759651571

Students should notice how quickly almost certainty is reached. With about 60 students in a room, the table indicates that it is almost certain (.99) that two students will have the same birth date.

Were one to do this with the death dates of the first 35 presidents, one would notice that two died on March 8 (Millard Fillmore in 1874 and William H. Taft in 1930) and three presidents died on July 4 (John Adams and Thomas Jefferson in 1826, and James Monroe in 1831).

Above all, this astonishing demonstration should serve as an eye-opener about the inadvisability of relying on intuition entirely.

99. HOW CAN ALGEBRA HELP US TO UNDERSTAND A PROBABILITY QUESTION?

This lovely little unit will show you how some clever reasoning along with algebraic knowledge of the most elementary kind will help you solve a seemingly "impossibly difficult" problem.

Consider the following problem.

You are seated at a table in a dark room. On the table there are 12 pennies, 5 of which are heads up and 7 are tails up. (You know where the coins are, so you can move or flip any coin, but because it is dark, you will not know if the coin you are touching was originally heads up or tails up.) You are to separate the coins into two piles (possibly flipping some of them) so that when the lights are turned on, there will be an equal number of heads in each pile.

Your first reaction is, "You must be kidding! How can anyone do this task without seeing which coins are heads or tails up?" This is where a most clever (yet incredibly simple) use of algebra will be the key to the solution.

Let us cut to the quick. Here is what you do. (You might actually want to try it with 12 coins.) Separate the coins into two piles of 5 and 7 coins each. Then flip over the coins in the smaller pile. Now both piles will have the same number of heads! That's all! You will think this is magic. How did this happen. Well, this is where algebra helps us understand what was actually done.

Let us say that when you separate the coins in the dark room, h heads will end up in the 7-coin pile. Then the other pile, the 5-coin pile, will have $5 - h$ heads and $5 - (5 - h) = h$ tails. When you flip all the coins in the smaller pile, the $5 - h$ heads become tails and the h tails become heads. Now each pile contains h heads.

100. WHAT KIND OF AVERAGES ARE BATTING AVERAGES?

Begin by asking students to explain what a baseball batting average is. Most people, especially after trying to explain this concept, will begin to realize that it is not an average in the way they usually define an "average"—the arithmetic mean. It might be good to search the sports section of the local newspaper to find two baseball players who currently have the same batting average but who have achieved their respective average with a different number of hits. We shall use a hypothetical example here.

Consider two players: David and Lisa, each with a batting average of .667. David achieved his batting average by getting 20 hits for 30 at bats, while Lisa achieved her batting average by getting 2 hits for 3 at bats.

On the next day, both perform equally, getting 1 hit for 2 at bats (for a .500 batting average); one might expect that they then still have the same batting average at the end of the day. By calculating their respective averages, David now has 20 + 1 = 21 hits for 30 + 2 = 32 at bats for a $\frac{21}{32} = .656$ batting average.

Lisa now has 2 + 1 = 3 hits for 3 + 2 = 5 at bats for a $\frac{3}{5} = .600$ batting average. Surprise! They do not have equal batting averages.

Suppose we consider the next day, where Lisa performs considerably better than David does. Lisa gets 2 hits for 3 at bats, while David gets 1 hit for 3 at bats. We shall now calculate their respective averages:

David has 21 + 1 = 22 hits for 32 + 3 = 35 at bats for a batting average of $\frac{22}{35} = .629$.

Lisa has 3 + 2 = 5 hits for 5 + 3 = 8 at bats for a batting average of $\frac{5}{8} = .625$.

Amazingly, despite Lisa's much superior performance on this day, her batting average, which was the same as David's at the start, is still lower.

There is much to be learned from this "misuse" of the word "average," but more important, students will get an appreciation of the notion of varying weights of items being averaged. What we call the "batting average" is in fact the relative frequency of hits with respect to the total at bats.

Index

CORWIN
A SAGE Company

The Corwin logo—a raven striding across an open book—represents the union of courage and learning. Corwin is committed to improving education for all learners by publishing books and other professional development resources for those serving the field of PreK–12 education. By providing practical, hands-on materials, Corwin continues to carry out the promise of its motto: **"Helping Educators Do Their Work Better."**